Backstage with Julia

Also by Nancy Verde Barr

Cookbooks
We Called It Macaroni: An American Heritage of Southern Italian Cooking
In Julia's Kitchen with Master Chefs (with Julia Child)
Make It Italian: The Taste and Technique of Italian Home Cooking

Fiction
Last Bite: A Novel of Culinary Romance

Backstage *with* Julia

MY YEARS *with* JULIA CHILD

Nancy Verde Barr

WILEY

Wiley Publishing, Inc.

This book is printed on acid-free paper. ⊗

Copyright © 2007 by Nancy Verde Barr. All rights reserved

Published by John Wiley & Sons, Inc., Hoboken, New Jersey

Published simultaneously in Canada

No part of this publication may be reproduced, stored in a retrieval system, or transmitted in any form or by any means, electronic, mechanical, photocopying, recording, scanning, or otherwise, except as permitted under Section 107 or 108 of the 1976 United States Copyright Act, without either the prior written permission of the Publisher, or authorization through payment of the appropriate per-copy fee to the Copyright Clearance Center, Inc., 222 Rosewood Drive, Danvers, MA 01923, (978) 750-8400, fax (978) 750-4470, or on the web at www.copyright.com. Requests to the Publisher for permission should be addressed to the Permissions Department, John Wiley & Sons, Inc., 111 River Street, Hoboken, NJ 07030, (201) 748-6011, fax (201) 748-6008, or online at http://www.wiley.com/go/permissions.

Limit of Liability/Disclaimer of Warranty: While the publisher and author have used their best efforts in preparing this book, they make no representations or warranties with respect to the accuracy or completeness of the contents of this book and specifically disclaim any implied warranties of merchantability or fitness for a particular purpose. No warranty may be created or extended by sales representatives or written sales materials. The advice and strategies contained herein may not be suitable for your situation. You should consult with a professional where appropriate. Neither the publisher nor author shall be liable for any loss of profit or any other commercial damages, including but not limited to special, incidental, consequential, or other damages.

For general information on our other products and services or for technical support, please contact our Customer Care Department within the United States at (800) 762-2974, outside the United States at (317) 572-3993 or fax (317) 572-4002.

Wiley also publishes its books in a variety of electronic formats. Some content that appears in print may not be available in electronic books. For more information about Wiley products, visit our web site at www.wiley.com.

Library of Congress Cataloging-in-Publication Data:
Barr, Nancy Verde.
  Backstage with Julia : my years with Julia Child / Nancy Verde Barr.
     p. cm.
  Includes bibliographical references and index.
  ISBN 978-0-471-78737-2 (cloth)
  ISBN 978-0-470-27637-2 (paper)
  1. Child, Julia. 2. Cooks—United States—Biography. 3. Barr, Nancy Verde—Friends and associates.
I. Title.
  TX649.C47B37 2007
  641.5092—dc22
  [B]
                                    2007001696
Printed in the United States of America

10 9 8 7 6 5 4 3 2 1

Interior Design: Lee Goldstein

To the memory of Julia, without whom...

Contents

Acknowledgments

When I began to work for Julia, my friend Jane Andrews told me to keep a journal so I would have a record of the dates and events of that special time. If I had followed her advice, I would now have a chronological, detailed accounting of the twenty-four years I knew Julia. I didn't and I don't. But somewhere I read that life is not about the dates that mark the beginning and end of one's life or the events in it; it's about the dashes between the dates.

Those dashes are indelibly recorded in my mind. And for those that needed illumination, I am grateful to friends of Julia's and mine who supplied the light. Zanne Stewart, Judith Jones, Sally Jackson, Dagmar de Pins Sullivan, Jody Adams, John McJennet III, Russ and Marian Morash, Debbie Moxham, Nan McEvoy, Mary Higgins, Hope Hudner, Philip Barr, my sons, Brad and Andrew Barr, Merle Ellis, Ed Dudkowski, and Ira Yoffe all ignited memories of events that made us smile when they happened and then again, when we remembered them. I am particularly grateful to Susy Davidson, who went so far out of her way to supply me with information, whether it was from her memory or the massive stockpile of materials she saves. She is, as she always was to Julia, "that darling Susy." For information I needed, and didn't have, I thank Jennifer Esposito for spending time with me at the Schlesinger Library hunting through the many boxes that contain Julia's papers.

When my agent Jane Dystel suggested this project to me, I vacillated and procrastinated. What would I write about a woman who was a friend to so many people and known to legions of others? Jane and her partner, Miriam Goderich, showed me the story that only I could tell. To Julia, saying someone was a "true professional" was high praise indeed and Jane and Miriam are true professionals. I am proud to be among their client list. Still, the process of writing this book had its traumas, and through them all Jane was always there to make the rain go away. For that alone, I wish her a life that is never without licorice.

I owe a huge debt of gratitude to my brother, Tom Verde, an award winning print and radio journalist, who was there, as he always has been, to help me say what I wanted to say a whole lot better than I might say it. I am particularly appreciative for his help since he took time from his Master's work and the production of a new radio show to read what I wrote and remind me when he thought Charles Dickens was in possession of my computer.

Many authors thank friends who read their manuscripts and give them valuable feedback. Others don't and I suspect they are like me. We hover over our works unable to reveal them to anyone until the publisher demands we pass them in. Instead, we share with friends our angst over what we are or are not writing, and for their patience in listening to my frustrations, I am grateful to Nelson Doubleday, my stepdaughters Vicki Cooley and Lydia Bailey, Lydia's husband, Dave Pac, Rosie Connors, and Nicky Nickturn. For some generous reason, they still answer my phone calls.

I hope Christine DiComo, Editorial Program Coordinator at John Wiley & Sons, knows exactly how much I appreciate the careful attention she paid to coordinating my materials into a book. And, thank you Justin Schwartz, Senior Editor at Wiley, for your enthusiastic support of this book. It was just like receiving one of Julia's postcards stamped with stars and bravos all over again.

Preface

The telephone rang just before dawn on August 13, 2004. Without opening my eyes, I rolled over and groped for the receiver. Tucking it under my chin, eyes still closed, I rolled back over and mumbled a sleepy "Hello."

"Nancy?"

More asleep than awake, I didn't recognize the voice. "Yes."

"It's Stephanie," was all Julia's longtime assistant said before pausing to let the early hour of the call register with me. She was in California. It was the middle of the night for her. I knew why she was calling.

"Oh, Stephanie," I said with resigned sadness but no exclamation of shock. Julia had not been well; it had been expected. "When?"

"A short time ago."

Stephanie told me that Julia had simply said it was enough and declined to go to the hospital yet once more; she passed away at home with her family and her kitten, Minou, by her side. It was two days shy of what would have been her ninety-second birthday. According to her wishes, there would be no funeral. I hung up the phone and allowed the tears to flow.

They flowed for the loss of a friend who had been part of my life for over two decades. Yet they were also tears of empathy. In that moment, I finally understood a feeling Julia had expressed ten years earlier when her husband, Paul, died. Her extreme sorrow at his loss was palpable and understandable, but when she wept to me, "It's the end of an era," I didn't fully understand, couldn't quite grasp her feeling. On August 13, as I lay there quietly weeping, I understood.

An era—a signal, definitive stage of history; a definable period in which a new order of things prevails; a special time. For Julia, Paul marked the beginning of her culinary awakening. Until they married, when she was thirty-four years old, she hadn't cooked at all, and she admitted that as a new wife her culinary attempts were mostly disasters that seldom made it to the table even close to a reasonable dinner hour. It was Paul who introduced her to French cuisine while they were living in Europe, and he did it with the knowledge and zeal of a man who was himself a connoisseur. She enrolled at the famous Paris Cordon Bleu cooking school in 1949, taking the first step that led to her long and equally famous culinary career. Paul walked with her every step of the path, accompanying her with enthusiasm, support, and devotion. Julia viewed her culinary birth and the course it took as the era of Paul and Julia.

For many of us, Julia was our culinary awakening. Our kitchen timers all started buzzing at once in 1963 when, at fifty years old, she debuted on public television with her show *The French Chef* and roused us first with the sound of her voice and odd galumphing about. Then she shook us awake and seduced us into her world with food that looked beyond delicious, even on black-and-white television and with names hard to pronounce. Were the recipes time-consuming and tedious to make? Were the ingredients hard to find? Who cared? Look at the fun she was having with it.

With eyes wide open, we went to great lengths to participate in the new order of her culinary world. We knocked down house walls and expanded our kitchens to accommodate monster-sized restaurant ranges and spacious Sub-Zero refrigerators with price tags that were startling. We purchased oversized sauté pans, fish poachers, stockpots, porcelain soufflé dishes with unglazed bottoms, and a *batterie* of small kitchen tools that we had never before seen or even knew existed. No longer was the one drawer that held a metal spatula, a handheld egg-beater, and a few mismatched knives enough. We needed room for a bench scraper, a bulb baster, several sizes of whisks, rubber spatulas, and flat-sided wooden spoons, as well as a place for a large set of well-honed knives. Kitchen counter space had to be generous enough to hold a K5A stand mixer, a food processor, and, for the truly passionate, a duck press. We stocked our refrigerators with "exotic" leeks, rare cuts of rare animals, and a very small glass jar that held two imported black truffles. Not only did the look of the home kitchen change, but so did its denizens. Once the domain solely of the housewife, it suddenly became a hobby center for men who embraced Julia's culinary world. At the same time, the previously male-dominated sanctum of the restaurant kitchen became the workplace for women chefs.

With a passion she sustained for over forty years, Julia continued to shape and influence the new order she had created, never allowing it to become stagnant. In addition to her monumental two-volume set, *Mastering the Art of French Cooking*, which provided a definitive education in traditional French techniques, she wrote nine more cookbooks that guided us through the application of those classic techniques to all good cooking of any ethnic genre. She headlined nine television series that followed the same progression from learning the proper foundation to applying it to "plain, good cooking." Over the course of her culinary life, she weighed in publicly and consistently with common sense and pithy wit on every food fad and culinary trend that caught our attention. She was the single most influential figure in the culinary world.

Her death was indeed the end of an era.

Like countless chefs, food writers, good home cooks, and even feckless pot-burners who would that day mourn her loss, I grew from cooking infant to adult culinarian in the age of Julia Child. Long before I began to work for her, I was already steeped in the era she created. I owned a large copper egg white bowl and an oversized balloon whisk, a conical fine-mesh *chinois* strainer, and a freezer full of homemade stock. I knew how to bone a whole chicken and how to make an omelet three ways. What I didn't know was what it took to be the kind of person who could define an era.

Julia always credited her success to timing: "I just happened to come along at the right time. If it hadn't been me, someone else would have done it." Perhaps. But could someone else have done it as well for so long? Could anyone else have made it as much fun to generations of audiences of all ages and interests, culinary or not? Would another person have devoted the time to developing the professionalism of gastronomy and provided such generous, personal mentoring to generations of culinary professionals?

Julia was right about her timing, though. At the beginning of the sixties, America was ripe for a new culinary age. After World War II, air travel to Europe was more accessible and affordable than it had ever been. Travel to France became increasingly popular with Americans who came face to fork with food the likes of which they had never tasted at home. The Kennedy's were in the White House and Americans became so enamored of their lifestyle that the First Couple became the country's standard for style. Jackie Kennedy brought a previously unseen elegance to state dining and entertaining and she did it with the aid of a French chef, René Verdon. French food became synonymous with fine dining, and the next best thing to hiring a Gallic cook was to learn how to make the dishes yourself. Julia was there to show us how. She was right: her timing *was* perfect. Still, she was not without precedent. James Beard and Dione Lucas had each published popular cookbooks, and Beard was on television with his *I Love to Cook,* while Lucas had her show, *To the Queen's Taste,* and could even occasionally be seen flipping French omelets in Bloomingdale's display windows.

So why Julia? Because more than the right time, she had the right stuff—what it took to go beyond simply filling a need and become synonymous with cooking itself. She had what the entertainment industry simply calls "it." On television her particular style of "it" told audiences that she was just like us, and if she could transform a large, unwieldy fish into dinner and turn common chunks of beef into a sophisticated Boeuf Bourguignon, then we could too. It was a masterly act of convincing, because in truth there was nothing common about Julia Child.

Everything about Julia was exceptional, from her strapping height and warbling voice to her zest for life, dauntless constitution, and interminable energy. To borrow a combination of phrases from George Carlin, she was "super-sized, long-lasting, high-definition, fast-acting, oven-ready, and built to last." She was unselfconsciously outspoken, smart, witty, and by her own admission a natural ham. Her discipline, work ethic, and organizational skills made me weep with envy, and her decisiveness and strong will sometimes just plain made me weep. She was curious and thorough, if not to a fault, at least to the point of making me beg her not to tell me another fact about the difference between sweet potatoes and yams. She was exceedingly practical, a trait that reflected her stern Presbyterian ancestry, and exquisitely nonjudgmental, which probably contradicted it.

Backstage with Julia is a memoir of the years I spent with Julia, years that showed me what kind of person could launch a culinary era. This book does not pretend to be a chronicle of her life and work. A detailed biography already exists; more may well follow. Neither does it explore Julia's culinary awakening. She told the definitive story of that time in *My Life in France,* the last book she wrote. These are my memories of the Julia who was my mentor, my colleague, my friend; my story of what made her so special.

That August morning, I lay in bed a long time thinking about Julia. I thought about the last time I'd seen her. It was a few months before the call, when I visited her in California. She knew I was writing a culinary novel loosely based on the television work we had done at *Good Morning America,* and she wanted to know all about it. I filled her in on the details of what I had written, and she thought it was a hoot. The events sparked memories that made us both smile.

"That's wonderful!" she said with genuine glee, and then she rested her hand on my knee. "We had such a good time. Didn't we?" she said. Oh, yes. Indeed we did.

1

*You live but once, you might
as well be amusing.*

—Gabrielle ("Coco") Chanel, French couturier

"It's an honor to have you on board, Mrs. Childs," announced the handsome flight attendant neatly clad in midnight-blue slacks, white shirt, and logoed tie. Bending over our seats, he whispered conspiratorially with a Texas drawl as broad as the state itself, "I'm such a *huge* fan. I have all your cookbooks."

Julia smiled demurely, tilted her head in acknowledgment, and said, "Thank you," without mentioning the erroneous addition of an *s* to her name. In the thirteen years that I had been working with her, the faulty pronunciation happened with curious regularity, and some years before, I'd remarked how odd I thought it that so many people put an *s* at the end of her name.

"Not really," she responded. "Before I was known at all there was a popular New York eatery called Childs. People knew of it and it helped them remember my name."

On that March day in 1993, three decades of public fascination with Child, the French Chef, had eclipsed whatever fame Childs the eatery had once enjoyed. That eclipse began the moment in 1963 when, from the display kitchen of the Boston Gas Company, she trilled her first WGBH-TV "Bon appétit." Cooking enthusiasts became dedicated fans, and even viewers who would never make friends with their stoves tuned in religiously to catch the antics of this Lucille Ball–like character with a rolling pin. I watched all—was it 134?—episodes of *The French Chef* for the cooking, but I reveled in her humor. Spontaneous humor—such as the time she pulled a bouquet garni out of a bubbling stock and said of the used bundle of herbs, "It looks like a dead mouse," and the time she announced, to cover for a bell that inadvertently rang during taping, "That must be the plumber!" Unable to resist, she licked a rich chocolate batter from her spatula and told us with a smile, "That's not part of the recipe." I laughed out loud when the long, slim baguette of French bread she planned to slice for onion soup slumped lazily in the middle when she held it up, so she declared it pathetically lacking in character and flung it dismissively over her shoulder.

She peppered her instructions for proper, classic techniques with frequent, amusing soupçons of sound: *blump, blump, blump* as she quickly sliced through mushrooms, *whomp* when she smashed her knife down on a clove of garlic, and a throaty, crackling sound when she broke off the claw of a lobster. In a distinctive voice that became one of the most recognized—and most imitated—voices in the country, she told us to be prepared to "shoot the wad" on buying the best ingredients and "go whole hog" in fearlessly cooking them. The combination of her off-the-cuff, madcap quirkiness and her deeply serious commitment to things culinary made watching her addictive. She catapulted to fame. When, in 1966, *Time* magazine featured her as its cover story, dubbing her "Our Lady of the Ladle," they wrote that her shows "have made her a cult from coast to coast and put her on a first-name basis with her fans."

Her name, sans the *s*, was unlikely to be forgotten.

"Want something to read?" Julia asked, reaching into her carry-on and pulling out an impressive stack of current magazines.

I held up the spy novel she had loaned me. "No, thanks. I'm just at the good part." Julia and I shared a passion for thrillers, mostly the ones that involved espionage. I could trace mine back to the Hardy Boys mysteries that I discovered when I was eight. Julia honed hers during World War II, when she worked with the Office of Strategic Services, the precursor to the CIA. She had just loaned me *The Spy Wore Red*, and although she insisted that during the war she had only typed and filed, I knew the government had cleared her for high-security work, and my overactive imagination kept plugging her into the role of undercover agent depicted by the heroine of the nonfiction book. Julia admitted that she had wanted to be a spy, but the "Oh So Secret," as she called the OSS, rejected her. "They said I was too tall," she would sigh. But of course, that's the sort of thing a spy would say.

I felt something brush by my foot. "Here comes the deluge," I said in a singsong voice.

"So much useless stuff," Julia said as she discarded several scented inserts, subscription forms, and coupon offers onto the floor. She didn't make neat piles; she unselfconsciously tossed the "useless stuff" around our feet. We were seated behind the bulkhead; there were no seats with pockets in front of us, so the floor was the only available receptacle for the mounting trash. I'd seen her do it often when in flight and, being infinitely more self-conscious, I always felt a compulsion to stand up and make a general announcement that we would pick them up before we left the plane. But Julia had no such compulsion. Delightfully uninhibited and completely comfortable with herself, she didn't worry about what other people might think.

"Do you know how many people actually pay attention to all that?" she asked pointing to the pile.

"No, I haven't a clue."

She cited an impressive statistic. "Isn't that amazing?"

"Amazing," I agreed, but more amazing to me was the fact that she was interested enough to find out. But then, after so many years with her, I was used to being amazed by her.

She continued to thumb through the magazines, paused intermittently to read articles that interested her, tore out several pages to read later, and tossed the pillaged remains into a heap on the floor. The litter at our feet was growing in scary dimension.

"Would you like me to take those?" the flight attendant asked, eyeing the mess and slipping a navy-blue apron over his head.

"Not now," Julia replied.

He looked at the pile at my feet and gave me a questioning look.

"It's *her* mess," I said with a shrug.

When he walked away, Julia gave me a quick, playful poke in the arm, and I responded as though she had broken it. I wasn't traveling with Julia Child the star—I was in the company of Julia McWilliams, the slightly naughty schoolgirl who took to elbowing and horsing around. Biographies, television programs, and articles about Julia often allude to the fact that in her youth she was a mischievous cut-up, a prankster, a party girl who loved to stir things up. But that fun-loving, mischief-causing character with a wicked glint in her eye was always very much there, elbowing and stirring up a little trouble whenever she felt like it.

We began our approach to Dallas, and the flight attendant returned to our seats. "We'll be getting ready to land soon, Mrs. Childs." And then, with a hesitant look at the clutter around our feet, "Shall I take these away now?"

"That would be very nice. Thank you."

"Is there anything else I can do for you?"

Julia gently patted both her knees with open palms and said, "We're supposed to have an airport cart pick us up. Where will that be?" Overall, Julia was blessed with remarkably good health, but stiffness in her knees often caused her extreme pain. "An old skiing injury and all that basketball in school," she'd say. Although bad knees are just in the cards for some people, all that jumping on her long, slender legs may well have compromised the joints. I'd realized just how long those legs were some years before, when a fan sent her an enormous box of Vidalia onions that contained the instructions "Store well ventilated in a cool place." When I asked her how she suggested we should store them, she handed me a pair of her pantyhose, saying, "These should do it. We'll hang them in the basement." The entire box of sweet Georgia onions fit into the one pair of her stockings.

When standing and walking seriously began to tax her knees, she reminded everyone around her to heed her call to arms: "Save the knees!" The Ritz-Carlton Hotel, our lodging in Houston, had rallied to the cause and arranged for an airport cart to pick us up.

"It will be at the gate at the end of the walkway. I'll make sure it is," the attendant informed us as he walked away with his armload of trash.

"There it is," I said, leading Julia toward the cart where a beaming woman driver was holding a sign that read, "Julia Child." We loaded our carry-on bags, our computers, and ourselves on board. When the cart began to back up, sounding its tooter to alert travelers that we were on the move, I said, "This is great. I've always wanted to ride on one of these."

Julia responded without missing a beat. "I've always wanted to *drive* one."

Her bright blue eyes smiled at me with a look I had grown to know and love in the more than a dozen years, and thousands of miles, I had been with her. It was the twinkling, teasing, conspiratorial smile that implied a connection, an understanding, a secret; it was a smile that she often gave me across a crowded dinner table when someone said something that we both knew more about but weren't going to tell. The one she flashed with a wink of her eye to me during long demonstrations that said, *Hold on, we'll be finished soon, and enjoying a cocktail and dinner.* That moment in Houston, the smile was saying, *Of course I drive. It's my cart.*

There never was any question that Julia drove the cart. I was just lucky to go along for the ride!

That ride began in Providence, Rhode Island, in 1980. I was thirty-six years old and married with two toddler sons, had graduated from culinary school, and was running two cooking schools of my own. The husband and the children were intentional; teaching cooking was a delightful fluke.

In 1969, I married Philip Barr and we moved to Washington, D.C., where he attended dental school and I found a job teaching hard-of-hearing children. I quickly became fast friends with a fellow teacher who was supporting her husband through law school.

"We can't just sit at home nights while our husbands study," she stated emphatically while turning the pages of the latest brochure of community classes. "Here's something interesting," she said, handing me the catalogue so I could read about the cooking classes a local woman gave in her home.

I signed up for the classes not because I had a particular interest in food but because it was something to do with a friend. But from the moment I placed a nugget of herb-infused butter on top of a boneless chicken breast, rolled it, and fried it into an elegant, stuffed Kiev, I was hooked. When I tasted the crisp explosion of unfamiliar flavor that a quick dip in hot olive oil made of a small, unimpressive bouquet of parsley, I wanted to know more about this food thing. I bought my first Julia Child cookbook, *The French Chef,* and watched her shows with a pad and pencil. Philip began to photograph our meals. When I watched Julia make something she called "Glamour Pouding," I took copious notes, invited friends to dinner, and wowed them with the "handsome molded dessert" that Julia promised me I would have if I did what she did on TV.

I became a community cooking class junkie, and one of my teachers suggested that I might want to assist. She put me in touch with Madame Teresa Colonna, a colorful Polish-French woman in her sixties who ran a cooking school from her home in Bethesda, Maryland. She had immigrated to the United States as a young woman with a certificate from the Cordon Bleu and training as a French milliner. When ladies' custom-designed hats became passé and cooking classes all the rage, she taught full time. For two years, I spent two nights a week at culinary boot camp—setting up the preparation for hands-on classes, fetching ingredients, adjusting students' grips on knives, and washing the dishes that remained. I couldn't have been happier. By the time Philip graduated from dental school in 1973, I knew I wanted to be Madame Colonna.

We returned to Providence, and I immediately enrolled in Madeleine Kamman's Modern Gourmet cooking school in Newton Center, Massachusetts, where I systematically worked my way through the classic techniques of French cooking. In 1975, I passed my Modern Gourmet exams, received my diploma, and opened my own schools.

I had been teaching classic French cuisine for five years when, in the spring of 1980, a friend, Tina Frost, telephoned me.

"I'm calling for my husband, Fred. He's heading up the committee for Providence's Planned Parenthood fund-raiser in October, and we'd like you to help out."

I'd done volunteer work for Planned Parenthood before. I knew there was a need. "Sure. What can I do?"

"Julia Child has agreed to come to Providence and give two cooking demonstrations. We need help organizing them."

Ta-da! I was not just going to meet the most important culinary figure in the country—I was going to work with her. It was akin to tossing a football around with Joe Montana or jamming on guitars with Eric Clapton. Tina was giving me dates and venues, and I was mentally kneading images of me standing next to Julia, passing her utensils and ingredients with the efficiency of an OR nurse. She would say, "Bismarck," and I would know exactly which pastry tip to pass her. "Brioche pan" and the fluted, tin mold would be in her hand.

I was lost in truffle heaven, but Tina's next words brought me back to earth. "Julia's bringing her own assistants, but she said we needed someone local with cooking experience who could take care of the food and the set. Do you think you can do that?"

Okay, I would be an orderly, not head nurse, but I would be there. "Absolutely! It's what I do," I said, stepping up to the plate with exaggerated confidence. True enough, it was what I did. I just didn't do it for *Julia Child*.

I made myself focus on the job and not the star. We needed food shoppers, dishwashers, and prep cooks. Since the demonstration site was to be the Rhode Island School of Design's auditorium, which in no way resembled a place where one could cook, we needed a cooktop, ovens, a refrigerator, small appliances, makeshift sinks, pots, pans, whisks, spoons, measuring utensils, food.

Julia mailed us detailed lists itemizing everything she would need, along with some specific instructions: the demonstration counter was to be thirty-nine inches high, four inches above the norm; the electric stand mixer should be a heavy-duty K5A—the "real McCoy"—and the rolling pin should be a proper ball-bearing one, at least sixteen inches long, and "not some toy." As did most Julia devotees, I'd formed my impression of her by watching her television shows. I'd seen the messes, the dropped potato pancake, the loaf of bread flung over her shoulder. She was someone who effortlessly winged it and didn't sweat the small stuff. Those lists said that there was a finely honed structure behind her madcap exterior.

Julia even told us precisely what she would like served for lunch on the set: smoked salmon with a "nice salad" one day and a "*real* Rhode Island red clam chowder" on the next. A popular local caterer volunteered to do the salmon buffet, and I asked my mother to make the chowder. It wasn't nepotism; her recipe was my great-grandma Feely's, and it was the best Rhode Island red clam chowder I'd ever tasted.

The day before the first demonstration, the Julia entourage arrived by train. The plan was for me to meet them at the auditorium, where Julia would check the set before going to the hotel. Sylvia Walker Quinn, one of my team of helpers, called me that morning.

"I told the committee we'd pick Julia up at the train station," she said.

"You're kidding!" I'm sure I must have thought a limousine would pick her up. At least it never occurred to me to offer to do it. Such things *always* occurred to Sylvia.

"Why would I kid you? I'll pick you up first."

The train was early, so when Sylvia and I arrived, Julia was already outside with her husband, Paul, Liz Bishop, Ruth Lockwood, and several pieces of mismatched luggage, some emblazoned with enormous, yellow masking tape X's for identification and others hand-lettered with a bold black P surrounded with the letter C. A few over-sized tote bags, bloated with an assortment of aprons, food, and cooking utensils, were leaning against the suitcases. This small culinary cortege looked more like an AARP group back from a weekend tour than a television star and her roadies. At a lofty six foot two, Julia towered over the group, and I realized why the counters needed to be so high. In later years, she became somewhat stooped, but on that day, the sixty-eight-year-old undisputed queen of cooking straightened up to her full height and greeted us with enthusiastic warmth.

"Hooray! You're here!" she warbled, taking Paul's arm with one hand and hoisting a tote bag with the other.

I smiled, or maybe I laughed. It is impossible not to the first time you hear that unmistakable voice in person—especially when it is accentuating the word *hooray*.

"We are," I said, accepting the bag she handed me. After multiple introductions, we squished ourselves into Sylvia's small blue station wagon, with Julia, Liz, Ruth, and me vying for space in the backseat.

"Up and back, Ruthie," Julia said. Ruth, a neatly coiffed, smartly dressed, efficient-looking woman, was Julia's friend, her original television producer, and clearly someone who had been squished into many backseats, because she'd devised the up-and-back seating arrangement that gave the derriere plenty of space. The person nearest the door slides well back in the seat, the next person sits just on the edge, the next back, and so on. Julia was sitting next to but well behind me, yet her long legs stretched out as far as mine. Many people dream of rubbing elbows with celebrities. There I was rubbing knees with Julia Child, who was telling us how happy she was to be in Providence. I guess we all have different reactions to being in the company of famous people. Mine was to ask innocuous questions about the trip and mention the weather. Sylvia's was to take a hostage. "Would you like to stop at Nancy's house to freshen up? It's along the way," she lied. It was close to the auditorium, but it was a roundabout way to go.

"Why not?" said Julia, demonstrating how delightfully ordinary my extraordinary idol was.

While I made coffee and rooted around in the cupboards for something to serve with it, Sylvia dragged my complete collection of Julia Child cookbooks off the shelf and asked Julia to sign them for me. All the books were food-spattered and dog-eared, and I half expected bits of parsley and pieces of onion peel to trickle out. I thought ruefully of the protective Plexiglas bookstand gathering dust in the closet.

"How nice to see that they are so used," Julia said, flipping through the smeared pages. Chalk one up for being a messy cook. Years later, after publishing my own cookbooks, I realized just how gratifying it is to see proof that someone actually cooked from them.

As she signed each book, she passed it on to Paul, who wrote his name in a fine bold hand, with a jaunty scroll beneath it.

"Thank you," I said, giving what I thought was a nice grateful smile and reaching for the book. He held it open in front of him and gazed reproachfully at me—for what, I didn't know.

"You have to wait for the ink to dry," he said authoritatively.

"Of course," I said, meekly sliding my hand away.

When he determined that the ink was dry, his tone became gentler and he directed my attention to the photographs and drawings in *From Julia Child's Kitchen,* or "JC's Kitchen," as I learned it was always called by all those who had anything to do with it.

"I took the photographs over her shoulder so readers would see the food from the cook's angle," he explained. It was an innovation in food photography, since most food photos aimed at tantalizing the appetite and not at teaching. Up until that moment, it had escaped my notice that the photographs and artful sketches in Julia's early books were Paul's. For all I knew about Julia's cooking, I knew little about her personal life. I'm not sure I even knew there *was* a Paul, so I certainly didn't know that Julia's husband, ten years her senior, had suffered a heart attack in 1974, followed by a small series of strokes from which he had never fully recovered. That day she made no apology or explanation for Paul's peculiar scolding tone.

He turned to the front of the book and pointed out what he told me was a favorite photograph—Julia silhouetted in shadow in front of the window in their Marseilles apartment. "Julie looks really good in this," he said, becoming the only person I would ever hear call her Julie. Somehow it instantly revealed the closeness that was

Paul, Julia, and me in my kitchen.

theirs and gave me a glimpse of the extremely charming man who had governed Julia's heart for some thirty-four years.

Meanwhile, on the other side of the kitchen, Liz Bishop was perched on a stool—knees crossed, top leg swinging sassily—surveying her surroundings. Liz had been working with Julia since the first television series. They were good friends. She was in her forties, brash and entertaining with a quick, bawdy wit and a sharp tongue that Julia found terribly funny. So did I. Then Liz said something that caught me off guard.

"You studied with Madeleine?" she asked, raising her eyebrows and tilting her head in the direction of my Modern Gourmet diploma in the bookcase. This was a touchy subject because I knew that there was bad blood between Julia and Madeleine. The times that Madeleine even mentioned Julia in class, it was to say, "She is neither French nor a chef."

"Yes, I did," I responded, and Liz gave me an inscrutable smile. I gave it my own read: I would be condemned by association and deep-sixed before I got to demonstrate my efficiency or serve my great-grandma Feely's red chowder. But no one said anything more on the subject. Not then, anyway.

We spent close to an hour in my kitchen, getting to know each other and smiling for Sylvia, who, being Sylvia, had her camera and was snapping photos. Julia talked mostly about the recipes for the demonstrations, describing in detail how she planned to mix this or assemble that. The words *perfectly, carefully,* and *impeccably* sifted evenly throughout her descriptions, and I knew she was sending me a message: *We don't rush through things.* As she spoke, her hands slowly pantomimed cooking motions, and I remember how their expressiveness captured my attention. Julia had very long, graceful fingers, adorned only by a lovely wide gold Tiffany wedding band. When she was imitating a culinary move, she cupped her palms slightly, tightened her knuckles a bit, and splayed her fingers gracefully in a most distinctive gesture. They were artist's hands, chef's tools that never ceased to captivate me. And her eyes intrigued me. They were the most delicate shade of pale blue and glistened as though tears were waiting to appear.

"The caramel gave us a lot of trouble in the past," she said, referring to the spun-caramel dome that would sit over the cake she was to demonstrate. Although I had never made a caramel dome, I knew the process involved swirling hot caramel with a spoon into a webbed pattern on the exterior of a bowl and, when it cooled, lifting it in one piece off the bowl.

"How so?" I asked, wondering what problems she had encountered.

"It kept breaking when we lifted it off the bowl. We tried different bowls, more butter, layers of plastic wrap. In the end, we found the difference was chilling the bowl beforehand."

It was obvious from her animated discussion that not only had she researched the releasing qualities of caramel with scientific precision, but she had thoroughly enjoyed the research process. It had been thirty-one years since Julia took her first cooking class at the Cordon Bleu, and yet there she was enthusing about learning a technique with the same passion of a first-year culinary student. Her enthusiasm was infectious.

That evening, at the patrons' gala dinner, I met Julia's assistants, Marian Morash and Sara Moulton. My copy of Marian's *The Victory Garden Cookbook,* the landmark, definitive work on vegetables, was as worn and stained as my copies of Julia's books. I had watched her on her own television show, *The Victory Garden,* but I didn't know that she is married to Russ Morash, the director responsible for Julia's successful burst into the television world. Sara, who would go on to become the star of her own shows on the Food Network, is a petite dynamo. I like to call Sara "petite." Since I am only five feet two inches, it's elevating working with someone who's even shorter. Sara looked like a teenager, but I knew she had to be older than that, because it took a lot longer than nineteen years to accumulate her degree of culinary expertise. Since both Marian and Sara had worked with Julia for a number of years and knew her routine well, I expected they would hardly need me for anything more than managing the dishwashing station.

The next morning, I stood back and waited for directions.

"Where should we begin?" Marian asked me. "You're in charge." How generous is that? Marian and Sara intended for me to be the onstage assistant to Julia during the shows, and their instant acceptance of me immediately endeared both women to me.

Liz seated and me getting to know Sara and Marian, while patron Nancy Taylor of Providence looks on.

Julia's demonstration that afternoon was to be devoted to fast puff pastry, a quicker but no less buttery version of the classically made, multilayered flaky pastry known in French as *pâte feuilletée*. The classic version calls for spreading masses of butter over a large sheet of pastry dough, *pâte brisée*, and then folding the two into a package. The butter and pastry package is then rolled and folded, rerolled, and folded again for a total of six times called "turns," with chilling necessary after each turn. Its success depends in great part on the cook's ability to handle the butter so that it maintains the ideal temperature to spread properly through the layers of dough: too cold and shards of it can pierce the dough, too warm and it can ooze out

Ramequin du Juste Milieu
for the uncooked insides of a vol-au-vent (for a 4-cup dish)

Purée the uncooked pastry (⅓ to ½ cup usually) in a blender or processor with 1 cup milk. Blend in briefly 2 eggs, ¼ cup grated Parmesan or Swiss cheese, salt and pepper to taste. Half an hour or so before you wish to serve, pour into a buttered baking dish and set in the middle level of a preheated 375°F oven and bake until nicely puffed and brown. Serve at once.

Copyright © by Julia Child. All rights reserved.

Julia's recipe for the inevitable bits of uncooked vol-au-vent dough.

the sides, sticking the dough together and preventing it from separating into flaky layers.

In 1980, we couldn't buy puff pastry in the market, so if we wanted it, we had to make our own. Julia did not invent the faster method, which she called "*pâte feuilletée express,*" but she heralded its use to her audiences so that they would not miss the joys of the layered pastry because they found the classic method daunting. With quick puff pastry, instead of a large sheet of butter spread on top of the pastry, diced pieces are added and blended directly into the flour and water in the bowl of a stand mixer. The dough is then ready for the traditional six turns and folds.

Julia would then demonstrate a number of delicious and inventive dishes you could cook up once you had rapidly made the dough. She would demonstrate two types of pithiviers, that wickedly rich, two-crusted tart that oozes sumptuousness: one with a sweet almond paste filling and the other with savory ham and cheese. There would be individual patty shells, called bouchées, and a large vol-au-vent shell.

Typically frugal, she also planned to show how to rework any leftover pieces of pastry into cheese appetizers. Then, a *truc* I'd never seen before, she would remove the inevitable bits of uncooked dough from the inside of the baked vol-au-vent, puree them with milk, eggs, and cheese, and bake the lot into a nicely puffed and browned sort of vertically challenged soufflé. She called this last dish Ramequin du Juste Milieu.

All that pastry with its turns and folds, rests, and shaping meant that we were up to our ears in flour and butter with a lot of work to be done before the show, and we all seemed to be in constant motion. Jody Adams, now the award-winning chef of Rialto in the Boston area, was then a young assistant at my cooking school and one member of my team. When I asked her recently what she remembered about those days on the set, she said, "Running. I remember all that running around." This was in no small part because the only water source was the ladies' room, a good distance away from the stage. Julia worked right alongside us, pausing only briefly to take in the aproned army around her and say, "Isn't cooking together fun?"

When Julia took the stage at two o'clock that afternoon, an excited, chattering audience warmed all six hundred seats of the auditorium. The house lights went up; Julia marched onto the stage and was greeted by a great thunderous applause. She clasped her hands together over her heart and bowed her head in appreciation. The clapping went on and on, and she raised her hands above her head and applauded the audience. Gosh, she was some showman. The audience loved it and rewarded her with louder clapping and several whoops.

Finally, Julia took her place at the demonstration counter and we assistants stood at the back of the stage waiting for her call to arms. Liz was perched on a stool off to the side. I realized that Liz was a non-cooking member of the team, a kind of majordomo in charge of Julia's arrangements and appointments. Unless need pressed her into action, she would remain perched. Ruth sat in the front row of the audience with Paul next to her. He held a small stack of handmade signs lettered with numbers on his lap. He was to keep track of the time and hold up a sign to let Julia know how much time she had left.

Assisting in a demonstration is all about anticipating. Good assistants know the recipes by heart, pay attention to the order of presentation, and keep their eyes on what utensils need replacing on the set. We were well on top of things as Julia was whizzing her way through making pastry.

"Ninety minutes!" Paul Child boomed in a loud voice that startled us all. Then the audience went dead quiet. Heads stretched and turned to see who dared cause such a disturbance. It well might have been an awkward, uncomfortable interruption, but Julia seemed neither uncomfortable nor interrupted. She never missed a roll of the pastry.

"Thank you, Paul," she said, smiling at him, before telling the audience that her husband was keeping time. Just as on the day before, when Paul had scolded me, Julia was not in the least bit embarrassed by his unconventional behavior. She was as unselfconscious and unpretentious in front of an audience as she had been in my kitchen. I had no idea of the years of partnership and romance that went into that simple exchange with Paul, but I saw clearly that Julia had a strong, secure sense of who she was, who they were, and she didn't need to explain or camouflage any odd behavior on or off the stage.

The demonstration continued smoothly, with all of us now nodding our thanks in Paul's direction for his periodic time reminders. When Julia got to the sweet almond Pithiviers, she put the filling ingredients—sugar, butter, egg, almonds, dark rum, and vanilla and almond extracts—into the food processor and pulsed them into a paste.

"This has to be well chilled before we put it into the shell to bake," she told the audience as she handed me the bowl. I, in turn, passed it to Brett Frechette, one of the teachers at my cooking school.

She was one of the best, a perfectionist. When I handed her the processor bowl, she looked in and whispered to me, "It's separated." I looked down, and sure enough, liquid was seeping out of the paste. It had been mixed too quickly for the flavorings to be absorbed.

"She can't use it like this," Brett said. I looked back to Julia to see if I could return the paste to her for fixing, but she was already on to the next recipe. And I didn't think I should I disturb her by removing the processor from the set.

"The blender," Brett and I whispered at the same time, looking at the brand-new donated Waring blender sitting on one of the workstations. The workstations were long, folding tables that we had swathed in green checked banquet cloths that draped to the floor. Brett grabbed the blender and scooted under the table near an electrical source. I gathered the ingredients and slipped them down to Brett, who turned them into a perfect, firm almond paste to replace the unusable, oozing one. The only person who seemed aware of the quiet whirring emanating from beneath the table was Liz, who smiled at me knowingly from her perch.

The theme for the next night's demonstration was filling and wrapping. The first recipe was an elaborate creation of artichoke bottoms stuffed with mushroom duxelles, topped with poached eggs, napped with béarnaise sauce, and served on a platter with large, homemade croutons. Whew! Then there would be a whole three-pound fish, cleaned and scaled but with head on, cloaked in brioche dough and baked—Fish en Cloak. The grand finale—and it was grand—was to be the construction of Mlle. Charlotte Malakoff en Cage, a most elaborate rum-soaked génoise, layered and frosted with a whipped-cream chocolate-hazelnut filling, and haloed with the thoroughly tested, perfectly spun caramel dome. That recipe alone covered five pages, and at the end was Julia's simple, understated instruction to "shatter the dome and cut the cake as usual."

Liz on her stool, me at the ready, and Julia with her cake.

As lunchtime approached, I found myself wondering if my mother's chowder was really as delicious as I thought. Too late to do anything about it. Volunteers had set up a long table with china, silver, linens, and an empty space for the large pot of soup that my mother was, at that very moment, carrying down the aisle. Rhode Island has three native chowders: a clear broth with clams and potatoes, a creamy white chowder usually called New England clam chowder, and a red one, which, since there are no carrots, celery, or herbs, is not at all like Manhattan clam chowder. Our Rhode Island version is made with salt pork, both quahogs and clams, tomatoes, and potatoes and served with a pitcher of hot milk and pilot crackers.

Julia stepped down from the stage to greet my mother, Billie Higgins Verde, who was beaming. My mother was Irish, and her family's food—primarily corned beef and cabbage and codfish balls

GREAT-GRANDMA FEELY'S RHODE ISLAND RED CLAM CHOWDER

$1^1/_4$ quarts hard-shelled clams, combination of quahogs and cherrystones, scrubbed

$^1/_8$ pound salt pork, diced

1 large onion, finely chopped

6 large russet potatoes, peeled, cut into $^1/_4$-inch cubes

6 to 8 large ripe garden tomatoes, finely chopped, or one 28-ounce can Italian peeled plum tomatoes, drained and finely chopped

Salt and ground black pepper, as needed

For serving:

Pitcher of warm milk

Pilot crackers

1. Bring 2 cups of water to a boil in a deep pot. Add the quahogs, cover and cook for 5 minutes. Stir in cherrystone clams and continue to cook for 5 to 10 minutes or until the shells open. Remove all the clams with a slotted spoon and set aside. Strain the broth twice through a fine-mesh sieve or paper coffee filters. There should be about 1 quart of broth; if not add warm water.

2. Render the salt pork in a large soup pot and when the fat melts, stir in the onions. Cook over medium-low heat until the onions are translucent and soft; do not let brown. Add the potatoes, tomatoes and broth and bring to a boil, then reduce the heat and simmer about 20 minutes or until the potatoes are tender. Meanwhile, finely mince the quahogs and coarsely chop the cherrystone clams. When the potatoes are tender, stir all the clams into the chowder just to reheat, about a minute. Season with pepper and taste for salt though none should be needed. Serve the chowder with the pitcher of warm milk and pilot crackers.

Note: Quahogs or quahaugs give chowder great flavor, but they are tough so be sure to chop them very fine. My grandmother put them through a meat grinder, and my mother pulsed them in a food processor.

served with homemade baked beans on Sunday mornings—took a lot of ribbing from my Italian father's family. For her to serve her

Irish family's chowder and not lasagna to Julia Child was a real coup—more so when Julia asked for a second bowl.

That evening, the demonstration began as it had the day before, with much applause and cheering. In spite of the elaborate menu, it was, so to speak, Child's play for Julia. She whipped through cloaking the fish, spinning the caramel, raffling off the finished dishes, and auctioning off the stage equipment.

But there was more. As I would come to know, a Julia show is not over when the Julia show is over. There were fans to greet, books and aprons to sign, and photos to be taken. Julia left the stage and sat at a table facing long lines of admirers waiting for autographs and a

Jody Adams, Marian Morash, Julia, Paul, Sara Moulton, me, Liz Bishop, and my assistants Jocelyn Hamblett and Sylvia Walker Quinn saying soufflé.

word with her. Some approached her laden with an entire collection of Julia Child cookbooks; others held only the program from the demonstration or an apron they had hastily purchased. They lingered, telling Julia how she'd changed their culinary lives, recounting tales of their own kitchen disasters, sharing family recipes, asking Julia what was her favorite recipe, favorite restaurant, favorite anything. Julia listened attentively, commented graciously, and answered all questions except those about favorites. "That's a media-type question," she'd say with her index finger raised. "I don't answer those."

It was taking a long time after an already long day. When one man babbled on, giving a cup-by-tablespoon description of his great-aunt Ethel's orange cake, I was ready to scream. Julia asked him what kind of baking pan Great-aunt Ethel used. Where did she get the energy?

At last, with all the books signed and the last fan satisfied, Julia gathered the kitchen teams together for a group photo.

"Say cheese," the photographer instructed.

"No. Say souf-*flé*," Julia corrected, overstressing the second syllable.

"Soufflé?" I asked, wondering if Julia had randomly chosen a French word. Could we just as readily say *quiche* or *canard*?

Liz, Marian, Ruth, Sara, Paul, and of course Julia were probably hoping someone would ask because, practically in unison, they looked at me, raised their voices, and said "Souf-*flé*! See? You have to smile to say it right."

We smiled our "souf-*flé*" together and then sadly said goodbye.

A few months later Liz Bishop telephoned me. I wasn't surprised to hear from her, since we'd made a nice connection when she was in Providence and had promised to stay in touch. She invited me to Boston, to lunch with Julia, and Julia had a question that did surprise me. Marian was working on a second book, was involved with her own television show, and had a growing family that needed more

ECOLE DES TROIS GOURMANDES
MASTERING THE ART OF FRENCH COOKING

Paris

SIMONE BECK FISCHBACHER
23 Bd. d'Argenson, 92000 Neuilly
(16-1) 624-74-78

Cambridge

JULIA CHILD
103 Irving Street, Cambridge
Massachusetts 02138
(617) 876-1072

31 October 1980

Ms. Nancy Barr
109 Williams Street
Providence, RI 02906

Dear Nancy,

How much we all enjoyed being with you and your marvelous group in Providence. We all said that was really the happiest time we've ever had on our demonstrations, just because of your charming, helpful, professional backing. And I think we had lots of fun together. We do look forward to another get together. Unfortunately, Paul and I are leaving for the west coast right after Thanksgiving, and are very much tied up with our ABC work, going back and forth to New York. But maybe something could be worked in before, or if you are going to be at DeGustibus, it would be great fun to see you.

With fond thoughts from us both –

Julia

PS: Loved our present, and am distributing it!

Julia's letter to me after the Planned Parenthood event.

of her time, so she could not commit to all the work Julia needed. Was I available to work with the Julia team? And, just like that, I hopped on Julia's cart. I would be saying "souf-*flé*" with her for the next twenty-four years.

*Look with favor upon a
bold beginning.*

—Virgil, *Eclogues*

My first assignment as a member of the Julia team was to assist her on *Good Morning America,* ABC television's morning news and variety show. Once a month, Julia spent two days at *GMA*'s New York City studios. Mondays were for prepping, and Tuesday mornings she appeared live for a cooking spot that ran two and a half or three and a half minutes. When the show went off the air at nine o'clock, she taped four or five segments of the same length for later airing.

Good Morning America was Julia's first contractual commitment with commercial television. Her primary loyalty would always remain with public television, but she felt snubbed when New York public television failed to air her series *Julia Child & More Company.* Astutely aware of the importance of "being out there," she wanted exposure in the city. As she put it, "If you're not on in New York, you ain't nowhere." So *Good Morning America* became her "somewhere" network home.

Several weeks before my first day on the Julia job, she called to give me my instructions.

"Meet us at the studios Monday at 6:00 A.M. sharp. Liz, Sara, and Paul will be there. We'll do a lovely pear tart for the live show." She then described what she would make for the taped shows and, almost as an afterthought, added, "That evening we'll be doing a demonstration for a school called De Gustibus." De Gustibus is now housed in a fully equipped kitchen on the eighth floor of Macy's, but in those days it operated in an auditorium, with all the limitations we'd faced at the RISD auditorium in Providence. "Very jolly people," Julia told me. "I think we'll make paella and a nice sabayon for dessert. Everyone's supposed to get a taste, and I think those dishes will go around nicely."

"How many people do they expect to attend?"

"About three hundred."

I was glad we were on the phone so she couldn't see my it's-never-gonna-happen expression. "That's a lot of people to feed. What kind of stove and equipment do they have?"

"No stove. Not much equipment. I've asked for two electric woks and a hot plate."

If it had been anyone other than Julia, my response would have been, *What? Are you crazy?* As it was, I mustered just enough confidence to say, "That should work."

"Sara will be our executive chef for the TV, but she can't be at the demonstration, so you're in charge. Can you find a good, reliable person in New York to help out?"

The answer came to me immediately. "My good friend Mary Higgins is the assistant food editor at *Ladies' Home Journal*. I'm sure she'd love to do it."

"That's wonderful. I think we should ask her to buy the shrimp for the paella. Oh, and dearie . . ."

"Yes?"

"Will you bring six perfect pears to the television set with you?"

I really wished she hadn't said *perfect*. Were perfect pears the same thing to me as they were to Julia? Certainly I'd bought my share of pears, but when Julia Child asks not just for pears but for "perfect pears," they cease to be produce. They are an aptitude test, graduate exams, the law boards. I knew I could spot perfection in pears, but would they be at the right stage of ripeness and still unblemished on the day they had to appear on television?

I took no chances. Every day for a week before the show, I bought pears—firm, unblemished Bartlett pears. I stored some in a bowl on the counter —my usual ripening method—and some in paper bags, a system I had read about in a cooking magazine. I needed them to be ripe but not too ripe, and I wondered what I would do if they all turned to brown blobs of mush by the time I needed them or, equally disastrous, did not ripen at all in time for the show. I thought about an incident when Philip was an undergraduate and had to evaluate the effects that environmental changes had on Venus flytraps. He had waited too long to buy the plants and there was not enough time to assess the consequences of long exposure to sun and heat. To speed the process he put the plants in the oven, but he wound up killing them all. I rejected the oven as a ripening option.

The counter did the trick, and the night before the show, I stayed at the upper Park Avenue apartment of my college roommate, Jane Andrews, and kept my perfect, precious fruit in my room lest one of her two children mistake them for a late night snack.

Early the next morning, cradling my pears, I prepared to leave Jane's. After assuring me that I would have no trouble finding a taxi at that early hour, she gave me some sound advice.

"This is a valuable experience," she told me. "Notice everything and write it down." Unfortunately, I did not heed her counsel; after all, it was Jane who in college had suggested that we climb out the dorm window after curfew to go get a pizza. And in eighth grade it was she who'd suggested that we skip school and go see *Marjorie Morningstar.* On both occasions she'd assured me, "It will be just fine." It wasn't!

Out on the early-morning street, which was quiet for New York, I worried a taxi into appearing immediately and gave the driver the West Side address of the *Good Morning America* studios, across town. I checked the address several times during the ride to be sure I had it right. When he pulled up to the very ordinary-looking side door across the street from Café des Artistes, I checked it again. Yep. That was it.

I walked up the few steps and knocked. A uniformed guard immediately opened the door.

"I'm Nancy Barr," I said, and then, just to be sure he didn't think I was one of the groupies who regularly hangs around outside the studio hoping for autographs, I told him I was with Julia. But he didn't need more than my name. "They're expecting you," he said, stepping back to let me pass.

Walking me the few steps across the narrow foyer, he led me into a small room. "This is the greenroom. You can wait here and I'll call someone to escort you into the studio." In no time at all, a young woman, perhaps a production assistant or an intern, arrived and led me down a short corridor, through a heavy door, and into the dimly lit studio.

Stepping over the jumble of heavy cables on the floor and peering though the army of cameras standing quietly, I saw the *Good Morning America* living room set that I had seen so many times on television. The studio itself was immense, and the suite of comfortable living room furniture arranged in one corner of that enormous space seemed dollhouse-like with all the production equipment hovering around it.

"They're in the kitchen," my guide informed me, and led me all the way through the studio to a hallway behind it. There were two kitchens at the *Good Morning America* studios. What television viewers saw was a small on-set kitchen that sat on a slightly raised platform behind the set's living room. Off the short hallway behind the studio was a staff kitchen, so small it could have been mistaken for a glorified utility closet had it not been for the four-burner electric stove, refrigerator, single sink, and about two feet of counter space. We could work on the set's kitchen before the show started at seven and again after nine when it went off the air. All other times, we would have to crowd ourselves into the dimensionally challenged room.

My pears and I entered the room where our team was assembled and nibbling on an assortment of items selected from what I discovered was a large buffet set up behind the studio. Paul was reading the newspaper and working his way down a banana. He ate one every single morning, claiming it was good for the constitution. Since he lived into his nineties, I have no reason to doubt him. Liz was sitting on a stool by the phone, also reading a paper, and I wondered if she traveled with her own seating.

"Well, here she is!" Julia hooted enthusiastically, exhibiting that most wonderful way she had of making people feel so happy that they had arrived.

"I am," I said just as enthusiastically. I saw that there was already a large pile of pears on the counter, and I added my every-bit-as-good-looking crop to them, glad to have the perfect-pear mission accomplished.

"Thank you," was all Julia said, "they're perfect." It would be some months before I understood that even if my pears had failed to pass muster, that would not have meant that I did too. Julia saw cooking as an ongoing learning experience—if you fumbled here and there, if your pears were lousy, she'd definitely let you know, but it would not cost you your job or diminish your competence in her eyes as long as you were willing to learn.

"Now here, meet Sonya," Julia said, directing my attention to her producer, Sonya Selby-Wright. Sonya was in her mid-forties, British, and had been producing for *GMA* for four years, during which time she developed a particular talent for producing food spots. She was blond and fair-complexioned and appeared to be a delicate, fragile person, but, as I would soon discover, she was an effective, insightful producer who had the ability to draw out Julia's natural ability for making instruction entertaining. Julia had a very strong-willed personality, and over the years I would see that she always did her best work with someone who was strong enough to take charge. Russ Morash was a genius at producing and directing her, with no equal, but Sonya was very good.

Me and Sonya on the set of Good Morning America.

My first day of work at *Good Morning America* was my initiation to what it took to produce a television food spot. Sonya, Sara, and Julia introduced me to the smoke and mirrors of television cooking—the swap or swap-out, a crucial component of the short cooking segment. On a half-hour-long cooking show, depending on the recipe, it is possible to demonstrate a dish from start to finish. Rachael Ray does this on her Food Network program *30 Minute Meals*. But unless it is the simplest of recipes or a single technique, this is not possible in the two or three minutes that morning television allots the talent. Therefore, the swap. A typical breakdown for a rice pilaf, for example, would begin with the talent mincing onions, carrots, and celery for a mirepoix. She'd then put the vegetables into a saucepan with melted butter, stir them around a bit, and explain that they must be sautéed slowly until translucent. There wouldn't be enough time to show the transition from raw to translucent, so she switches from that pan to an identical one sitting on the stove with an already cooked mirepoix and pours in a cup of rice. After a few seconds of sautéing the rice, the talent pours in stock, adds seasonings, and covers the pan. The pilaf then needs fifteen minutes to cook, fifteen minutes morning television can't provide, so the talent swaps to an identical pan containing perfectly cooked rice that is also on the stove. She uncovers it, shows the audience what the pilaf looks like fully cooked, perhaps transfers it to a serving dish or a plate that holds meat and vegetables, and in Julia's case says, "Bon appétit." Some recipes require several swaps, and it takes careful planning to know where the switches are most effective so that viewers get a good, clear idea of what is happening and can confidently say to themselves, "I can do that!" or, better yet, "I *want* to do that!"

Julia was a master at breaking recipes down into the necessary steps to entice the audience into trying them. She hated what she called "dump TV"—a cooking spot in which the talent dumps the unidentifiable contents of several bowls into a pan and then proclaims it will look like the dazzling finished dish all nicely decorated with hibiscus blooms that sits on the counter. She wanted to show the steps, explain the techniques, produce sizzling sounds, and create some steam. Consequently, her demonstrations usually involved a number of swaps, which she carefully spelled out in her scripts.

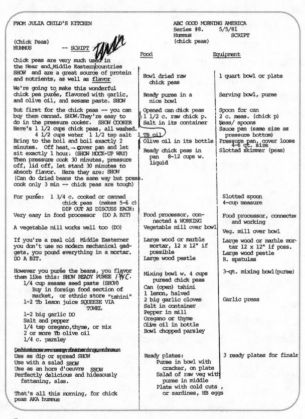

FROM JULIA CHILD'S KITCHEN		ABC GOOD MORNING AMERICA Series #8. 5/5/81 Hummus SCRIPT (chick peas)
(Chick Peas) HUMMUS -- SCRIPT	Food	Equipment
Chick peas are very much used in the Near and Middle Eastern countries SHOW and are a great source of protein and nutrients, as well as _flavor_	Bowl dried raw chick peas	1 quart bowl or plate
We're going to make this wonderful chick pea purée, flavored with garlic, and olive oil, and sesame paste. SHOW	Ready puree in a nice bowl	Serving bowl, puree
But first for the chick peas -- you can buy them canned. SHOW.They're easy to do in the pressure cooker. SHOW COOKER Here's 1 1/2 cups chick peas, all washed. 4 1/2 cups water 1 1/2 tsp salt Bring to the boil and boil exactly 2 minutes. Off heat, cover pan and let sit exactly 1 hour: (SHOW MOCK-UP WAY) Then pressure cook 30 minutes, pressure off, lid off, let stand 30 minutes to absorb flavor. Here they are: SHOW (Can do dried beans the same way but press. cook only 3 min -- chick peas are tough)	Opened can chick peas 1 1/2 c. raw chick p. Salt in its container 1 TB oil Olive oil in its bottle Ready chick peas in pan 8-12 cups w. liquid	Spoon for can 2 c. meas. (chick p) Meas/ spoons Sauce pan (same size as pressure bottom) Pressure pan, cover loose 4-6 qt. size Slotted skimmer (peas)
For purée: 1 3/4 c. cooked or canned chick peas (makes 5-6 c) DIP OUT AS DISCUSS EACH: Very easy in food processor (DO A BIT)		Slotted spoon 4-cup measure
	Food processor, connected & WORKING	Food processor, connected and working
A vegetable mill works well too (DO)	Vegetable mill over bowl	Veg. mill over bowl
If you're a real old Middle Easterner you don't use no modern mechanical gadgets, you pound everything in a mortar. DO A BIT.	Large wood or marble mortar, 12 x 12" if possible Large wood pestle	Large wood or marble mortar 12 x 12" if poss. Large wood pestle R. spatulas
However you purée the beans, you flavor them like this: SHOW READY PUREE 1¾C. 1/4 cup sesame seed paste (SHOW) Buy in foreign food section of market, or ethnic store "tahini" 1-2 Tb lemon juice SQUEEZE VIA TOWEL 1-2 big garlic DO Salt and pepper 1/4 tsp oregano,thyme, or mix 2 or more Tb olive oil 1/4 c. parsley	Mixing bowl w. 4 cups pureed chick peas Can (open) tahini 1 lemon, halved 2 big garlic cloves Salt in container Pepper in mill Oregano or thyme Olive oil in bottle Bowl chopped parsley	3-qt. mixing bowl (puree) Garlic press
Use as dip or spread SHOW Use with a salad SHOW Use as an hors d'oeuvre SHOW Perfectly delicious and hideously fattening, alas.	Ready plates: Puree in bowl with cracker, on plate Salad of raw veg with puree in middle Plate with cold cuts , or sardines, HB eggs	3 ready plates for finale
That's all this morning, for chick peas AKA hummus		

Sample of detailed Julia script for Good Morning America.

FROM JULIA CHILD'S KITCHEN		ABC GOOD MORNING AMERICA Series #8. 5/5/81 Cole Slaw Script
COLE SLAW -- SCRIPT	Food	Equipment
What's one of the best accompaniments to broiled fish, hamburgers, hot dogs and barbecued ribs???? Cole slaw -- homemade crisp wonderfully seasoned cole slau. Here's my favorite way of making it. SHOW READY, SPOON IT UP	Ready cole slaw	Bowl for ready cole slaw Salad spoon & fork
For 6 to 8 people Best, I think with hard-headed cabbage, about 1 1/2 lbs. CUT IN HALF THROUGH STEM CUT HALF IN HALF = QUARTERED CABBAGE CUT WEDGE OF STEM OUT OF QUARTER	1 hard headed cabbage	Big chopper knife Cutting board
Now want to shred it. SHRED WITH KNIFE SHRED WITH FRENCH CUTTER SHRED WITH BABY CUTTER	French Mandoline cutter Feemster baby cutter (both from Julia)	
We have about 4 cups shredded cabbage here	4 cups shredded cabbage	Very large mixing bowl (shredded cabbage)
Now for the additions 2/3 cup diced celery 1/2 cup grated carrot 1/4 cup diced scallions 1/2 cup diced gr. pepper 1 small apple, peeled, cored, diced 1 medium cucumber, seeded diced 4 Tb minced fresh parsley	2/3 c. diced celery 1/2 c. grated carrot 1/4 c. diced scallions 1/2 cup diced gr. pepper 1 grated apple (or diced) 1 diced cucumber 1/4 c. minced parsley Whole examples of each of the above	Bowls or cups for veg. at left Big bowl or plate for whole veg.
Make the dressing like this: 1/2 Tb Dijon type mustard mixed with 2 Tb vinegar 1 tsp salt 1 tsp sugar 1/4 tsp caraway or cumin seed 1/4 tsp ground bay (if have it) 1/4 tsp celery seeds MIX, AND TOSS WITH CABBAGE	Mustard (Dijon) Wine vinegar Salt & pepper Caraway seeds (or cumin) Celery seeds Ground bay (if available -- or do it in blender)	1 qt. bowl (mix dressing) Wire whip R. spatula
I like to let it sit, tossing several times for 30 min. Keep tasting for seasoning until just right. Flavor gets into cabbage.		
Can eat just like this -- fine for dieters		
OR, Drain out juices and toss with mixture of sour cream and mayonnaise 1/3 c. s. cream 1/2 c. mayonnaise DO	Mixture of 1/3 c. sour cream 1/2 c. mayo	Cover for bowl (to drain out juices) Bowl or cup for mayo/cream
SHOW READY (OR JUST MADE) COLE SLAW -- Serve	Plate with cole slaw and spare ribs; and one with ribs only	2 plates

Sample of detailed Julia script for Good Morning America.

Sonya introduced me to blocking, which is planning where the equipment and food will sit on the set when the spot was on air. I had no idea such a thing was necessary but soon realized that blocking is as vital a step in food television as it is in theater and movies, and one that Sonya worked on with the diligence of any Broadway stage director. Before the show went on the air, we brought all the food and equipment to the set and walked through what the talent would do with it. We decided where the items should be laid out, put them there, pretended to cook them, and then laid them out again until we decided where they best worked. Then we drew pictures of the layout and took everything away, transferring then to carefully marked trays. Nothing could stay on the kitchen set during the first two and a half hours of the show. In the brief time of a commercial break, we would have to return everything to the set, and we couldn't bring it there. Union rules demanded that stagehands move the items from the prep kitchen to the set, hence our need to mark the trays as to the position. The blocking and rehearsal meant that when the spot was on the air the talent would not have to move repeatedly back and forth, making it difficult for the cameras and audience to focus on the food. It thwarted any need to reach awkwardly over a hot stove or across the host's midsection to pick something up. It also ensured that tall items would not block shorter ones from the camera's view.

Every time I watched another morning show's production and saw a chef zigzagging around the set or I struggled to see an unidentifiable object hidden behind a tall bottle of wine or olive oil, I thought about how Sonya's diligent blocking never would have allowed it to happen.

From seven until shortly after eight-thirty, while the show was on the air, we crowded into the prep kitchen, working over and around each other under a sign on the wall that said, "Clean up after yourself. Your mother doesn't work here." When the kitchen monitor alerted us to the commercial break, several stagehands picked up the marked trays and carried them to the set. Sonya, Sara, and I followed right behind them and moved the items from the trays to their designated places, obsessively checking to be sure that everything was there and exactly where it should be. There is no wiggle room in live television: if something is missing, the talent has to wing it. Winging it was never a problem for Julia; she was truly unflappable. On one of our earliest shows, Julia sautéed veal cutlets and made a lovely pan sauce for them. Joan Lunden was by her side, and the spot ended—as always, unless it was oysters, which Joan wouldn't touch—with tasting the finished dish and making appropriate appreciative sounds. Julia put the veal on a plate, napped it with the sauce, and handed it to Joan. Joan looked down, turned to the right and then the left, and then glanced back at Julia. Somehow, in spite of all our careful blocking and obsessive planning, we had forgotten to put a fork and knife on the set. As I stood on the sidelines, wondering in horror if I could crawl under the camera's line of vision and pass utensils up to them, Julia picked up the large wooden spoon she had used to stir the sauce and told Joan, "This will work." Joan struggled a bit to cut the veal, managed to remove a small piece, and ate it with the spoon, which was considerably larger than her mouth. Neither she nor Julia behaved as though it were anything unusual.

Once the live shows were off the air, we began our prep for the next day's tapings. Stagehands set up several long tables in the studio and we went to work dirtying more dishes and preparing more food than I had ever seen in one place before. Taped segments involve so much more preparation than live ones, since no matter how wrong live segments may go, they will happen once only. With taped segments, the director or producer can ask for a retake, so we needed enough food for at least three backups—three for every swap. The same rice pilaf recipe that needed two cups of rice to make the swap in a live segment required eight cups to allow for backups in a taped segment.

And that's just one recipe. We were doing five or six. That meant a lot of food, a lot of equipment, nonstop work, and always more cafeteria trays and little glass bowls than we could seem to muster up. And if we weren't going out for lunch, Julia always insisted that we stop at noon and sit down together for a "nice, proper meal" with carefully prepared food—and wine! Using whatever food we didn't need for the tapings, we'd prepare handsome meals to which Julia often invited guests—cookbook authors and teachers, several family members, her editor, Judith Jones, and, to the delight of all of us, her dear friend and colleague Jim Beard. The work it took to ready the food for shows *and* prepare a sit-down lunch for eight to twelve people was a bit staggering. In fact, Julia often looked over the mounds of food and nonstop chopping, peeling, and mixing and pronounced with obvious glee, "We're a regular sweatshop." But those meals were what food was about for Julia. It was not a vehicle to stardom or something to fill the pages of a cookbook. It was about the joys of sitting down at a table, sharing, and communicating. The fame she achieved was firmly rooted in the passion she felt about dining well with good friends.

In a letter Julia wrote after my first day, she acknowledged the incredible amount of work Sarah and I had accomplished, writing, "I don't see how you two did it." She should have said "how *we* did it" because she was right in there cooking and sweating with us. In fact, everyone cooked, except for Liz, who was always at the ready if we needed her. Paul did whatever we needed of him, and even Sonya helped, although her knife skills were limited—and positively worrisome, since she was prone to gashing a finger or two. We also had two or three stagehands who willingly peeled onions, washed vegetables, trimmed herbs, and cleaned up after us. For the most part, it was the first time any of them had touched food they weren't about to eat. Later on, Julia hired another skilled assistant to help with the preparations and asked that the construction crew build a portable butcher-block work counter in the center of the room. The counter cramped our movements, but at least we had an ample work surface.

On my inaugural day of work with Julia, we left the studio at noon with the preparations for Tuesday's shows sitting on and tucked into every available space of the prep kitchen. Following Julia's instructions, we labeled everything with clearly marked Post-it notes: "DO NOT TOUCH!" The studio's night staff was notorious for hungry raids on the kitchen. My thoughts then turned to the upcoming De Gustibus demonstration and paella for three hundred in two electric woks; Julia's turned to lunch.

"Perhaps they can take us all across the street at Café des Artistes," she mused. Before we could say "roast duck and a good Chablis" we were savoring them. While the gregarious Hungarian restaurant owner, George Lang, stood by our table and talked about the current culinary scene in New York, I began inventing concerns about the De Gustibus demonstration. Had I given my friend Mary the right address? Would she remember the shrimp? Had buying the shrimp become a "pear thing" for her? Would we leave Café des Artistes in time to finish the prep for the demonstration? Julia, on the other hand, was savoring duck and trading gossip with George.

As it turned out, Mary was at the auditorium when we arrived around three o'clock, but when she handed me a plastic bag that held one small butcher-paper-wrapped package nestled in melting ice chips, I couldn't stop myself from asking, "Is that *all* the shrimp you bought?"

"That's all you asked for." God, I love people who don't worry.

The demonstration didn't exactly go off without a hitch, but the snag had nothing to do with the number of shrimp. The culprit was the sabayon dessert. While Julia attended to the twin woks, which were gurgling encouragingly with tomato saffron rice, sausage, chicken legs, and the shrimp, she asked me to make the sabayon. That meant standing in full view of the audience using a makeshift double boiler set up on a small hot plate, sitting atop a folding table and praying that I could whisk the egg yolks, sugar, and white wine into the sumptuous foam it should be and not into scrambled eggs. I had made sabayon countless times but never under such conditions. It was my first Julia-like experience in winging it.

Liz perched, Julia attending the wok, and me getting ready to make sabayon on the hot plate at the De Gustibus demonstration.

Marshaling a positive pose and determined attitude, I spun my whisk around the bowl nonstop, like a windmill in a hurricane. Lo and behold, the ingredients uncharacteristically emulsified immediately. *Wow,* I thought, silently crediting my rather decent tennis forehand for giving me the needed arm strength. Julia looked over.

"That's amazing," she said of my record-breaking eggs-to-sabayon conversion. She stepped closer and dipped her finger into the egg foam. "It's beautiful," she said just before putting her finger in her mouth. She tasted and then, with an exaggerated grimace, boomed, "Ugh. It's salt!" In setting up for the demonstration, we had emptied all the ingredients from their original containers into several identical bowls, and I had obviously mistaken the salt for the sugar. The audience roared, and Julia gave me a conspiratorial wink as though I had staged the mistake. "You'll have to make another—this

70 Seaview, Montecito Shores, Santa Barbara CA 93108

NANCY:

I finally found out about the "strange sweet taste" in the
fish mousse -- there was sugar in the salt container!
Seems to me we have run into that kind of thing before,
but in reverse order!

Love to all —

Julia

805-969-3662

*After my fiasco at De Gustibus, there was some comfort in knowing
that even Julia could make the same mistake.*

time with sugar," she teasingly instructed. Never again, in all the
demonstrations I did with her, did I ever put similar ingredients in
unmarked bowls. One salt-for-sugar mistake is sufficient to the wise.

In the end, my second sabayon was as it should be. Let me
revise that: there actually was no end. When the demonstration was
over, the crowd swarmed the set to receive mouthfuls of paella, tea-
spoons of sabayon, autographs, and several words with Julia. It was at
least ten o'clock by the time she gave her final autograph and the last
vestiges of the audience left the auditorium. Then the party began.
The De Gustibus owners produced several bottles of chilled champagne, and suddenly we were toasting the success of the night with
several glasses of bubbly appreciation.

I distinctly recall that at the time my thoughts were running
more along the lines of pillow and bed than of champagne. But the

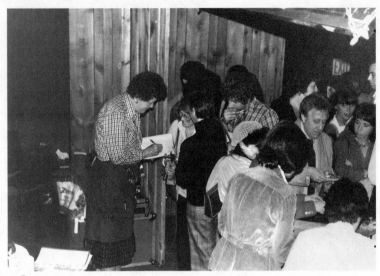

Signing books and tasting paella at De Gustibus.

day had gone well, we were in good shape for the next morning, and Julia had arranged for me to have my own room that night near hers at the Dorset Hotel, so I didn't have to worry about getting across town on my own at that late hour. Voilà! I indulged in the champagne, gratified that I would soon be lost in a sleep devoid of nightmares about rotten pears. I had made it through my first Julia Child workday, and I was gratified. Julia was hungry.

"Where should we go for dinner?" she asked without so much as a fleeting glance at her watch, which would have told her it was already well after ten-thirty at night.

Dinner? Who's thinking dinner? I almost said aloud. I didn't need food; I needed rewinding.

Liz, who of course knew this was coming, was already on the phone seeking a restaurant that was still serving dinner and was near our hotel. Even Paul, ten years older than Julia and so much frailer than any of us, failed to suggest that perhaps since we had to be at the studio the next morning at five-thirty, it might be a good idea to go directly to bed.

"Doesn't Julia ever get tired?" I asked Liz.

A look of horror seized her face and she came close to slipping off her stool. "We *never* say the T-word," she warned.

The restaurant was Mercurio's, just around the corner from our hotel. It was Italian, unpretentious, and attentive without being fawning. I sat next to Paul and for the first time I had an opportunity to talk with him at some length. He fascinated me with stories of an urbane life. Of moving with his identical twin brother Charlie and his mother to Paris when he was three years old, of playing the violin and his mother singing in Parisian cafés. Of art and his own painting. Bits and pieces of his work in the diplomatic corps. He both charmed and fascinated me.

At the end of what was a copious meal, I ordered a decaffeinated espresso and Julia ordered coffee, raising her finger to emphasize that she wanted "real coffee." I felt like a wimp, having ordered decaf. The cups arrived with a plate of amaretti, and since I was in a somewhat relaxed mood thanks to the champagne and the wine at dinner, I showed Julia how to light the thin paper cookie wrappers so they floated in wisps of quickly fading color toward the ceiling. She had never seen it before, and her first several attempts at amaretti-paper arson came close to burning the tablecloth before she got the hang of it and began merrily to share her new trick with the waitstaff and several patrons.

"How do you know how to do that?" she asked me.

"I don't know. I guess it's an Italian thing."

"You're Italian?"

"Half Italian, half Irish. My maiden name is Verde."

"Verrr-de," she repeated, pronouncing it operatically, trilling the *r* in the Italian way. She had studied Italian in college and could still demand a bottle of wine *subito* while simultaneously thumping the table with her fist. "Do you teach Italian cooking classes at your school?" she asked.

My culinary training had included a smattering of Italian, but classic French cuisine was what intrigued me. Of course, I had grown up on Italian food, but it was Italian American and in my mind not worthy of study. How foolish of me!

"A few Italian classes," I responded.

"Well, you should. You have to meet Marcella Hazan. You should go to her class in Italy. I'll call her tomorrow. And you should use your full name, Nancy Verde Barr, so everyone will know you know what you're doing."

"Do you speak Italian?" Paul, who was multilingual, asked me.

"Only dialect, and most of it not suitable for company," I admitted.

A very happy me in class with Marcella Hazan in Bologna.

> HOTEL
> MILANO
> EXCELSIOR
>
> Bologna 12 Maggio 1981
>
> Cari Amici,
>
> Come state? Sono molto bene. Bologna e bellissimo!
> Io mangio troppo!! I'm afraid that I haven't gotten
> much further than that with my Italian, Paul.
> No loose tongue here.
>
> Regardless, we are having a wonderful time. I
> haven't set fire to any Italian tables — perhaps
> that should be my parting gesture.
>
> The course is very well planned. There is
> a good mixture of time in the classroom and
> trips to good restaurants, vineyards, Parmesan
> cheese factory and the like. One of our most
> enjoyable evenings was a "festa in campagna."
> We had a country dinner at a farmhouse, Il
> Gaidello near Modena. The meal was rustic
> and flavorful — wines (local, Lambrusco, a little
> too rustic) — the farmhouse simply bursting with
> charm. Marcella had asked three of her friends
> to play music for us and that they did —
> with mandolin, mandola and a strange guitar.
> The farmhouse is owned by friends of Marcella and
> they produce jams and relishes which Marcella hopes
> to export to New York. We sampled the relishes and
> the tomatoes and they were very good.

Part of one of the two enthusiastic, long letters I wrote to Paul and Julia from Bologna after my classes with Marcella. Both contained Italian for Paul, and this one had an affirmation for Julia that I hadn't set fire to any tables in Italy.

"Well, I'll teach you some," he said.

That night I began my first Italian-language lesson and professionally became Nancy Verde Barr. The next day, as promised, Julia called Marcella. A month later, with the smattering of the Italian Paul taught me, I was off to Bologna to take the first of many classes with Marcella and her husband, Victor, who expanded my knowledge and love of Italian food to the extent that it became the area of my culinary concentration. The first cookbook I published, *We Called It Macaroni*, was on Italian American food.

I don't remember what time we left the cozy dining room at Mercurio's and walked around the corner to our hotel, but I do remember it was after lots of food and wine, and long after Julia had exhausted the restaurant's supply of amaretti wrappers. I was not used to consuming that much alcohol in one night (in college I'd

70 Seaview, Montecito Shores, Santa Barbara CA 93108   June 15th

Dear Nancy:
        We are finaly quite well settled, with rented furniture until
our own slowly arrives (which will not be completed before we leave),
but the kitchen is pretty well set, and we can eat, sleep, and entertain
in a most simple way. And we are so happy in our new abode - - I am at
this moment overlooking a soft green meadow with the waves lapping
the other end of it, only 4-5 stones' throw away. We can just walk
out onto the beach at anytime, stroll there after dinner, and the
breezes play through our apartment which is light and airy. We feel very
lucky indeed.
        Your 2 letters did arrive, and were gobbled up with great enjoyment.
I was so very happy that you had a really fruitful time with the Hazans, and
that you responded to them. (I'm sure all our briefing did some good, because
you knew what to expect.)   You are just the right sort of person for
that course, and it certainly is not for fluffies! I'm delighted, and
I know others will be too, because there has been severe criticism of
Marcella's manner of doing things from some quarters. Mary O'Brien, from
Andover, who also worked with us on the PBS shows, felt just as you did.
Good! And thank you so much for giving me all the details with such loving
care.

Part of Julia's letter to me in which she acknowledges receipt of my letters from Italy and tells me why she's glad I went.

TROIS GOURMANDES
PRODUCTIONS, INC.
FROM
103 IRVING STREET
CAMBRIDGE, MA. 02138   October 15, 1981

TO   NANCY BARR   19

ADDRESS   109 William St., Providence RI 02906   ORDER NO.

CITY   STATE   TERMS

	Taping of ABC GMA series #13,				
	Oct. 4,5,6,7.				
	Consultant's fee for 3 days	300.00			
	Tavel expenses per slip submitted	49.00			
	Total herewith				349.00
	Addendum: 1 day's subsistance allowance	30.00			
	Ammended total				379.00

Julia Child

#106

Julia's payment statement to me for early GMA work. I'm not sure why I received a sustenance allowance because someone fed us every meal.

acquired the nickname "Thimble Belly"). I floated, much like the amaretti papers, back to the hotel and fell into bed.

At five-fifteen the next morning, I was no longer floating. As I approached our waiting car, I felt more like the ashes of the previous night's burned-out amaretti wrappers.

Julia, already seated in the back of the car, looked refreshed and eager to get on with the day. Through the fog in my head, I had impressions of having acted somewhat less than professionally the night before, and I wondered if I needed to apologize for anything. Just in case, I said, "I think maybe I had too much to drink last night. I feel as though I was dancing on tables."

She put her hand on my knee and smiled. "You were. But you were very good." I'm pretty sure that was the exact moment that I stopped seeing Julia Child the culinary idol and saw the person—and I really liked her.

Chapter

3

What is the recipe for successful achievement? To my mind there are just four essential ingredients: Choose a career you love, give it the best there is in you, seize your opportunities, and be a member of the team.

—Benjamin F. Fairless, industrialist

When I began to work for Julia, her appearances on *Good Morning America* occupied but a few dates of a full schedule that was at most mind-boggling and at the least . . . well, mind-boggling. Demonstrations, media appearances, and book signings all over the country kept her on the move at a relentless pace, and her time at home was just as busy. In addition to writing a monthly column, with recipes, for *McCall's* magazine, she planned and outlined her programs for live demonstrations and TV shows. Although she often recycled recipes for her demonstrations, tweaking them to fit the time and situation, she liked to develop new ones for print and for TV. Creating and testing recipes takes time. Some ideas that taste good in one's head fail to meet one's expectations when completed—perhaps the derivation of

"The proof is in the pudding." Even when the pudding is good, the recipe may need adjustments to make it perfect—a little more sugar, less flour, longer cooking, a different pan. That means retesting, and if that doesn't go just right, testing again, and sometimes again. Once Julia was satisfied that the recipes were exactly as she wanted them, she then spent hours typing them in her impeccably clear and detailed Julia style, wrote headnotes for *McCall's*, and broke down the television and demonstration recipes into scripts and lists of required food and equipment. So when she wasn't on the road, she was usually in her office writing, or up to her apron strings in groceries in her kitchen—one of her kitchens, that is, since she divided her time between her homes in Cambridge, Santa Barbara, and France. In her "free time" she attended national culinary conferences and participated in a slew of professional events at local restaurants and cooking schools.

I don't think the term had entered our vernacular back then, but Julia could have invented it: *multitasking*. And she could have taught classes in how to do it. She had the organizational skills necessary to manage her complex and demanding workload. Moreover, she had the energy, she relished being busy, and, most important, she loved what she was doing. I've no doubt that she could have whisked her way through all that work by herself, but as she said, "cooking together is such fun," so she employed a number of people to share in her good time. Depending on the task, one or a number of assistants joined her on the road or cooked with her in her spacious, slightly funky lime-green Massachusetts kitchen, her smaller but efficient California space, or her charming, quintessentially Provençal *cuisine*.

Even book signings required some assistance, since the crowds were usually too large for bookstore personnel to handle alone. A personal assistant at her side helped move the lines along by passing her the books already opened to the page she would sign. This seemingly minor expediency saved time and allowed Julia to concentrate on her fans until every person had a signature and a word with her, regardless of the fact that the lines inevitably wound out the door and around the block and the signings took hours. Someone recorded the bodies at one signing as fourteen hundred, and Julia stayed until the last smiling fan departed with a book inscribed, "Bon appétit! Julia Child." Of course, authors are expected to stay, but we did all gasp at stories of some who just up and left after a certain amount of time. Julia cared far too much for her audiences to allow them to shuffle slowly through a long line only to be left hanging with unsigned books. Besides, Julia was generally interested in people and loved hearing their stories. Initially I thought she engaged fans in conversation just for the show, but then sometime later in the day, or the week, she'd say something like, "Isn't it remarkable that the woman in the wheelchair went back to college with ten children at home and an infirm father to take care of?" Gosh! I hadn't picked up on that. But as in every crowd, some people just wore out their welcome, and when they lingered a bit too long in front of her, she artfully used her assistant to help graciously shuffle them away from the table. "That's fascinating," she would say to the fan. "Here, now tell [designated assistant] all about that," thereby forcing the lingerer to step out of line and redirect attention to the assistant.

It was at book signings and culinary gatherings that I realized one of Liz Bishop's most valuable assets as an assistant—running interference. Since Julia believed that it was "part of the job" to speak to each fan who approached her, it was no easy task to get her from one end of a crowded room to the other. Some of those who approached her were friends, and Julia wanted to ask them about their families, or how their books, schools, or new shows were going. Others were strangers, but Julia felt no less need to give them her attention. Talking to everyone was impossible on those occasions when she was on a tight schedule, and that's where Liz came in. The two of them would perfectly orchestrate their moves through a crowd, with Julia smiling but

A dog shows up to meet Julia at a book signing.

not making eye contact with approaching fans and Liz close at her side, tersely reciting a litany of efficient brush-offs: "We are in a hurry. I have to get her to an appointment. We don't have time. Please let us pass." They did it so well.

Julia essentially divided her assistants into East Coast and West Coast teams, and for all the years I worked with her, she varied and alternated the team players and their positions. No one ever participated in every Julia event. Sometimes a team member might fly to the working coast, but, being the practical, frugal person she was, she usually employed the person or people geographically closest to the job. In a letter she wrote to me from California a few months after I started at *GMA*, she described classes she had taught at Mondavi Vineyards and referred to Rosemary Manell as "my West Coast Liz." Rosie was more demure than Liz but, at six feet tall, probably more effective at blocking tactics. Since the *GMA* studios were in New York, I was part of the East Coast team. From April through June of 1981, when she suspended her taping until fall, that once-a-month gig and the one demonstration at De Gustibus were the only work I did with her—the only direct involvement I had in the industry that was Julia Child Productions.

Then, early that summer, Sara was offered a chef's position at the New York restaurant La Tulipe to start the following October. Julia was delighted for her, but she also wondered if Sara would be able to meet the demands of both late-night restaurant and early morning television work, so she promoted me to executive chef and gave me more responsibility for the shows. As it turned out, Sara's restaurant schedule and her energetic personality allowed her to continue working with us at *GMA* until 1984, when she left La Tulipe to work in *Gourmet* magazine's test kitchens. When, in 1987, she became the executive chef for *Gourmet*'s dining room, she once again had the flexibility to return to *GMA*. She eventually became the show's regular food editor, a position she still holds today.

"Executive chef" is the title Julia chose, and I have always felt a bit squirmy about using it. Traditionally "chef" refers to someone who works in a professional kitchen or restaurant, and the executive chef is the one in charge. Unlike Sara, I had trained not for restaurant work but for teaching, much as Julia herself had, and I never call myself a chef, nor did Julia. Regardless of the title of her *The French Chef* series, Julia considered and called herself a "cook" and often a "home cook." So I was surprised she used that title for us. Sara explained that years before, while they were working on the PBS television series *Julia Child & More Company*, there was a bit of a muddle on the set because no one knew exactly who was responsible for what. Julia thought of her assistants as a team of equals, all Indians and no chiefs, and originally did not create a hierarchy of positions.

Sara said it caused confusion, so Julia, master of organization, decided to assign a title to everyone. She named her body of assistants "Julia Child associates" and, most likely for want of a more explanatory term, bestowed the title "executive chef" on the person who would tell everyone else what cooking needed to be done and be responsible for seeing that it was. Julia was pleased with the order the titles gave. Liz was officially "executive associate," and when Rosemary Manell worked as the food stylist and not the "West Coast Liz," she was the "official food designer." An artist with her own quirky sensibilities, Rosie disliked the more common term "food stylist," so she suggested "food designer"; Julia added the "official."

After she promoted me to executive chef, my involvement with her work increased. We spoke and wrote more often about what recipes she would do for her television shows. In a letter she wrote me that summer, she said, "Recipes, script, etc for the Gd. Morning are on their way to you via Judy Avrett. Please give them a harsh look through, and any critiques, corrections, suggestions, most welcome. I won't pick new shows, but am happy to change details, like spinach topping for the oysters Rockef, giant cookies, etc. etc. (No spinach here, which is strange.)" Me, give a harsh critique of Julia Child's recipes? Seemed to me that she'd done pretty well for herself so far without benefit of my comments. I did thoroughly scrutinize the equipment and food lists; seldom was anything missing, but I did not alter her recipe choices even when some of her ideas sounded a bit weird, such as her suggestion in a later letter that we substitute sauerkraut for the spinach on the oysters. I responded more with curiosity than with criticism: "You will have to show me oysters and sauerkraut—never experienced that!" (Since we never did make them, I'm guessing that Julia tried and discarded the suggestion on her own.)

When Julia asked specifically for suggestions, I gave them. Let me amend that. I zealously gave them. I recently had a good laugh when I discovered copies of my letters to Julia among her papers at the Schlesinger Library in Cambridge. In offering my suggestions, I was, as Liz Bishop would say, like the man who knew how to spell *banana* but didn't know when to stop. In response to her program list that began with "I have thought of the following eleven for Gd. Morning (but haven't done anything more than think, as follows: 1) Lentils 2) Sausage cakes 3) Meat Loaf (Do you have any great ideas?? I like beef and sausage, and think it useful for leftover meat)" and ended with "But I don't have any desserts here—any ideas?? ... would welcome the comments from our Exec. Chef!" I sent back three handwritten pages that contained every thought I had ever entertained about the subjects: "I adore lentils—didn't Esau sell Jacob his birthright for a bowl of lentil soup? My grandmother used to make the most wonderful *pasta e fagioli* soup with lentils, macaroni, sausage, tomatoes, onions—heavenly. Cold lentil salad is good—and of course just lentils hot with butter, walnuts or pine nuts." I droned on about sausage cakes and meat loaf, even suggested having *GMA* purchase a meat grinder, and then I went on to desserts. "You have never made a *crème anglais* on *GMA* ... you could serve it over poached fruit or macerated orange slices—or stabilize it for something like those wonderful individual size *tarte St. Tropez* . . . or a trifle with bananas and nuts." I wasn't finished. I still had Indian pudding, the great American brownie, applesauce, flummery, and a fruit fool to suggest. Had I been Julia reading my rambling list of suggestions, I would have thought the fool particularly appropriate. In spite of my babbling suggestions, Julia never stopped asking me to "send them along."

Team is a real feel-good word—team effort, team spirit, team goals. Biographies can better discern at what point in her life Julia developed an appreciation for and keen understanding of what constituted a team. But she did, and in every sense of the word, she thought of herself and her associates as one team. She was always right there in the thick of things, working along with us. We never questioned that she was in charge, but she made it clear that she valued and trusted our opinions (babbling suggestions and all) by involving us in all aspects of the work we did together. She even created a team motto—"EOT" (eye on target)—and she set very high standards for that target and gave us very large responsibilities in seeing that it was met. But she never sent us onto the field alone; she was always in the game with us.

As soon as she promoted me to head of the kitchen team, she assigned me my first major task. We needed an additional kitchen associate for the fall, and she asked me to choose one. "Whomever you would like to work with would be fine with me—it's you who will be in command, anyway, and must have someone you like and trust there," she wrote me from France that summer. I began to search but was having difficulty finding someone with the necessary experience who had the job flexibility to take two days off every month. Plenty of friends who were gourmet cooks offered their services, but we needed a professional, and in 1980, there was not the large number of trained professionals in Rhode Island that there is today. My contacts in New York and Boston were few. Just as I was beginning to feel that I might not be able to accomplish the task, Julia called me.

"I've asked someone named Susy Davidson to call you. She studied with Anne Willan at La Varenne and worked with Simca [Simone Beck]. Simca's very fond of her and she may be just who we are looking for. Talk to her and see what you think." Perhaps it's a subtle bit of leadership, but it did not go unnoticed to me. Julia did not relieve me of my responsibility to find a new associate because I hadn't accomplished what needed to be done; she left it in my hands while giving me the assistance I needed.

I liked Susy immediately when she called, and could tell that she was more than qualified to be a JC associate. I relayed my opinion to Julia, and we agreed to give Susy a trial run. That fall when Susy joined us, I quickly saw that she was truly qualified for the job. Moreover, the minute she walked into the prep kitchen, I was immediately aware of just how eager she was to do her job well—and how resourceful she was. On the mornings that Julia was on live, we were at the studio no later than 5:30 A.M., so there was no time to eat at the hotel beforehand. Not a problem. There was always a huge buffet waiting for us; Paul could have his banana and Julia usually some melon and maybe an English muffin, "well toasted, please." I had relayed this information to Susy during our phone conversation, and at five-thirty that morning, into the kitchen walked this tall, striking twenty-nine-year-old brunette carrying an artfully arranged platter of neatly sliced bananas, melon sections with the rind carefully cut away, and a thoughtful assortment of other fruit. Whether or not there were decorative garnishes, I don't recall; I only know it was a presentation decidedly more attractive than the simple whole banana and half melon I regularly served Paul and Julia. When had she had time? How had she found the buffet and the utensils?

"Good morning, America!" she exclaimed, lighting up the tiny kitchen with her smile. Julia had invited her to join us "on trial," and Susy came prepared to do the best job possible so that we would keep her. And she was a keeper. She became a cherished friend to Julia and still is to me today; I always think of her as Julia wrote and spoke of her: "that darling Susy."

Susy was young, effervescent, and ready to gobble up, in the dearest way, all that New York had to offer. A native of Portland, Oregon, and just back from Paris, she seemed a bit like Audrey Hepburn's Sabrina—a sweet, generous girl who had been broadly painted but not tainted with Parisian sophistication. I suspect that Susy's joie de vivre reminded Julia of herself so many years before when she had discovered the joys of Paris.

Julia queried Susy about every detail of what was going on in the Parisian food world, and Susy filled her in on who was who and what was what in culinary France. Julia would recall—as she said, with "trembling nostalgia"—her early days in Paris, when she first sampled the evocative flavors of French cuisine that had so overwhelmed her appetites. She spoke with wistful reverie of the lessons she had learned under the tutelage of chef Max Bugnard at the Paris Cordon Bleu. I didn't have much to contribute during those conversations since my one trip to France had occurred prior to my epiphanies with chicken Kiev and deep-fried parsley and I had spent more time drooling over haute couture than haute cuisine. But I was a greedy listener, and when I returned to Paris a few years later, the passion of their conversations inspired my trip. I ate in their suggested restaurants and purchased so much cookware at E. Dehillerin and foodstuffs at Fauchon that my customs inspection back in the United States was interminable.

Talking about Paris seemed to stimulate Julia's memories of the useful French *trucs* or tricks that Bugnard had shown her, and she decided she should show more of them on the show. Throughout her television and teaching career, everything Julia cooked followed the principles of classic French techniques according to Escoffier. Legendary among chefs and gourmets, George Auguste Escoffier simplified, modernized, and wrote down the lessons of haute cuisine that Antoine Carême had pioneered before him. Escoffier's 1903 *Le Guide Culinaire* became and remains every serious culinary student's definitive text on how to cook. Julia's way to cook always adhered to the Escoffier method, but in the years following her original shows and initial books, she expanded her recipe repertoire to show that those techniques could and should be applied to "good, plain old cooking," whether it was American fare, Mexican cuisine, or that of Timbuktu. She made meat loaf, hash, guacamole, and hummus with the same Gallic care with which she made the staples of classic French cuisine.

When she decided to demonstrate some of the useful lessons from Chef Bugnard, she chose a French *truc* of how to make end-of-the-season, slightly over-the-hill garden peas taste sweeter by cooking them with a few of their pods and some shredded lettuce, and I ran into my first snafu as executive chef.

It was a taped segment, and that meant we needed three back-ups for every stage of the recipe Julia would demonstrate. The script called for her to begin by shelling a few peas and adding those to a pan of peas sitting on the stove. So we needed four times enough peas in their pods for her to shell, four times enough shelled peas to fill the pan on the stove, and one set of cooked peas to put on a serving plate. The problem was that it really was the end of the season, so we could find only enough peas in the market for one backup for every stage instead of our normal three. But it was a simple spot—what could go wrong? Scary words in television.

Paul Child offered to shell the peas and sat on a stool quietly removing the pods and then dividing the peas into the two setups. At one point, I heard him say, "Forgive me, but I'm peeing on the floor."

Excuse me? Had I heard right? I turned and immediately saw the twinkle in his eyes. He was referring to the occasional wayward pea that slipped from its pod onto the floor. He was pea-ing, not pee-ing, and I thought it was a terribly funny thing to say, but Julia, who usually gave such comments her great hoot of a laugh, merely smiled, and I realized it was probably a quip they had shared many times while shelling peas. I also realized that we needed those peas that were scattering hither and yon, and I crawled around on my hands and knees to capture them as they rolled under stools and nested next to cable wires. Such is the lot of an executive chef.

With the cameras rolling, Julia shelled a few peas, put them in a pan with the ones we had placed there, added pea pods and a healthy handful of finely shredded lettuce, and then something—I don't recall what—went wrong. The director yelled, "Cut," and asked that she start again. Starting again meant using the last of the pea crop. If something went wrong with the next take, we had no backup, and directors and producers don't want to hear that the segment has to be scrapped because someone (me) has run out of peas. Furthermore, when the director tells the talent to start again, he or she means immediately. Time is money in network television.

Stagehands rushed our one and only backup to the set and then raced the "used" peas to the prep kitchen, where I tossed them out onto a cookie sheet. As Julia began her second take, we began frantically and painstakingly to pick pea pods and tiny shreds of lettuce out of the peas that she had started to cook in the first take. Again, after making it through the addition of lettuce and pods to the second pan of peas, something went wrong, and we whisked *those* peas back to the kitchen for lettuce removal. That oh-so-simple spot took five takes, and today I have a Pavlovian reaction to cooking old peas: I add the lettuce and pods to the peas and then immediately pick them out.

"Hooray! We did it," Julia said, enthusiastically cheering her team for hitting the target in spite of the chaos. It was, of course, what she expected her team to do, and no more than she herself always did. What felt so good about her response to overcoming what could have been a failure was the way she acknowledged that it was a team effort. Other than having us jump on the field in a large pig pile, she couldn't have done more than exclaim, "We did it!"

No segment we did for *Good Morning America* gave us more trouble or more satisfaction than the one on the complex making of a Tarte Tatin. The famous upside-down apple dessert, known classically as *tarte des demoiselles Tatin* in honor of its creators, the spinster Tatin sisters, is a lovely dessert with a good story. Supposedly, the two Loire River restaurateurs forgot to put the pastry in the bottom of the pan before layering the apples in it, so they put it on top instead and reversed the dessert after it was baked. Another version of the story says the sisters dropped the tart after it was baked and it landed upside down—a more amusing story but doubtful.

Making the dessert calls for a number of steps—swaps in our case—and, because it was a taped segment, three backups for each swap. The first step is to melt sugar and butter in a cast-iron skillet until it turns to a bubbly brown caramel. The next step is to arrange several layers of sliced apples in a decorative pattern of concentric circles over the caramel, then cook and baste them with the caramel until the apples are soft and the juices are thick and syrupy. After a brief cooling period, on goes a circle of pie dough and the tart is baked until the crust is golden and the caramel rich and thick. Then the drama: turn the pan upside down on a large plate and lift it away to reveal buttery, caramelized apples sitting atop the crisp pastry crust.

Tarte Tatin is not a difficult recipe to prepare in one's own kitchen, but showing all the steps in three and a half minutes was a challenge. Our calculations told us we needed ten cast-iron pans and a seeming orchard of apples.

Early Monday morning, we all got to work on the setup for the Tuesday taping. We peeled and cut apples until our fingers ached, then sprinkled them with sugar and lemon juice so they wouldn't turn brown overnight. Then we set up the pans: a pan for Julia to show the ready caramel and how to start layering the apples (only one backup since we would have time to wash out the pan and pour in caramel if things went wrong); a pan with all the apple layers in place and cooking on the stove to show the texture of the cooked apples and perfect thickness of the caramel (three backups); a ready-cooked tart for Julia to unmold (definitely three backups in case she dropped it).

(This is probably a good place for an aside on Julia dropping things. The truth is, she never did drop all the things people claimed they saw her drop on her shows. I've heard viewers describe in great detail how ducks, chickens, and éclairs slipped from her grasp and landed on the floor at her feet when it really was only the potato pancake that flipped from her pan to the stove. Anything else that landed on the floor she threw there on purpose.)

We were all proud of ourselves when we arrived at the studio the next morning and examined our flotilla of pans and apples all perfectly at the ready for their audience presentation. They looked great. It would be a fabulous spot—just not that day. As we began to assign the pans to trays, Sonya came into the kitchen with the news that assassins had killed Anwar Sadat, the president of Egypt, in broad daylight and in front of crowds of people. The entire *GMA* studio and all its staff were to be turned over to the news division of ABC immediately, and we couldn't tape.

We were all stunned at the news. And then we were in awe as a sort of controlled, practiced chaos erupted around us and several producers jumped into action to change their focus from a morning variety show to world-altering news. They hung on every phone desperately trying to contact authorities on Mideast affairs who could get to the studio as quickly as possible. ABC news anchors rushed into the studio to replace the *GMA* hosts.

Julia found the news as shocking and the studio changeover as fascinating as we all did, but being the exceedingly practical person she was, she felt that such events did not mean that everything else should stop—and at that moment, everything else to her was the makings of a Tarte Tatin sitting in the ten pans around us. "Well, see if we can do it tomorrow," Julia told Sonya. "Otherwise it's an awful lot of work gone to waste."

After several discouraging minutes of staring at all those expectant apples, we were relieved when Sonya returned with the news that we could return the next day and tape the spot. We remained at the studio long enough to tuck the pans and apples back into safe places.

The chaos we faced the next day was far from controlled and in no way practiced. The long wait in new cast-iron pans had turned all the apples a hideously unappetizing shade of gray. They were unusable. Racing against time, we sent out for apples—any apples—and repeated the entire setup, trying not to believe that the segment was doomed—and it wasn't. We filled all the pans for swaps and backups in time for the show, and Julia whizzed through the spot in one take. When the Tarte Tatin recipe appeared in her book *The Way to Cook,* Julia described the taping: "Whether many of our viewers were able to follow the final intricate proceedings, I don't know—but we did it all in one take, in $3^1/_2$ minutes, and we felt triumphant." Our team effort did manage the chaos and we shared in the triumph, but ultimately it was her game plan that made it work. She was the one who broke a multistep recipe into stages that fit into three and a half minutes. We just kept our eyes on the target she set, and when we thought the game was lost, she stepped in to carry the ball.

After the episodes with the peas and Tarte Tatin, Susy and I felt pretty savvy and confident about television food preparation. After all, we had mastered swaps and backups and even conquered the occasional snafu. But no one told us about the beauty shot.

A beauty shot is a close-up of a finished dish—usually without the talent—and it's used to entice audiences to stay tuned. A set designer arranges the food on the set along with decorative accompaniments such as napkins, appropriate utensils, perhaps flowers—anything that makes it look appealing. During the first and or second hours of the show, the dish appears on the television screen while the host tells viewers to "stay tuned because Julia Child will be here to show you how to make this delicious dish." If the dish is part of a live segment, it has to be cooked and shot early in the morning, before the show; otherwise, the cameras wait until after the show has been taped. They don't take beauty shots for every recipe, and Susy and I had not heard of it. What we did hear every time we finished taping was the delicate stampede of stagehands and camera operators into the kitchen to get a sample of Julia Child's cooking, and we gladly laid the remains of the day out on large platters so that everyone could have a taste.

We were introduced to the beauty shot on the day Julia taped a segment on how to roast a turkey. When the spot was over, the usual suspects filtered into our prep kitchen to pull bits and pieces from the juicy bird. They had made it through one entire side when the word came into the kitchen that the director wanted a beauty shot.

"What's that?" Susy asked.

"I have no idea," I said, and didn't until Sonya hurried in and told us to bring the turkey to the set to have its picture taken. Oh, my God! Julia had roasted a whole turkey, and we only had half a bird left.

It was Liz who saved the day. She must have faced this before, because she propped the turkey up with a small can and grabbed a bunch of parsley to cover the devoured side. The set designer finished the camouflage with tools from his bag of tricks. Essentially, those tools are spray bottles of water and/or oil to make food glisten, colorful napkins, and objets d'art to direct the eye to a specific part of the picture. I worked with Liz for many years after that, and always when I looked in panic at some dish that didn't seem quite as it should be, whether it was soup or custard or cake, Liz and Julia would tell me to "cover it with parsley."

With so much to absorb about setups and swaps and deflection of problems for short food segments, I spent most of my early months on the job either prepping in the small kitchen, checking and rechecking setups and backups, or running back and forth between the kitchen and the set. I rarely saw Julia's performance except for snippets on the prep kitchen monitor. It was only weeks later, on my home television, that I would see the entire segment from start to finish. But once our team had mastered the game of swaps, backups, and the ominous beauty shot, we found the time to remain in the studio and watch Julia in action in front of the camera. That was when the real show began, and what a thrill it was to be in the live audience!

Those Julia-shows-within-the-shows explained so much of why she was a television success. She had such a remarkably keen sense of timing. Three and a half minutes is not a lot of time, and even though Julia carefully planned beforehand what steps she needed to demonstrate the recipe from start to finish, sometimes something unpredicted ate into that valuable time. They were usually simple things such as a stove not being hot enough to begin a sauté, an unexpected question from a co-host, or searching for a dish or utensil that was misplaced. A floor manager stood near the cameras signaling how much time was left, and Julia paid close attention. She knew what she had to squeeze into the remaining time to make the segment work, so she adjusted her actions to fit. She did it so smoothly that the finished segment never appeared truncated. Because we had the scripts in front of us, we knew what she had skipped or altered; audiences never would.

Watching her in action, we saw that Julia was truly and utterly unflappable. No matter what complications preceded a segment or what disaster might befall it while the cameras rolled, she flowed with it and made it work. Moreover, she was able to pull energy out of some secret source even as those around her dissolved into used dishrags.

One morning, after arriving at the studio at five-thirty, doing a live show at eight forty-five, and then taping four shows, Julia started in on her fifth taped segment—showing how to cut up a roasted chicken so it would feed eight people. We didn't start the segment until after eleven forty-five, and the *GMA* budget required that our work be completed by noon, since every minute after that sent the production crew's pay scale into a staggering rate of overtime. Sonya suggested that we hold the spot for another day, but Julia wanted to do it. The cameras rolled, Julia cut up the chicken, and she finished by saying something like, "Now that will feed eight people." There were flaws; the director asked for a retake. She did it again and finished with the same tag line. Again, there were problems with the spot, and now there was only five minutes of studio time remaining. Sonya again suggested that we postpone the spot, but Julia assumed an authoritative stance and said, "I'll do it again." Sonya stepped aside and we put the backup chicken in place. Members of the crew standing near me began to mutter their doubts aloud: "She'd better hurry—she'll never do it." *Just you wait,* I said to myself. With a remarkable burst of energy born from sheer determination, she cut up that bird, added a witty "or two hungry teenagers" to her tag line about it feeding eight people, and finished exactly two minutes before noon. The studio erupted in clapping and laughter. She'd done it, and what's more, she'd showed them the Julia way to do it. You don't just hit the target; you hit the bull's-eye. Who else would have thought of equating two hungry teenagers to eight adults at that tense moment?

British author and poet Rudyard Kipling said it best in his 1895 poem, *If*: "If you can keep your head when all about you / Are losing theirs . . . / Yours is the Earth and everything that's in it." Someone in the studio passed out copies of a parody of that poem that read, "If you can keep your head when all about you are losing theirs, you clearly do not understand the situation"—apropos for the hectic world of television production, but not for Julia. She always most clearly understood the situation, yet was always able to keep her wits *and* her wit about her.

No matter what was going on behind the scenes or how many times the director or Sonya asked for retakes, Julia's humor never failed her. Hers was such a quick wit; it was smart and natural, never corny, sarcastic, or strained. She could ad-lib at the drop of a hat and define a situation or create an image with a few well-chosen words. In response to questions about her opinion of a low-fat diet, she retorted with such pithy statements as "You'll get dandruff and your fingernails will fall out," and "The only time to eat diet food is while you're waiting for the steak to cook."

For the most part, her on-camera humor was spontaneous, but she also enjoyed inserting an orchestrated bit of funny business into her shows now and then. She was good at it. She said that her fondness for both producing and performing began in the family attic when she was a child and wrote and performed in her own plays. From then into adulthood she acted in a number of amateur performances for her local Pasadena community theater, for the Junior League, and in school plays, always pleased to take a role that required some manner of goofiness. I don't think that Julia ever aspired to an acting career, but if she had, she would not have received much support from her fellow amateur actors. Shortsighted as they were, they felt she didn't have a serious chance of making it in the performing arts because of her unconventional height and unusual vibrato, which tended to sound somewhat like yodeling when she was excited. It's nice to know that her theatrical passions and abilities played out in a different venue, and best of all, she got to play herself.

No matter how humorous she made her shows, she always maintained the integrity of what she was doing—teaching cooking. So by the time she said, "Bon appétit," audiences had not only had a good laugh but had a recipe. I remember as a kid how I loved to watch pianist and humorist Victor Borge. I thought him so funny, but I also wanted him to finish playing the song, and he never did. The humor, not the song, was the point of his performance. For Julia, the recipe, not the humor, was the point of her performance, but she well understood that television is entertainment and if you want to get your message across, you need to be entertaining.

The first "Julia shtick" I recall her producing for *GMA* involved cheese. Besides being our new Julia Child associate, Susy worked at Hay Day Country Farm Market in Greenwich, Connecticut, as a cheese consultant. When Julia decided to demonstrate a recipe that used Emmental cheese, she decided that we should open the spot with an entire wheel of the Swiss-made cheese. That's a lot of *fromage*. How would we get one? Susy had one at the market. So on the day of the show, a limousine gathered Susy and the humongous, two-hundred-pound wheel of cheese in Connecticut at four in the morning. I don't know if they tied the cheese to the roof, roped the better part of it into the trunk, or crammed it with poor Susy in the backseat, but I do know that when they got to the studio it took several stagehands to wrestle it to the set. Julia loved it. She had a prop— one almost as large as she was—and she knew it was amusing. Just as it had so many years before when she held up an entire horrid-looking monkfish for the opening of a *French Chef* episode, the prop caught the audience's attention.

Unaccompanied, Julia was a very funny one-woman show, but she went into comedic high gear when she had a straight man, and *GMA* provided one. She did most of her live spots with one of the show's co-hosts, and when I started at *Good Morning America,* the hosts were David Hartman and Joan Lunden. Both Joan and David loved working with Julia, and she with them, but her rapport with David was special. She liked working with men and she never hesitated to say so. Some years later, when David left the show, Charlie Gibson took his place, and Julia was as enamored of him as she had been of the former host. But there was something very special about her connection with Charlie. Her off-camera exchanges with him were downright cute, a word not often said in the same sentence with Julia Child's name, but she was. Her demeanor was blatantly coy, flirty, and charming, and on the screen it was magic.

Charlie obviously adored her back. At one point he said to Paul, "I hope you don't mind, but I'm in love with your wife."

"Not at all. I'm in love with her myself," Paul responded.

When Julia scripted a segment that would include one of the co-hosts, she gave a good deal of thought to what would make it most entertaining. The blowtorch was a good answer. Today there are small blowtorches made especially for kitchen use, but when she discovered its usefulness, it was the ordinary, three-foot-long hardware-store type. Without waiting for the broiler to heat up, she could caramelize the top of crème brûlée, ignite wine sauces, and brown the meringue on a baked Alaska. She loved her blowtorch and immediately saw its appeal for television. On one hand, it meant that food could be "broiled" directly on the set, without ever leaving the camera's view to go to the oven. On the other, it provided Julia with an infinite number of humorous opportunities to surprise. She liked to keep the bright red, utilitarian tank hidden under the counter and whip it out, startling her TV host. "Now you will need your trusty kitchen blowtorch," she'd announce before lighting it with a loud whoosh.

Knowing it made for such good television, she thought in detail about how and when she'd use it for the best effect. When she sent me her ideas for an upcoming gig at *Good Morning America*, her list started out with the names of what she wanted to do without any specifications until she got to number ten, which was more detailed: "Baked Alaska with blowtorch & David." The blowtorch spot turned out to be all the more entertaining because at first the flame actually incinerated part of the meringue and then it went out altogether. David tried to relight the torch and then tried to turn off the gas, but he was laughing too hard to get a handle on what he was doing. Meanwhile, Julia forged ahead, explaining what she was doing, and then poured even more liqueur on top of the meringue. The piece of cake she served David would have inebriated ten men. Relaxed and unflappable, Julia had turned a goof into a hilarious piece of television.

Steve Bell inadvertently became her ultimate straight man. Steve was an ABC anchor who was accustomed to reporting serious news from behind a desk. Occasionally he filled in for David on *Good Morning America*, and one of those times happened to be a morning when Joan Lunden was also away. I don't think he expected that cooking would be part of his duties that morning, but he approached it with good humor.

Julia was making crepes, and the script called for her to have one pan on the stovetop in front of her and a second pan a few feet down the counter on a hotplate for Steve. As usual for our setups, there was a crockery pot of utensils sitting between their stations. With the cameras rolling, Julia poured batter into both pans and began to explain to the audience how to proceed and how simple it was to make crepes for a crowd. It's a good guess that Steve didn't spend a lot of time in front of a stove. As his batter turned black on the bottom of the pan, he tried in vain to flip it over as Julia was doing. Even if he'd had the flair to flip a crepe, it wouldn't have done him any good at that point because the once light and shimmering batter was now smoking like a teenager behind the gymnasium at a school dance. In a desperate attempt to salvage the crepe, Steve reached for a tool from the pot of utensils, but his crepe was already history. Unruffled, Julia swooped down on the situation like a fire brigade that's seen it all and simply lifted the crepe from the pan and flung it to the floor. "That's okay," she said, pouring more batter into his pan. "Just start over." Then the problem escalated beyond that of a burnt crepe. Steve had chosen a rubber spatula as his tool and because he was laughing so hard at Julia's crepe toss, he left the spatula resting directly on the surface of the hot pan and the rubber melted, gluing the tool to the pan. Steve and the entire control room were convulsed in laughter, but Julia continued on as though nothing unusual had happened—and I'm not sure she did know exactly what had happened until we tied a bow around the sadly deformed spatula and asked her to sign the handle for Steve.

Julia was never shy about tossing a few risqué ad libs into the mix—not surprising, considering she was the same person who in 1956 sent a Valentine card to friends that bore a photo of her and Paul in a bathtub covered only with bubbles and inscribed with the message, "Wish you were here." Given her nature, it was natural that her provocative playfulness would surface when the cameras were rolling. So we may have gasped, but we weren't altogether surprised, when at the end of a segment, after David smiled warmly, clinked his wineglass against hers, and wished her "Bon appétit," Julia smiled back and responded, "Or as we often say, bon appe-titty." Cookbook author and television personality Merle Ellis told me that it was Julia's unselfconscious naughty side that had landed her the regular gig on *GMA* in the first place. Before Julia became part of the *GMA* family, he was a regular on the show, appearing weekly in a popular spot as "The Butcher." Merle, of whom Julia was very fond, invited her to join him for a tour of a meatpacking plant. Julia, a butcher wanna-be, jumped at the chance. When the small group that included Merle's *GMA* producer came to the "kill room," the consensus was to pass it up, but Julia wanted to see all aspects of the butchering and insisted that Merle escort her into the room.

Merle, Julia, and the producer viewed the killing, gutting, and skinning operations and then arrived at the tenderizing station. They watched as men placed two large paddles on either side of the carcass. When a large bolt of electricity shot through the paddles, it caused the animal's tail to suddenly shoot upright and rigid. "I can think of other uses for that!" Julia gleefully exclaimed. A few weeks later the producer called Merle to ask for Julia's phone number, and she soon had a contract with ABC.

In spite of the usually overwhelming amount of work, the very early hours, and the occasional snafu, it didn't take me long to realize that I loved—no, adored—television food work. What's more, I seemed to have a knack for it, because Sonya soon hired me to work on segments with other visiting chefs and celebrities. For the next seven years I worked with more celebrities, cookbook authors, and chefs than I can recall. It was all such fun, but no one ever brought the same magic to the show as Julia did. Julia Child plus food plus television was simply a winning combination.

And there were perks involved in working with her. Not the kind of employee incentives associated with health plans, retirement benefits, or the right to participate in office football pools, but the sort that expanded our knowledge of what was notable in the food world, what was evolving into becoming notable, and who was making it happen.

When Julia arrived in New York for her monthly gigs at *GMA*, she did so with a stack of invitations to restaurant openings, wine tastings, book parties, luncheons, and dinners. There were always more invitations than time allowed, but she accepted the ones she could, and always requested that she be able to bring her assistants as guests. I ate my first lunch at the famed 21 with Julia, as well as my first dinners at Union Square Café and Montrachet, which then were not famous but would become so. It was with Julia that I tasted my first, exquisite bite of American foie gras and met the delightful Ariane Daguin, who was just establishing her foie gras business, D'Artagnan, in the United States. As I savored the delicacy in front of me, Julia gave me a brief history lesson about Ariane and her renowned father, André Daguin, who was then chef-owner of the Hôtel de France in Gascony and a towering figure in the gastronomy of that area. And, being Julia, she stretched her neck way up and gave me a visual description of *gavage* (the way geese are force-fed). She finished by giving all of us at the table her opinion that it does not offend the hungry birds to be fed in such a way, contrary to the views of many people in the business and virtually everyone who was an animal rights activist. *Gavage* remains a point of controversy, and whether Julia was right or wrong in her opinion will most likely never find a definitive answer; it's been argued since Egyptian times. But the point is that before she made her determination about its cruelty or lack thereof, she made sure she had all the facts and saw the process for herself. I think I was a bit on the fence on the subject, probably because I adore foie gras. So on a trip to California, she decided we should visit a Sonoma foie gras producer so I could see for myself. Unfortunately, the owner said they were not feeding the geese at the time of our visit, so I was unable to make my own analysis. It would have been futile for me to give an opinion after that, since Julia would have said, *You haven't seen it for yourself, so you can't say.*

Perhaps the party that most beguiled me was a dinner at the Four Seasons where I met the legendary British culinary writer Roy Andries De Groot. I needed no explanation from Julia of who he was. My copy of his book *Recipes from the Auberge of the Flowering Hearth,* published in 1973, was tattered and worn, not from my use but because I had only learned of it when I discovered it in a used-book store. I was so taken with it that I read most of it sitting cross-legged on the dusty bookstore floor. His story of how he went to France seeking the history of the liqueur Chartreuse and in the process discovered the existence of two women who cooked with the seasons is not only an influential culinary classic but also one of the most beautifully descriptive accounts of gastronomic discovery—all the more incredible since De Groot was blind.

Julia was extremely generous and thoughtful to include us in all that her culinary status afforded her, and when James Beard invited her to a tasting of champagne and chocolate ice cream that he was hosting, Susy and I saw just how far her thoughtfulness extended. We were working at the studio and had not quite finished all the prep we needed for the next day. But Julia had to leave, since she was expected to say a few words with Beard at a given time and then had to go on to another event. Her afternoon schedule was crowded, and a limousine was already waiting outside to take her to the Beard party and then on to the next and the next. "I hope you can finish in time to make Jim's party," she said. "Leave as soon as you finish all this."

Almost an hour later, Susy and I finished. Looking at the time, we realized that unless we found a taxi immediately we would probably miss the party. As soon as we opened the door to leave the studio, we saw the downpour and we knew that finding a taxi at all would be nearly impossible. We had no raincoats, no umbrellas, and several blocks to go. As we descended the stairs, a driver stepped out of the limousine parked at the curb and asked, "Are you Susy and Nancy?"

"Yes," we answered.

"Mrs. Child sent me here to wait for you and said I should bring you to the party."

It was a thoughtful, generous thing to do, but when I look at the larger picture of who Julia was, I know that her efforts to include us in her many outings were not solely out of her generosity. She wanted to introduce us to the entirety of the culinary world—a world she had the foresight to know was undergoing important and exciting changes.

4

My advice to you is not to inquire why or whither, but just enjoy your ice cream while it's on your plate—that's my philosophy.

—Thornton Wilder, *The Skin of Our Teeth*

*W*ysiwyg. That's what Russ Morash said when members of the press and fans asked him to reveal exactly what the real Julia Child was like in person. Those in search of a juicy story most likely hoped to unearth tales of a misanthropic madwoman who hurled pots and pans at kitchen assistants, or hear stories of a prima donna who lazed about conceitedly watching reruns of her own programs while kitchen slaves served her coq au vin and croquembouche on a tray emblazoned with her image. Russ, who was not only her director but also her good friend, was in a better position than most to know, and he gave the true and definitive, succinct and explicit answer—"wysiwyg." It may sound like a word from Lewis Carroll's "Jabberwocky," but don't reach for the dictionary. *Wysiwyg* is not a word. The letters stand for "what you see is what you get." And that's the truth of it. Julia was just as down-to-earth, unpretentious, and unselfconsciously outspoken in the company of friends as she was with the cameras rolling. She was just as humorous and deliciously quirky. The *real* Julia Child was right there to see, whether you watched her on a TV screen or sat next to her at the dinner table. She was always Julia.

To say that Julia was always the same person does not mean that she was without depth or breadth. There were many prismatic dimensions to her personality, many layers. Discovering those layers did not require a special guidebook or road map. You only had to spend time with her. And I was getting to do just that.

If I had to describe my working association with Julia, I would say that at first it was gradual, and then it was simply all of a sudden. When she made me executive chef at *GMA*, she also asked me to assist her at a few of the many demonstrations that she gave on a regular basis to promote her own work and to raise funds for charitable organizations. That meant traveling with her and seeing her out of the public light. Then Julia offered me another job. In 1981, she gave up her *McCall's* column and accepted an offer to be the food editor for *Parade,* the popular Sunday newspaper insert. Her monthly features were much more elaborate than her column had been and they would reach a much wider audience, a fact that greatly appealed to her. *Parade* shot the photos for the first series of "From Julia Child's Kitchen" in Santa Barbara, California, where Julia and Paul had just purchased a condominium. Julia worked it out with *Parade* to have the shoots take place on whichever coast she and Paul were living at the scheduled time, and she asked me to serve as her executive chef for the East Coast team when she shot the next series in Cambridge in the spring of 1982.

Up until *Parade,* Julia and I had communicated primarily by phone or mail, but when our work became more involved, she suggested I come up to Cambridge to go over things with her. There I observed my first at-home, in-person Julia-isms.

Actually, the first was before I even got there. We were on the phone working out the time I should be there, and she asked me how long it took me to drive from Providence to Cambridge. I told her that the drive should take a little over an hour, depending on traffic.

"Well, how do you go?" she asked.

I described my route. "That's all wrong," she said. "You have to take the little eekie off Memorial before the garden center and then the eekie off Kirkland before the fire station."

"Uh, is Eekie the name of a street?" I asked, thoroughly confused.

No, it was the term Paul and Julia gave to the shortcuts they used that resulted in the quickest drive to their 103 Irving Street home. On my one previous trip to her house, with a reliable map as my guide, I made turns onto clearly marked streets. Julia's route called for zigzags onto barely noticeable, seldom labeled, and often poorly paved streets. To this day, I can find my way to 103 Irving Street with those eekies, but I couldn't tell you the name of the streets I took, because Paul and Julia simply called them "eekies." What's more, if they did mention street names, they used their own appellations: the street with the tilting chimney was "Slanted Chimney Way," and the one with the white fence was "White Picket Street" regardless of what the street signs said.

So I followed the eekies and pulled into her driveway having cut a good eight minutes off my trip.

Julia let me in the back door—she never used the front—and I followed her up a short flight of stairs, through the high-ceilinged hallway, and into her kitchen. It was not glamorous. In fact, it was downright funky. Pegboards, painted the shade of fading grass, hung floor to ceiling on nearly every bit of wall space. Attached to them was a *batterie de cuisine* that would tax the capacity of a Williams-Sonoma warehouse. Knives, carbon- and stainless-steel-bladed, stood at the ready in descending order of size from large chef's knives to small paring ones along two magnetic strips attached to either side of the

Julia in her Cambridge kitchen.

kitchen window, where a person who was more interested in decoration than function might have hung café curtains. There were more knives, including a very large Chinese cleaver, nestled in a hollowed-out groove next to a wooden cutting block abutting the counter. "I'm a knife freak," Julia confessed.

A professional six-burner Garland range that Paul and Julia had purchased used in 1956 for $429 dominated one wall, and above it hung a handsome set of long-handled, flat copper lids designed to cover any size pot or pan. Linoleum, in a spattered pattern common in the 1950s, covered the floor. Yellow Post-it notes inscribed in Julia's hand clung to numerous surfaces and instructed how things worked. The one on the dishwasher told exactly how much soap to add and which buttons to press; on the electric coffeepot were detailed calculations on how to measure the coffee (both per pot and per cup); the note stuck to the door of the small under-counter freezer used for baking ingredients listed what was stored inside. A Post-it on the bathroom door asked departing occupants to leave the door ajar, "to air the joint out." And, because at one time someone had inadvertently left a scoop in the icemaker, causing it to break down with a scrunching noise that Julia imaginatively imitated for me, that note said, "DO NOT leave scoop in ice machine."

The kitchen was the epitome of Julia's no-nonsense approach to cooking and to life—a visual expression of her practical personality. The pegboard organization, a system Paul and Julia first devised for their small French kitchen in Provence, was a sensible solution to storage constraints. Paul cut and painted the boards, and then, after each pot, pan, and tool was in place, he outlined it with a thick tracing of black marker, so when an item was lifted off the peg, the remaining ink shape told exactly where that tool and only that tool fit. The boards not only provided ample space for equipment but prevented the problems that can arise from having revolving teams of workers in the kitchen. It annoyed Julia to no end if someone used a piece of equipment and then put it where it didn't belong, thereby forcing her to hunt all over for it when she needed it. The pegboards and the knife strips showed exactly where those tools belonged, and there was no excuse for not putting them there. The Post-its prevented newcomers from clogging the dishwasher with an excess of soap or putting odor-exuding ingredients into the freezer with odor-absorbing bits of pastry and sticks of butter.

Julia Child's culinary sanctum may not have been worthy of a center spread in *House Beautiful,* but it was one of the most functional kitchens I ever worked in—except for the counters. Just as she always requested that her demonstration counters be higher than the norm, she'd had her home counters designed and built to accommodate her height. It was practical for her but a bear for me. I could manage most things at the awkward height, but I simply could not roll pastry on them. I was too short to get the leverage I needed, so Julia provided me with a child's stool to stand on. It was effective, but standing on the stool made me feel like a kid, and I couldn't help but laugh at myself as I pushed her massive rolling pin over sheets of pastry dough. Liz loved to emphasize my little-girl-in-Mama's-kitchen feeling by dragging into my vision a small sign that Julia kept in the counter corner. It read, "I wasn't there. I didn't do it. It was the little people."

The "little people" sign did not charm me nearly as much as the paintings and photos of cats that decorated the few smidgens of free wall space. When I asked Julia about them, she told me she loved *poussiquettes*. She didn't have one in Cambridge, just the wall images, but she had Minou in France, and she reached into her daybook and pulled out the cat's photo that she always carried with her. Some

My sons, Brad and Andrew, at Julia's house in France with poussiquette Minou.

years later, I discovered why Julia was so fond of Minou. She was a lively ham of a cat. My sons and I stayed in Julia's house in France when she was not there, and *poussiquette* introduced herself to me in the middle of a pitch black night while I was sound asleep in Julia's bed. She entered the room from outside by leaping up to pull down the handle of the bedroom's French door and then pounced on me, frightening me nearly to death. I called Julia from France to tell her that her cat was diabolical; she told me to give her some fresh hamburger and she would stop assaulting me.

Each trip to Julia's Cambridge house was like opening a surprise package that held another dimension of her personality. On one visit, when I walked into the hallway I immediately saw a very elderly, stooped woman walking up the stairs to the second floor. She had a firm hold on the banister and was obviously struggling with each step.

"Should I help her?" I whispered to Julia, assuming she was an elderly relative.

"No. That's my housekeeper. She's used to it." The woman had to be ninety! And she did the laundry, ironed, and dusted that enormous, three-story house with a small dust rag that she kept clutched in her arthritic hand. Julia had employed her for years and wouldn't for a minute let that loyal woman feel that she had outgrown her usefulness. Julia was much too kind to let her go because of details as insignificant as poor posture and a halting gait. She did hire a professional cleaning company, however, to come in on a regular basis to wipe up what that dear old woman missed.

The two questions I am asked most frequently about Julia are "Did she ever see the Dan Aykroyd spoof of her on *Saturday Night Live*?" and "What did she think about it?" An early visit to Julia's answered both: yes, she saw it and she *loved* it. She kept a videotape copy of Aykroyd's 1979 performance under the television in her kitchen so she could show it to anyone who had missed it. Usually when people ask me about the tape, they wonder if Aykroyd's stumbling about while taking swigs from a bottle of booze offended Julia. Not at all. She had a marvelous sense of humor that was expansive enough to include all well-done parodies about her. What never did amuse her were the countless attempts to imitate her voice, as impossible as it was to resist doing. Those she dismissed with a curt "I don't sound like that." In fact, most people's imitations sound more like Aykroyd than Child.

When I admitted that I had never seen the tape, she immediately popped it into the VCR, and she and Paul laughed with me as though they were seeing it for the first time. When Stephanie Hersh began to work for her years later, Julia didn't show her the tape but acted it out, giving her impersonation of Dan Aykroyd's impersonation of her staggering around a kitchen trying to stop the profuse, fatal bleeding from a thumb gash while shrieking "save the liver" from the chicken she was cutting. Stephanie said Julia did her own staggering around her office and ended her skit "by sprawling herself across her desk and exclaiming, 'And then I died!'"

Since Julia was, by her own admission, a born ham, my guess is that she enjoyed acting out the skit as much as she liked watching Aykroyd's performance. Sometimes she planned her spoofs into her performances; often they were spontaneous.

Julia the ham took me by surprise for the first time in New Haven in the fall of 1981 when we did a benefit demonstration for the Long Wharf Theatre. Named for the wharf that ran beside New Haven Harbor, the theater occupies a previously vacant warehouse that sits in the middle of what was once a busy terminal. Two Yale alumni created the theater as a home for a resident acting company in 1965, and like all such theaters across the country, it relied on benefactors' support. Betty Kubler, one of the theater's benefactors, had been a classmate of Julia's at Smith, and her husband, George, and Paul Child shared a longtime friendship, so when Betty called Julia and asked her to help raise money with a demonstration, Julia said yes without hesitation.

The night of the show, Julia walked out on the stage, smiled, and bowed to the cheering audience. I stood behind her knowing that as soon as the cheering part of the program ended, she would walk around behind the counter and I would move forward to stand by her side. But when the applause died down, Julia didn't walk anywhere. She turned around, picked up a breadbasket from the set, and with the exuberance of a relief pitcher warming up in the bullpen began tossing the dinner rolls into the audience. There was mayhem as hands stretched up and out to snag one of the starchy missiles. Cheering and applause broke out again with renewed vigor. You could just see what a kick Julia got from doing it.

Tossing things was nothing new to Julia. It was obviously something she loved to do. She did it often on her TV shows. In fact, long before she developed a reputation as a food maven, she had one as a food tosser. As a kid in Pasadena, she hurled mud pies at passing motorists and then had to scale a fence in order to escape their wrath. And it didn't end there. When she was a student at Smith College, she and her roommate would get into such "giggle fests" that they couldn't concentrate on their studies, so they stretched a rope across the center of the room and draped a green rug over it. That way they could no longer see and disturb each other. It should have done the trick—but it didn't, because Julia couldn't resist repeatedly tossing jelly doughnuts over it.

Her slapstick performances, like the layout of her Post-it-annotated kitchen, were not convoluted attempts at eccentricity. They were, as Russ noted, wysiwyg—just who she was. Spending more time with her, I was seeing the varied ways that her public persona played out in her private life. Those ways were not always necessarily loveable.

Most viewers would agree that she came across publicly as an outspoken, opinionated woman, and she was. We loved it when she gave the "food police" hell for trashing cream and butter. During a pre-Thanksgiving radio interview with a vegan host, he repeatedly expressed his distain for the "dead meat" Julia planned to eat on the holiday. She asked him what he would cook. "I fashion a bird out of whole grains," he said, and Julia gave him a raspberry—loud and clear over the air. Her immediate, unguarded response was hilarious, but that same bluntness could be insensitive. She was often curtly dismissive of old people who acted old, "fluffies" who referred to every dining experience as "gourmet," and "housewifey types" who were not "serious" about cooking.

She had an appealing openness about her own personal life and an insatiable curiosity about the lives of others. But she loved to gossip, and unless you made her swear on her life not to tell, she'd throw your personal issues into the storytelling mix without thinking that you might be more sensitive about revealing your private matters than she was about sharing hers.

Professional organizations sought her involvement because she was a strong, effective leader who had no problem writing scathing letters to anyone who stood in the way of her causes. In her personal life, her strength often translated to stubbornness, and when she dug in her heels, there was simply no talking to her. At times it was terribly frustrating; usually it was just plain funny. Ironically, for all her strength and directness in her public affairs, in her personal life she hated to deal directly with conflict, and usually refused to do so even when she was the one who had caused it in the first place.

Strong, admirable people are still, of course, only human and not without their share of shortcomings. Yet people such as Julia are venerable because their shortcomings never override their qualities. Certainly, Julia's faults never diminished my admiration for her or dissuaded me from wanting to be like her in many ways. Of course, I never could be exactly like her, but my years in her company clearly rubbed off on me, as my sons, who were raised with Julia in my life,

Me with Brad and Andrew in Julia's kitchen.

often remind me. Recently I was embroiled in a conflict that was driving me to distraction. My son Brad listened to my blithering complaints for a length of time that would try anyone's patience. When I paused in the midst of my tirade, he calmly said, "Mom, think for a minute. What would Julia do?" It was all I needed to hear.

Brad and Andrew were four and two years old when I began to work with Julia, and books by Benjamin Spock, T. Berry Brazelton, and several other child-rearing experts shared shelf space with Irma Rombauer, Jacques Pépin, and Julia Child. I pretty much had weaning, toilet training, and separation anxiety down, but I was in search of the absolute, definitive, no-fail method of instilling self-confidence in children. Julia abounded with a secure sense of self and a can-do attitude. I wanted the same for my boys. So I asked her how she got like that.

On a visit to Julia's, three-foot-tall Andrew took an entire roll of film of her that never captured anything above her waist.

"My mother thought we could do no wrong," she answered immediately, referring to herself and her younger siblings, Dorothy and John, who like Julia grew to be over six feet tall; Mrs. McWilliams liked to say that she raised eighteen feet of children. "She was always telling us we were special. When you hear it all the time, you can't help but feel good about yourself." From that moment on, I never missed an opportunity to tell my boys that they were the best, and today, at twenty-nine and thirty-one, they are!

Perhaps it was Mrs. McWilliams's enthusiastic cheerleading, maybe it was all genetic, but Julia *was* special, and her uniqueness came wrapped in all that self-assurance. No wonder she was able to inspire passion in at least three generations of amateur and professional cooks; along with each technique and morsel of French cooking, she served up a generous helping of confidence.

"Have the courage of your convictions," she told her audiences. "If I can do it, you can do it." And we believed her. We were like Mrs. McWilliams's eighteen feet of children—we could do no wrong. If, perchance, we did make a mistake, it didn't matter. "Remember, you are alone in the kitchen." Long before Nike made it a call to action, Julia gave us the message "Just do it!" In New Haven I would soon realize that she wasn't just talking about flipping potato pancakes, crepes, and omelets; she was talking about dealing with life.

We arrived at the theater early in the morning on a glorious fall day. A historic old port, this particular section of New Haven had all the weathered charm of a classic New England dockside market, where vendors sold food from burlap bags and wooden boxes. That day there was a farmers' market in front of the theater. For me, the produce of fall outshines that of any other season, including the much-touted summer offerings. Plump purple eggplants, deep green and brilliant red bell peppers, long and narrow pale green frying ones, lush plum tomatoes, and lacy Italian parsley all scream, "Cook me!" The brilliant display was not to be ignored, and Julia, who admitted that some of her fondest memories of France were the outdoor food markets, did not intend to.

We strolled the stands pinching, sniffing, admiring the wares, and chatting with the vendors. Julia told me that talking with the vendors was her favorite part of visiting an open market. After assuring us that his plump, perfect eggplants had been picked just that morning, one vendor directed our attention to the food shops that lined the wharf.

"Best meat in the country," he told us, pointing to an Italian market behind him.

"We should go in," Julia said, already striding toward the store.

Busy at work, carefully arranging cuts of meat in a display case, were the owners, a middle-aged Italian American couple who were as proud of their store as they were obviously surprised and delighted to see Julia walk into it.

"Why, that's just beautiful," Julia said, admiring the well-marbled steaks, neatly sectioned chicken parts, long ropes of sausages, and tied roasts.

"Thank you," the man said. "We cut and prepare all our own meat and make all the sausage, sweet and hot, right here." He invited us into the back room where they hung the meat ready to be cut and then showed us into another room where the sausage was made. Julia was like the proverbial kid in a candy shop, and on the way back to the theater she told me that she could be content being a butcher; the whole business of meat fascinated her. That was probably why she was so visually descriptive of meat cuts on television, pointing to her own body parts and moving her arms about to show how some parts became tough with use and needed long, slow braising while other parts remained relatively unused and would be tender enough for a quick sauté.

The format for the Long Wharf demonstration was much the same as it had been in Providence when I met Julia: Liz sitting and organizing, Paul keeping track of time, and Julia, Marian, and me prepping all day for an evening's demonstration. Lunch would be on the set, and I expected that some eager volunteer would arrive with a favorite dish. But at about eleven o'clock, Julia spoke up. "What should we do about lunch?" There was some muttering, and then she decided, "Why doesn't Nancy fix us lunch?"

I'm sure I must have hyperventilated or at least blanched. If they are honest, most chefs who find themselves having to feed Julia for the first time will admit that the mere thought of it is enough to obliterate everything they ever knew about food and cooking. Over the years, many told me so. I'd known that eventually I would prepare a meal for her, but I always expected that it would be at home, and that I would spend days shopping, cooking, and fashioning frilly paper booties for the bone ends of rack of lamb. To cook spontaneously for Julia Child, let alone Marian, gave me the same feeling I had during those dreams when I walked into a final exam and I hadn't read the text or attended a single class.

"What would you like to eat?" I asked, hoping my tone conveyed that I would fix whatever she liked and not the feeling of "why me?"

"Something good. You decide," she responded.

I looked around at what was available. We had plenty of staples—eggs, flour, butter, a variety of cheeses. My mind began to entertain a frantic jumble of possibilities. Maybe a quiche or a soufflé . . . but would they be as good as Julia's or Marian's? Maybe just a good old egg salad. I had enough eggs to make mayonnaise, and what's better than homemade mayonnaise? Would Julia think that was too simple?

Then it occurred to me just to fix something I wanted to eat, and I immediately knew what that was.

"I'll be right back," I told Julia, grabbing my purse and running out the door. I went back to the meat market first to be sure they still had some of the sausages they'd been making that morning. I left with a plump package and then stopped at the outdoor market for peppers, garlic, onions, tomatoes, and parsley. Back on the set, I prepared my nonna's sausage and peppers, a dish I could make with confidence, with my eyes closed, and without stopping my prep work for the evening's demonstration.

"This is delicious," Julia said, genuinely relishing the standard Italian fare.

Her delight with it encouraged me to admit my initial total lack of confidence in my ability to cook for her. "You know, I was very nervous when you asked me to make lunch. I almost couldn't do it."

She looked at me with a warm twinkle in her eye and told me, "I knew you could." At that moment I had a sense of what it had been like to be one of Mrs. McWilliams's children. More than having the ability to do something, having the confidence in that ability, the courage of your convictions, is what makes it happen. Whatever confidence I have in myself today is mine, but Julia set it in motion, and I've never forgotten that. In the acknowledgments for my first cookbook, I wrote, "In her [Julia's] ever practical and endearing way she simply assumed that I would do this—and do it well."

For Julia, having the courage of your convictions also meant being willing to speak those opinions frankly. That same positive outspokenness, which appealed so to her audiences, was visibly deflating in person. I found that out before our New Haven demonstration, when we visited the meat market. When Julia was admiring the meat in the display case, she commented on the quality of the delicate white veal.

"It's real veal and not all that small cow people are feeding us," she said.

"That's right," the owner said. "I buy the animals whole and cut them up myself."

Sure enough, when we went into the meat rooms, there were the carcasses of several small calves hanging on meat hooks. I still don't know why I said, "Poor babies," when I saw the tiny animals, but I immediately regretted it. Julia turned straight toward me and with a stern look and a raised index finger said, "That is unprofessional!" I blushed. "They wouldn't be born if they weren't meant to be eaten," she added firmly.

"I know," I said, and I did. I had no problem with veal at all. It was a staple in my home growing up. My grandfather owned a meat store and cut up calves just like those. My comment did not express any underlying aversion I had to veal; it was just a foolish muttering, I suppose, to say something. Julia's direct reproach took me by surprise and embarrassed me. But that was the end of it. She spoke her mind, and the next time veal came up, she made no reference to my previous remark or seemed even to recall that I had said it.

Julia spoke just as directly to others who worked with us, whether it was to challenge a comment she thought was unfounded or to interrupt an improper technique. It was just her manner and she usually accented her stern words by raising her index finger, turned out in a stop motion, in front of her chest. In restaurants she was bluntly honest about the food she was served. If it wasn't right, she said so, and I always felt sorry for the waiter or chef who offhandedly asked her how everything was when something was not as it should be. "Well, it's not good at all," she would reply, and then would proceed to explain exactly what was wrong with it—in one way or another as I discovered during that same New Haven trip.

Our demonstration had ended late and we were all desperate to find someplace where we could sit and quietly eat dinner. We found a nearby family eatery that boasted of large steaks and real baked potatoes.

"Perfect," said Julia, leading us to a table and immediately ordering the largest steak on the menu and a baked potato. When the meal came, Julia took a large mouthful of potato slathered with butter and made a face.

"Ugh. It's sweet!" At first I thought she meant that she had been served a sweet potato by mistake, but I leaned over the table to peek in and could see that hers was white like everyone else's.

"What do you mean?" I asked.

Marian, the vegetable expert, explained it to me. "When potatoes stay too long in storage, the starch begins to turn to sugar."

"It makes them sweet and unappealing," Julia added, just as our very young waitress came to the table to ask how everything was. Julia told her that the sweetness of the potato was unacceptable, and just as I had done, the waitress looked at it, saw it was white, and didn't know what to say, so she left to get the manager. He was only slightly older than our waitress, and in a gesture too grand and serious for his age, he knelt down next to Julia. I think he even laid his hand patronizingly on her arm. "Is there a problem, Mrs. Child?"

"The potato is sweet," she said, and for the third time someone looked into the vegetable to see what color it was.

"I don't understand," he said.

Julia was obviously finished with having to explain. She asked him to open his mouth, and when he did, she shoveled a large forkful of potatoes into it. "Here, taste it," she said. I'm not sure he detected the offending sweetness. It was impossible to know if his shocked expression was a response to the taste of the potato or to being spoon-fed by Julia Child.

Having the courage of one's convictions does require, of course, that you have a good fallback strategy if your convictions turn out to be wrong. I don't know if Julia uttered those words for the first time on television during the infamous potato pancake show, but I remember them best from that episode. She said them just before she started to shake the pan so the potato pancake would jump up, turn over, and flop back into the pan. But it didn't; it landed on the stove in front of the burner. Julia's fallback strategy was to pick up the pieces, put them back in the pan, and admit, "That didn't go very well." She didn't beg the cameras to stop so she could do it again, she didn't complain that someone had given her the wrong pan or the wrong potatoes, and she never expressed even the remotest sense of agony that she had flubbed up in front of an untold number of viewers.

Whether it was flipping a potato pancake or something life-altering, Julia had a remarkable ability to put her mistakes behind her and move ahead. She refused to get all twisted up about something that she couldn't change. It was done. Over. Move on. It wasn't that she didn't learn from those mistakes; she did. But once she decided what had gone wrong and why, she dropped it and refused to dwell on the consequences or belabor whose fault it was. "Shoulda, coulda, woulda" were not in her vocabulary. A reporter once asked her, "What is your guilty pleasure, Mrs. Child?"

"I don't have guilt," she responded, and she did not. Moreover, she did not expect that we should either. And that was a beautiful thing, because I had my share of flubs that made me cringe and it was good to know that Julia would make light of them and not banish me to the dishwashing station. Not even when I single-handedly trashed one of the most beautiful covers for *Parade* magazine did she blame me.

Parade was my initiation to food photography on a grand scale. Each of the articles occupied four center pages of the magazine and contained several recipes and plenty of full-color how-to photographs. The cover was a knock-'em-dead full-page photo of all the recipes that followed. Each production session required a week's worth of work and a large team. I served as executive chef and Marian as co–executive chef when she was on the East Coast, and together we supervised a kitchen staff that consisted of one or two assistant cooks and a dishwasher/cleaner-upper. When Julia wasn't upstairs in her office writing the recipes that we would prepare, she was part of our kitchen team. Liz was there, of course, organizing the schedule and making certain that we had what we needed—from her stool. When a shoot called for a pan that we didn't have but she did at her home across town, she crossed her legs, put on her glasses, and phoned for a taxi to go to her house, collect the pan from her son, and drive it back to Irving Street. When I answered the door, there was a rather confused taxi driver asking if someone was expecting a pan.

Someone of course had to take the photos, and our East Coast photographer was the delightful, keen-eyed, and oh-so-easy-to-work-with Jim Scherer, who had worked with Julia before on the cookbooks that accompanied her *Julia Child & Company* and *Julia Child & More Company* books. *Parade's* art director, Ira Yoffe, and senior editor David Currier joined us for the week and we all fell madly in love with both men. They were excellent at their jobs, great at fostering and maintaining a team spirit with everyone, and—probably what made us love them most of all—they ate everything we fed them with the appreciative appetites of hungry teenagers after lacrosse practice.

Because Julia wanted the look of the food in each issue to be consistent, she asked Rosemary Manell to work with both the East and West Coast teams, and so I met the "official food designer" for the first time. Rosie and Julia's friendship began in the 1940s, when Paul Child worked with Rosie's late husband, Abe. About ten years younger than Julia, Rosie was almost as tall but with a much larger physique, and she lumbered with slow, plodding steps around the kitchen. She had a great long mane of white hair that she pulled back

Rosie Manell in Julia's kitchen in France.

into a ponytail with a rubber band. She eschewed makeup, wore sensible shoes, and was not into clothes, as Julia was. Paul called her "earth mother," and I thought of her as an aging hippie.

Rosie had a fine artist's eye, knew exactly what look she wanted to create for the covers, and was so fastidious and exacting about getting there that we all learned to stay out of her way when she was creating. It was her painting, and we didn't mess with it. Had she not been so open to our good-natured teasing about her fussiness, her rigidity might have spoiled our fun.

She, Ira, and Jim collaborated to create some astonishingly artful and often award-winning covers—but they took a great deal of time. For each session, they cleared out Julia's large dining room and swept yards of colorful cloth onto the floor, which became the photo's background. Atop that, they constructed a virtual collage of the food we cooked, and then they accented it with decorative serving pieces from Julia's large collection.

All that did not happen in a one-two-three motion. Ira often tried several colors of cloth for the background before finding the one that he felt best complemented the food; Rosie chose and rejected a series of dishes; Jim checked and rechecked the lighting, opening and closing blinds and moving his lights around the room. During this setup phase, we used stand-ins, just like movie stars use stand-ins to frame a shot, but ours were look-alike food dishes that resembled the real ones waiting in the kitchen.

When the stage was set, they called for the food, but it would still be a long time before we were finished. In the days before digital camerawork, taking a magazine photograph was not the simple snap-edit-and-upload it is today. First Jim had to take several Polaroid pictures to check the lighting, positioning, and multitude of other I-haven't-a-clue-what details that food photographers check with such tedious and meticulous care. *All* food photographers. I've never worked with a food photographer who was speedy, and Jim was no different. That is how food stylists got so popular in the first place: after a lovely, glistening chicken had sat for hours and endured endless moving hither and yon into position, the photographer would remove his frowning eye from the lens and announce, "That chicken looks dull." The stylists then pulled out a trusty basket of tools and sprayed, brushed, oiled, and blowtorched the glow back onto the bird.

So, to return to my story about trashing the cover, on that day, the subject of the article was a summer wedding lunch, and the design team had transformed the dining room floor into a captivating flurry of pink lace and romance. But Rosie wasn't satisfied.

"We need something else," she said. "It needs more celebration."

"How about the Baccarat champagne glasses?" Julia asked, referring to two exquisite crystal glasses she'd received as a gift the day before.

"Perfect," agreed Rosie, who asked me to retrieve them from Julia's office upstairs. Although Julia always appreciated the many gifts that fans and industry personnel sent to her, she seldom kept them because there simply was not enough room in her house—despite its ample size—to accommodate the nonstop deliveries that arrived at her door. But she wanted to keep those particular champagne glasses, not only because she appreciated their beauty and value but also because they were a gift from a French official who was dear to her. So when the glasses arrived, Julia put them upstairs in her office, out of harm's way.

I ran upstairs and then tiptoed carefully back downstairs with one costly glass in each hand, as if I were afraid to wake them. Rosie cleared a spot for them and, keeping my eyes on the empty space, I moved toward it. I should have kept one eye on my feet because I didn't see the upturned edge of the cloth on the floor. It caught my toe and sent me headlong on top of the artful arrangement of petit fours and tea sandwiches. The once beautiful setting of pink lace and dainty delicacies was smashed to smithereens and, worse, so were the

Julia with Ira Yoffe, creative director and now vice president of Parade Magazine, who cleans up the set around the meat before having the how-to photo taken.

glasses. Shards of what had been once finely cut crystal were everywhere. I was horrified. With a good bit of effort, I knew, we could replace the food, but Julia's precious Baccarat was history. Rosie let out the most excruciating wail, and I could tell by the look on her face that she was getting ready to hang me upside down from an upstairs window and leave me dangling there by my felonious foot.

"I'm so sorry about the crystal, Julia," I nearly wept as I wiped bits of pink icing and homemade mayonnaise off my clothes.

"What would I have done with just two anyway?" she said without the tiniest hint of remorse for her loss or blame for my blunder. "We'll use my old champagne glasses." And then, winking at me, she added, "I have plenty of them."

Over the days, weeks, and eventually years I spent with Julia, the many layers of her personality constantly unfolded, and I can express no more simply what I felt about her than to say I adored her. Moreover, so many of her attributes amazed me. Right up there at the top of my list was her energy. Anyone who worked or played with

Julia couldn't help but be awed by how energetic she was. As Russ Morash observed, "energy was her secret weapon."

I was aware of her incredible energy from the first day I worked for her, but I eventually learned that it was more than a genetic inheritance; it was a mind-set. She simply did not allow herself or others around to consider the T-word. It visibly annoyed her if they did.

One late night, after a hideously long day at a conference where Julia participated on a panel, gave a demonstration, and hosted a reception, a woman, brow furrowed and head shaking, approached Julia to express her concern. "Oh, Mrs. Child. You did so much today. You must be exhausted." The pathetic whine in her voice emphasized the level of distress she felt for the septuagenarian and sent Julia into a stern, defensive stance.

"I *don't* exhaust," she brusquely snapped back before abruptly turning away from the startled woman and leading our small entourage into the hotel bar for a nightcap. Julia didn't just not exhaust; she steadfastly did not *want* to exhaust.

Also noted in my mental inventory of what fascinated me about Julia was her total lack of pretension and nonchalance about her fame—how unaware she was of her own celebrity. She certainly never acted like one. She lived her life in a most ordinary fashion, taking daily walks to the local variety store for her newspaper, pushing her own cart through the supermarket, scooting around town in a very recognizable red car with a wooden spoon taped to the radio antenna—ordinary daily activities (except perhaps for the antenna spoon) that made her seem just like the neighbor down the street. She liked it that way because that was how she thought of herself.

Her lack of affectation surprised many a journalist whom she invited to interview her over lunch at her house. I have seen many of the resulting articles and can't help but smile when I read the writers' account of how they arrived with great, hungry expectations of a gourmet lunch and instead got a tuna fish sandwich—albeit a very,

very good tuna fish sandwich. My own brother, Tom, who is a writer and radio journalist, was assigned to interview Julia. She invited him to lunch, and he skipped breakfast in preparation for his meal. When he arrived, Julia opened a can of hash and together they fixed one of her favorite meals. He said she made it better by adding a bit of good beef stock to it as it sautéed—but it was still canned hash.

Before her assistant Stephanie Hersh came on board and fixed things up, Julia traveled coach class and stayed in simple hotel rooms even though she was often donating her time to organizations that easily could have arranged for upgrades. Julia never asked. At hotels, she would wash her lingerie in the sink and hang it on the shower rod, and set up an ironing board in her room so she could do her own ironing. She even offered to iron my clothes. I borrowed the iron and the board instead. Maybe that was shortsighted of me; who knows what a skirt ironed by Julia Child would be worth today on eBay.

On one occassion I thought she took housekeeping too far. We were in Memphis, Tennessee, to do a demonstration for Planned Parenthood and it was minutes away from show time, but there was no Julia. She had been there a few minutes before, and I hadn't seen her leave the stage area.

"Where's Julia?" I asked Liz, who was coolly organizing herself on a stool.

"She went to the loo. Better tell her we're ready to begin."

When I entered the ladies' room, I saw two women standing by the sinks, gazing toward the stalls, looking confused and uttering some vague words of agreement to a voice that was coming from one of the stalls. It was Julia's voice.

"Women can be such slobs," she protested from an open-doored stall. I looked in. She was wiping down the toilet seat.

"Julia? What the heck are you doing?"

"I'm wiping the seats. I don't know why women have to go all over them. It's revolting," she said, going into the next stall and grabbing more toilet paper to wipe that seat.

I honestly didn't know if I should wipe seats with her, wash out sinks, or do what I was sent to do. "Um . . . we're ready to begin."

"It's all right. I've finished. I'm coming." As she washed her hands, she told the two women that they should tell the auditorium to put up a sign: "No Peeing on the Seats!"

No. Julia did not behave like a star or demand to be treated like one. In fact, she was usually surprised when she was. On a trip to Dallas, our hotel checked us into its grandest accommodation, even though Julia had reserved "two nice, roomy singles." When we entered the suite, I gluttonously digested the enormous living room with its glorious view of the city from a wall of full-length windows. There was even a meticulously polished grand piano. A long wallpapered dining room was elegantly set with two places, and the galley kitchen was generously stocked with food and beverages. No question about it—it was the presidential suite, reserved for our leader and those deserving the same grandiosity.

"Gosh, Julia," I said when I could close my mouth enough to get the words out. "I had no idea you were such a big deal."

"Neither did I," she responded, looking even more awed than as I was.

Not even at restaurants did she expect special treatment, in spite of the fact that having her as a patron was money in the bank. One morning during our prepping at *Good Morning America,* she decided it would be good fun to call Betty and George Kubler and see if they would like to come into the city and meet us for lunch.

"Great idea!" I said.

"I'd like some serious French food," she said. "Have you ever eaten at La Grenouille?"

"No, but I'd love to," I responded with genuine enthusiasm, envisioning the elegant dining room with grand floral displays, which I had seen only in photographs. Those photos always showed a dining room filled to capacity with, as they say, "those who lunch." "But how will we ever get in at this late hour?" I needled her as she left the room to call the Kublers and the restaurant.

"We're all set," she said when she returned. "They were fully booked, but we managed to get a table."

"How *ever* did you manage that?" I teased.

"I called my hairdresser at Elizabeth Arden's. Her brother is the dishwasher there, and he got us in."

I stopped cooking long enough to see if she was serious. "Did it ever occur to you to just tell them who you were?"

"Oh, they wouldn't care. They get big celebrity types all the time." There was absolutely no sense in trying to convince her that when it came to restaurants she was in a celebrity class all by herself. She wouldn't buy it.

Without a doubt, I saw the most unpretentious side of Julia during one of our outings from work at *GMA*.

In 1984, there was much chatter about an excellent cooking school opening on Broadway in New York's Soho area. The school's

Julia with chefs and students at the French Culinary Institute.

mission was to combine classic French techniques with American ingenuity, and Julia was fascinated. "We have to go," she announced after Sara Moulton told her about it. At that time Sara had left La Tulipe for *Gourmet* and had an in, so even though the school was not quite ready for business, she wangled an invitation to lunch. Our *GMA* producer, Sonya, called for a car to drive Sara, Julia, Paul, Susy, and me some sixty blocks south to the school, where the owner, Dorothy Cann Hamilton, welcomed us with open arms and much appreciated kir imperials, those timeless Parisian aperitifs made with champagne and eau de framboise.

When we left the school, sated with allumettes au Gruyère, sole bonne femme, and fresh fruit with sabayon, it was dusk. Sonya had dismissed the car and driver earlier when we arrived, and there were no taxis in sight. Seasoned New Yorker that she was, Sara valiantly dashed from corner to corner in a vain attempt to spot one. Meanwhile, Sonya, visibly nervous about having her star entertainer stranded anywhere in New York, let alone the not-quite-yet-gentrified area we were in, tried unsuccessfully to contact the car company and see if they would come to our rescue immediately. Julia spotted the nearby subway entrance.

"Why, we can take the subway. I used to do it all the time when I worked here for Sloane's." That was in the forties, when subways were not gathering grounds for what Sonya believed were villainous, psychotic weirdos who'd as soon push you onto the tracks as look at you. She was adamantly opposed to the idea, but Julia was already heading for the stairs.

The last car of the train was practically empty, and we paraded in, and plopped down together toward the back. Julia and Paul sat opposite us, with Julia a few spaces away from a woman who can be described kindly as having seen better days but more accurately as a very down-and-out bag lady. She had the requisite grimy shopping bags, and we could smell her across the aisle. I suspected the odor was why the car was empty. She looked at Julia and then moved down the seats to be closer to her.

"Hello," she said, revealing a few discolored teeth. "I know you." Obviously, her better days had included a television set.

Sonya immediately went into retreat mode, tapped my knee, stood up, and said, "Come on. We're moving."

I started to stand, but Julia wasn't budging from her seat, wasn't sliding away from the woman or paying any attention to Sonya's impending flight. She was talking to the woman—about where she was going, about how this had happened to her, about *cooking*. Their conversation lasted all the way uptown, and all that way I watched and thought, *How kind, how gracious.* But it was more than that. Julia didn't think of it as being a star showing kindness to a poor nobody. They were both just people who'd wound up in different places.

Julia honestly wanted to know that woman's story, just as she wanted to know those of the many people she met. Her genuine interest in other people was one of her most outstanding qualities and right up there at the top of my list of attributes fondly remembered. Moreover, it was one I knew was worth instilling in my boys. If I could not inspire in my children the actual quality of interest in others, then at least I could teach them the graciousness and value of the characteristic. My son Brad was always shy when he was very young. (Hard to believe today when I see him onstage playing guitar and singing with his band to a thousand or more people.) So when he was no more than four or five, I told him that when he found it hard to say much, he should ask other people about themselves and take the pressure of having to talk off himself. Not long after, we were in the market and I saw an elderly woman, perhaps in her early eighties, who was a friend of my mother's. I greeted her and introduced her to Brad. Dottie had been an art teacher, and she immediately asked Brad where he went to school. "Gordon School," he replied, and then I could see him grappling a bit before he came up with, "Where do you go to school?"

5

Do or do not. There is no try.

—Yoda, *Star Wars*

On my first week at *Good Morning America*, Julia asked me, "How much do you charge? What is your fee?"

Fee? I'd never thought about charging her a fee. ABC reimbursed me for all my travel expenses, paid for the hotel, and even gave me a daily food allowance. It didn't cost me a penny to work for her, and I considered it a plum of an opportunity to apprentice in television production with the best in the business. If she had asked me to pay her, I would have thought it a fair price for the education.

"You don't have to pay me, Julia. I'm just thrilled to have the opportunity to work with you," I said, and honestly meant it. I suppose I expected her to accept my zero-an-hour offer. I couldn't have been more wrong.

Immediately her index finger jutted out and she spoke sternly. "Don't *ever* say that! You are a professional and should charge accordingly. I pay $12.50 an hour. Will that be okay?"

Until the moment she decreed me a professional, I'm not sure I ever thought about what I did as an actual, honest-to-God career or really even as a job. I was serious about my teaching, but it was more a passionate hobby turned paying hobby than an occupation. Working with Julia was just icing on the cake.

Julia saw what we did quite differently. It was a business, and we had to think of it as such. I didn't know it at the time, but her quick reproach of my offer to work for nothing was sparked by her years of determination to see that a career in the culinary arts received the recognition and respect she felt it warranted. Next to actually cooking and teaching, her ultimate passion was the development of the "profession of gastronomy," and few in the field devoted the time and effort to making that happen. Yet I doubt that even Julia could have predicted the extent to which it would grow.

The directory of the International Association of Culinary Professionals (the food professional's equivalent of the American Bar Association or the medical or dental associations) lists over seventy networking categories for those who earn their living in food-related careers. There are the groups you would expect to see in such a directory: chefs and restaurateurs, culinary educators, nutritionists and dieticians, vintners, food writers and cookbook authors. But there are other members not commonly thought of as food professionals, and their diversity attests to the enormous breadth to which the food industry has grown. Food photographers, culinary historians, radio and television producers, and program hosts fill the lists of a constantly expanding membership roster, as do editors and indexers who specialize in cookbooks, literary agents who concentrate on selling them, and publicists dedicated to promoting them. There are professions that did not exist in pre-Julia years: freelance food stylists, recipe testers, and culinary media escorts, who greet cookbook authors at airports around the country and prep the recipes required for television appearances.

Of course, Julia did not personally create all those categories. What she did do was change the image of the profession so that it became a desirable one. Before Julia, outside of the commercial food industry that fed America, a culinary career usually meant cooking in a restaurant or teaching those who did. Neither was considered glamorous. Julia used to say, and rightly so, that "the cooking end of gastronomy was strictly a blue-collar job." The celebrity chef was nowhere in sight. And although Americans could list their favorite restaurants, they could rarely name the person in the kitchen who was turning out the meals that made them swoon. They fondly named Delmonico's, the 21 Club, and the Palm as places not to be missed, but the man—and it almost always was a man—behind the stove remained nameless. There were but a few professional culinary schools in the country, and they were not well known. Today's prestigious Culinary Institute of America with impressive campuses on two coasts was in the 1960s located in a nondescript building on a New Haven, Connecticut, street that I walked along every day when I was in college in the same city. We all thought the CIA on the building meant it was a Secret Service outpost. Johnson and Wales University, now one of the world's largest cooking schools, with campuses in six states, did not exist until 1973.

Back then, the prevailing benchmark for a great meal was lots of food at a reasonable price, so few Americans noticed the lack of culinary erudition. Moreover, the food industry as a whole was dedicated more to getting the housewife out of the kitchen than to putting her in front of the stove. Television commercials spoke of ovens that turned themselves on and off and efficient electrical appliances that "got you out of the kitchen in a jiffy." Those too busy to cook at all were encouraged to reach not into the prepared-food section of a gourmet specialty store—of which there were few to none—but into the freezer for TV dinners.

The culinary scene that Julia discovered in France when she fell in love with gastronomy was entirely different. Eating well was a national pastime for the French and Julia thought that was exactly as it should be. The yardstick for fine dining was the careful selection of excellent ingredients cooked with care—at home and in restaurants. Although a chef's position was artisanal as opposed to professional, it was more respected in France than in America. Boys of twelve, thirteen, and fourteen—they were always boys—considered it a great coup to gain an apprenticeship under a known chef.

Julia was acutely aware of the differences between the French and American attitudes toward what they ate and who prepared it, and she devoted her professional life to obliterating those differences. As New York columnist Regina Schrambling wrote in her column headlined, "Julia Child, the French Chef for a Jell-O Nation," Julia "brought cassoulet to a casserole culture." Julia not only wanted to raise America's awareness of and demand for good food, she wanted to bring the French concept of cooking as a respected career to America. The one notion of the French kitchen she had no desire to replicate was the sex of the chef. She saw no reason why women as well as men should not pursue that career.

Julia did not begin her career with the intention of changing an entire profession. She had learned something wonderful about eating well and wanted to share it. But her very presence on television inspired young men—and women—to choose culinary careers. At book signings across the country chefs, teachers, writers, and several food industry executives thanked Julia for being responsible for their careers. Numerous authors whom she had never met credited her in the acknowledgments of their cookbooks as the person who made it happen.

When Julia realized how much she could bring to gastronomy, she used her renown to mentor not only the industry as a whole but the individuals in it. She gave chefs and cooks the respect she felt they deserved. Seldom do I recall a restaurant meal that did not end with her going into the kitchen to speak with and encourage the chef and the entire staff, most of whom removed sweat-covered hats or food-stained aprons and asked her to sign them. She listed her telephone number in the local directory and answered the phone herself; anyone could call and ask her questions, whether it was about how to stabilize whipped cream or what to do with their professional lives. She personally responded to the multitude of letters she received from those who wrote to ask her advice on topics from what to serve for Thanksgiving or where to go to culinary school.

Where did all this mentoring lead? Today, chefs are megastars. No longer are restaurants staffed with a diffident group of cooks who remain nameless in the kitchen. We speak of Mario, Jasper, Wolfgang, and Emeril and sometimes have to ask ourselves, "What *are* the names of their restaurants?" We have a cable television station totally devoted to food, twenty-four hours a day. In 2006 alone, cookbook sales were projected to reach $519 million. Dunkin' Donuts sells croissants—of a sort. Culinary education, food writing, and product development are big business. Unlike in the days when it was a blue-collar job, a great many of those who enter the profession are augmenting already-earned college degrees in history, literature, art, engineering, biochemistry. Like Julia herself, the "new culinary professional" is intelligent, well educated, and above all, passionate.

If Julia had a conscious strategy in establishing a new culinary order, it was to organize the troops. While she was introducing TV audiences to the joys of fine cooking, she was also rallying a new generation of food professionals to prepare and educate themselves to meet the needs of an eating public with higher expectations. "Ours is a really serious profession and a discipline and an art form," she said in an interview for the video magazine *Savor*. And Julia did all she could to validate her comment. Together with Rebecca Alssid and

Boston University, she succeeded in establishing the first American degree program in gastronomy. She joined and supported the growing numbers of national, international, and state culinary organizations that cropped up to support those flocking to culinary careers. In some cases, Julia was an active worker bee in these associations. At the very least, she made it a point to attend as many meetings as she could. To neatly tie together professionals with nonprofessional but dedicated culinary advocates, she joined forces with Robert Mondavi of Mondavi Vineyards in 1981 to form the American Institute of Wine and Food, open to anyone serious about gastronomy.

The extent of her influence is impressive, but it was futile to suggest to Julia that she was so remarkable as to be responsible for altering the culinary path of America. While she never denied her influence, she claimed that luck had just put her in the right place at the right time. Luck and timing undoubtedly played a major role in making her famous, but her exceptional attributes were what changed the face of the culinary world.

Julia did not see herself as exceptional. If you said she was, she'd reply, "I'm just good old pioneer stock," alluding to the fact that her grandfather, as a teenager, had headed West in a covered wagon. It often surprises even some of her most ardent fans that Julia was a California girl, born and raised in Pasadena and not in Boston, as so many thought. She did have a New England air about her, most likely inherited from her mother, Julia Carolyn (Caro) Weston McWilliams, who was descended from a long line of blue-blooded New Englanders of impressive pedigree. But Julia was not one to assume airs about lineage. She preferred telling stories about her grandfather, John McWilliams, instead of dry and dusty accounts of her Massachusetts colonial ancestors. When he was only sixteen, McWilliams attached four oxen to his wagon laden with bacon and flour and set out to pan for gold in the Sacramento Valley. "My grandfather was a good, tough old boy who fought in the Civil War and died at ninety-three."

Paul was less reticent about his wife's outstanding qualities, and he said it well in Julia's debut *Parade* issue in February 1982. The magazine published an interview that included Paul's answers to what attracted him to her. Along with "the sound of her voice" and "I thought she was beautiful," Paul said, "Brains . . . guts . . . ability . . . I liked that she was tough and worked like mad and never gave up on things." Those were the strengths that converted culinary hobbyists and blue-collar cooks into professional culinarians.

For those of us working with her, the conversion was personal. We had a private Merlin, a one-on-one mentor, our own Yoda. She never stopped encouraging and promoting us along a path that would grow our professional lives, never stopped introducing us to the infinite opportunities that the cooking business provided. Being a Julia Child associate was the culinary equivalent of being a graduate student, and I was right to have thought that I should pay her for the education.

"Aren't we lucky to be in this profession?" Julia said repeatedly over the years. Well, yes! She made it stimulating and exciting far beyond the challenges of mastering the art of cooking. She offered us the opportunity to be part of the new world of American gastronomy.

For all I knew about cooking techniques when Julia hired me—and believe me, Madeleine taught us well—I was a neophyte in the new world of Julia's vision. I was completely unaware of all those culinary organizations that existed. Julia not only let me know about them but encouraged me to get involved. And she made me want to. Once alerted to the expansive nature of the profession that I'd begun as a hobby, I was a most eager soldier under her command. Her goals became mine, not just because they were hers but because she so ably convinced me of their wisdom and necessity.

I joined and began to attend meetings with her of the Boston Women's Culinary Guild, which Sara Moulton had helped found; a few years later, because we worked in New York, we qualified for and became charter members of the New York Women's Culinary Alliance, of which Sara was also a founder. Julia introduced me to the International Association of Culinary Professionals (at that time called the International Association of Cooking Schools) and I became a member, traveling with her to meetings across the country where I met large numbers of people who had also turned cooking hobbies into culinary professions. When the IACP instituted a professional certification program, Julia and I both took the exam and passed, thereby giving us the right to place the professional affirmation CCP (Certified Culinary Professional) after our names. When the Boston chapter of the American Institute of Wine and Food was formed, I was there with my checkbook, and I eventually worked on establishing a chapter in Rhode Island. Within two years of meeting her, I had become an actively involved culinary professional.

Seeing that I was such an avid convert to the cause, Julia involved me in her objectives, which she always clearly defined. Better food in America was her overall goal, but she concentrated her efforts on education—teaching, writing, and learning. She demonstrated her commitment to that area of gastronomy in her own work and in her financial support of organizations that shared that goal. She donated an annual scholarship to the IACP's foundation, stipulating that it was available only to those seeking to further their culinary educations. In the summer of 1982, she wrote asking me if I "would be so kind in helping to interview a prospect for our scholarship—we've changed it from 'fellowship' and are directing it to those interested in teaching, writing, or research of a scholarly nature—no restaurant types . . . Seems simpler to make limits, and those are my interests, anyway—and yours too."

So characteristic of who she was, she didn't just urge others to educate themselves but continued to school herself, and encouraged me to do the same. When conference programs and registrations arrived in the mail, she would call me and we would go over which lectures and seminars sounded most interesting. Together we attended several sessions of the Symposium for Professional Food Writers at The Greenbrier in West Virginia, where she participated fully in the required writing exercises. We attended numerous cooking classes at which she listened attentively and took notes. In England, we joined the culinary intelligentsia at the Oxford Symposium on Food, where we attended lectures on such topics as the significance of the shish kebab skewers in the corner of the ancient 214-foot-long Bayonne Tapestry and the prevalence of cannabis (marijuana) as an ingredient in biblical-era cooking.

"That was fascinating" and "I always learn something," she would say after classes, and always learning something was essential to her.

Julia sitting in on a late night study session at the writers' symposium at The Greenbrier.

CHAPTER 5

Samuel Johnson wrote, "Curiosity is one of the permanent and certain characteristics of the vigorous mind." Vigorous indeed, and keen. She was curious about so many things, not just about food. She was interested in and savored every substantial morsel of life, whether it was about people, politics, or technology, and hers was not idle curiosity. At a time when even those in the industry were saying home computers would never catch on, she was already using one. She was intrigued with the remote to my Jeep and would ask me to test its range in parking lots, from the windows upstairs and downstairs in her house, from her car to mine. The exacting, minute details of a person's life, the state of the country, and the love life of Pamela Harriman were all equally interesting to her. If the story involved sex, all the better. She by no means dwelt on prurient things, but she was unashamedly void of prudery and things of a sexual nature did not embarrass her. She loved a good raunchy joke and a bit of lascivious gossip.

When it came to food, her curiosity was especially inexhaustible. She planned lunch and dinner parties around local or visiting chefs and cooked the meal alongside them, not only because she found it such fun but because she learned from them. "That's fascinating. Show me how you did that," she'd encourage whenever she saw a technique that was new to her. Playful bickering and differences of culinary opinion aside, she adored working with Jacques Pépin, her dear friend and the ultimate master chef, because the good-natured competition kept her mind agile.

She did not reserve her interest in techniques for chefs. Philip Barr has a most unusual way of eating a fresh pear. He begins by inserting a sharp paring knife straight downward, parallel and close to the stem, until he feels the tip of the knife touch the core. He then removes the knife and makes additional cuts around the stem until he can lift a neat circle of pear out of the top. Then he turns the pear over and slips the knife into the blossom end, angling it out slightly to reach beyond the wider bottom core. He continues making incisions around the core at the blossom end until it is free of the flesh and he can push it out. Then he turns the pear right side up and makes neat horizontal cuts, leaving him with perfect, ½-inch-thick, donut-shaped slices. When Julia saw him do this sitting at her kitchen table, she was fascinated. She picked another pear out of the fruit bowl and handed it to Philip. "Here. Do it again. More slowly."

I marveled at her curiosity, and I teased her about it. Once when we were making a simple salad in her kitchen and I said, "We are now going to consider the forty-two or so possible ways to trim and wash a head of lettuce," she came right back at me with, "There are fifty-four ways and I think we should try them all." Mostly I envied it, and I once asked her if she had always had such a keen interest in so many things.

"Not at all," she responded. "It was Paul who taught me to really look at everything around me. When I met him, he thought I was a scatterbrain. And I was." I might think that she was exaggerating, but Paul's assessment of Julia's lack of attention to detail is forever stored in the archives of the Schlesinger Library. Shortly after meeting her, he described her to his brother Charlie in a letter: "Her mind is potentially good but she's an extremely sloppy thinker." Paul made it his mission to correct that, and he obviously did a bang-up job. When he introduced her to the joys of the table, particularly the French table, she found her passion, and with it a sense of direction. With intense curiosity and dogged determination, she spent the rest of her life perfecting her culinary knowledge.

"[Cooking] takes all of your intelligence and all your dexterity," Julia said in a 1984 interview, and she always gave it her all. She wanted to know exactly how things worked, why they didn't, and how many ways they could be made to work. She delved into the origins and uses of ingredients the way Einstein studied relativity. She attacked questions of technique scientifically through research, multiple rounds of testing, and querying authorities.

Those of us who worked with her, especially when she was developing recipes for her cookbooks, became part of the research team. We shared her enthusiasm, but I don't recall that any of us were prepared to approach all subjects with Julia's thoroughness. Hard-boiled eggs come to mind. HB eggs, in Julia-speak, are not something we think of as particularly difficult. Most cooks can and have made them, yet Julia felt they warranted extensive, exhaustive research. To prick or not to prick, how much water, how long to cook to avoid that "dolefully discolored, badly cooked yolk" with its telltale green-hued ring, how to peel, and how to store were all issues to which Julia wanted definitive answers. She tested several methods, contacted a number of authorities, and liked the method suggested to her by the Georgia Egg Board. It was fail-safe but fussy, and few of us were as excited about it as Julia was. First the eggs must be pricked a quarter inch deep in the thick end, then covered with an exact amount of water depending on the number of eggs, brought just to the boil, immediately removed from the heat, covered with the pan lid, and left to sit for *precisely* seventeen minutes. When the time is up, the eggs are transferred to a bowl of ice water and chilled for two minutes, then, six at a time, returned to boiling water for ten seconds, and finally put back in the bowl of ice water to chill for fifteen or twenty minutes before peeling. They were perfect HB eggs and a perfect pain to do—for everyone but Julia.

Whenever our work called for them, we anxiously looked at each other, hoping someone else would do them. If Julia was out of the kitchen, whoever picked the short straw was always tempted to cook them according to his or her own favorite method. The one time she caught me using my technique instead of hers, she didn't tell me to stop, didn't insist I use hers. She cautioned me with one of her favorite warnings: "When all else fails, read the recipe."

Turkey received the same thorough research as HB eggs. At some point in the eighties, high-heat roasting became the in technique. Magazines and cookbooks devoted a considerable number of pages to the procedure, purporting to tell the reader "everything you ever wanted to know about roasting"—unless you were Julia Child.

"I think we should test all these methods," she said to me over the phone one day in July. "Would you get five turkeys and roast them five different ways? I'll do the same and we'll compare results." She was particularly interested in the best way to roast poultry since there is always the problem of having the dark meat fully cooked without the white meat drying out.

So for several days, as the temperature stubbornly hovered at record-high levels, I cooked turkeys in my un-air-conditioned summer home—one after the other, because I had only one oven. I roasted one at a moderate 325°F, another at a frightening 500°F. I started turkeys three, four, and five at one temperature and finished them at another. Julia called me midway through her testing.

"Well, the 500°F turkey smoked up the whole house!" she reported. "And the oven was a horrid mess. The meat was juicy but I think a bit tough. I'm going to try it again and reduce the heat after the initial browning. Maybe add some water to the pan. What did you think?"

What I thought was that no one should roast anything when the oven and the kitchen are at the same temperature! In the end, she continued to cook her turkeys as she had always done, at a steady 325°F, but she was satisfied in knowing exactly what each method would produce. Meanwhile, I couldn't get anyone in my family to eat roasted turkey for months. At Thanksgiving, they begged for roast beef.

Cooking, when approached Julia's way, was without question the serious discipline she said it was. It required time, thoroughness, and impeccable attention to detail. We worked hard, and she worked hard right alongside us. She could have given us a list of chores and taken off to lounge in her room—who would have called it bad form? But she loved nothing more than being in the thick of all that chopping, sautéing, whisking, and testing. And that's where the fun came in, because Julia was Julia.

Multitasker that she was, when we were working at her Cambridge home, she'd put the kitchen phone on speaker and deal with necessary business at the same time she was cooking. When someone called, she'd introduce the phone person to the kitchen people—"Now say hello to Nancy, Marian, and Liz"—and she'd expect us to engage the faceless voice in conversation. When the voice belonged to one of her favorites, we'd be privy to delightful exchanges such as her sign-off to Cuisinart founder Carl Sontheimer, "Give yourself a big, wet sloppy kiss for me," and his to her, "An even wetter, sloppier one back to you."

When she wanted a more private conversation, she didn't leave the kitchen. She'd sit on the stool in the corner and pick up the receiver. The one-sided conversations we heard were no less engaging. When her friend and lawyer Bob Johnson was in the hospital, Julia called him often. One day as Susy Davidson and I cooked, Julia sat on the stool, picked up the phone, and dialed the hospital. "Robert Johnson's room, please," we heard, and then, after a pause, "Hi, Bob, it's Julia." There was another very brief pause and then Julia said she was sorry to have disturbed the person. She hung up, dialed again, told the answering party that she had been given the wrong room, and again asked to speak to Bob. This time she knew right away that the person who answered was not Bob because she immediately said she was extremely sorry and called the hospital switchboard a third time. Amazingly, the mix-up occurred again, but this time we heard her say, "Well, I'm awfully sorry that I have bothered you again. I was trying to reach a friend who is there also. But tell me, how are *you*?" She spoke to the unknown patient for at least five minutes, and Susy and I had to leave the room to prevent our giggling from disturbing the call.

Working with Julia on her projects provided all the professional stimulation I thought I needed, but she was not about to let me make a career just being a Julia Child associate. Even during those periods when our work together was time-consuming and extensive, she encouraged me to continue with my own work. She suggested classes for me to take, introduced me to people I should know, and brought me out front onstage with her to give me exposure to her audiences. And, for which I am so very grateful, she encouraged me to write.

"It's publish or perish," she told me about a year after I began working for her. We were riding in the car on a long trip somewhere and talking about college. She told me that when she went to Smith she'd intended to be "a great novelist," but when she graduated and applied for a job at the *New Yorker*, "they had no interest in me whatsoever." After trying *Newsweek,* she finally got a job in public relations and advertising for the W. & J. Sloane furniture store in New York. Eventually, of course, she achieved success as a writer; cookbooks were her novels. And she was a fine writer, with a full, colorful vocabulary, meticulous attention to grammar and syntax, and an enviably natural way of expressing her thoughts. She was careful about her text and fluently descriptive with her recipes.

During that ride, after she told me her college story, I told her mine. I had also aspired to be a writer, although—typical of the differences in our personalities—I'd never thought "great novelist," simply "writer." My aspirations were sideswiped not by the *New Yorker* but by a classmate in my junior year. We were in Mr. Taylor's creative writing class and one by one we had to read essays we wrote. When the boy sitting next to me read his, I had an epiphany, and not a good one. *He's a writer,* I said to myself. *I'm not.* That boy was Tom Griffin, who went on to be a noted playwright *(The Boys Next Door, Einstein and the Polar Bear)*. Had Julia been my friend back then, she would never have allowed me to give up my dream just because someone else was better at what I wanted to do.

After that conversation, she began to encourage me to send articles to culinary magazines. I did, and when I proudly announced that I had sold my first one to *Food & Wine* magazine, she said to send more, to all the magazines. *Gourmet, Cook's Illustrated,* and *Bon Appétit* bought my articles, and as soon as the issues arrived at her door, she called or wrote to tell me how much she enjoyed what I had written.

When I told her of an idea I had for a book, she wrote back: "Glad you got through your last classes and that you are really in there writing—that's the way to do it. Yes, for the book—but get lots done first so you'll have something to show, including a complete outline for all of it. The illustrations sound good and original. (We rewrote our Mastering I three or four times—so never get discouraged whatever happens.)"

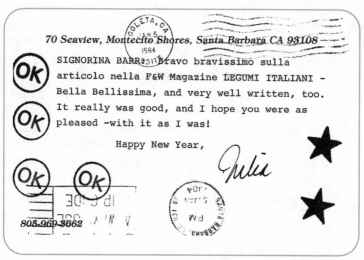

70 Seaview, Montecito Shores, Santa Barbara CA 93108

SIGNORINA BARR: Bravo bravissimo sulla articolo nella F&W Magazine LEGUMI ITALIANI - Bella Bellissima, and very well written, too. It really was good, and I hope you were as pleased -with it as I was!

Happy New Year,

Julia

805-969-3662

Postcard from Julia congratulating me on my first magazine article.

It was three years before I decided I was ready to propose the book. I got "lots of it done," as Julia suggested, included a "complete outline," and sent it to an agent in spite of the fact that many friends suggested I ask Julia to show it to her editor at Knopf, Judith Jones. But by the time I was ready to pitch my book, I had learned an important fact about Julia. She did not lend her name easily, did not write forewords or blurbs for other people's books. Unless she herself had tested every recipe in that book, she wasn't going to imply approval of it by having her name associated with it. Companies asked her constantly for endorsements, and she always said flat out, "No. How do you know that company will still be good in six months? If it goes downhill, my name goes with it."

So completely did I understand and respect that about her that I never considered asking her even to suggest to Judith that I might be able to write a book. Suppose I couldn't? Then Julia would be barreling down a hill with me. Since Julia's lawyer negotiated her contracts, she never used an agent and couldn't recommend one. Cookbook author Jean Anderson generously loaned me hers, Julie Fallowfield, and ironically, the first publishing house Julie pitched was Knopf. And it wound up being the only one she pitched, since Judith bought it. Julia was thrilled, not only that I had sold the book but that I would be working with Judith. "None better," she said as she opened a bottle of champagne to toast my success. That was the celebrating part of the book, the part before the actual dogged work of writing it.

At the time I sold that book, *We Called It Macaroni*, I was still working on a typewriter—an electric typewriter, but a typewriter—and Julia's immediate advice to me was "Get a computer." She was already using one.

So I invested in the computer; I bought a printer and reams of that old computer paper with yards of attached sheets folded on top of each other and tiny holes running down the sides to move it through the rollers. I loaded the paper in the printer, installed a word-processing program, and composed my first work—a letter to Julia. Her return letter was an enthusiastic response to my computer efforts.

"Dearest Nancy," she wrote in July 1985. "Delighted to have your letter on your WP, and aren't they wonderful! I'm getting really used to mine, and can do pretty much what I want—but do I know all that it can do? That will be an eternal question. Certainly, once you've gotten onto the processor (like the food processor), you'll never go back. However, I still have my electric typewriter, and use it for corrections on sticky tape."

Letters to Julia were easy; the book was hard. Not the recipes— I knew which ones I wanted to include, and I was as exacting as Julia was about testing and retesting. The problem was all that copy around the recipes. It did not exactly flow onto the computer screen, and I understood what Gene Fowler meant when he said, "Writing is easy. All you do is stare at a blank sheet of paper until drops of blood form on your forehead."

Judith was a no-nonsense, thorough, and exacting editor, and quite honestly, she scared me to death. She wanted cookbooks that told a story or at least said something, and that something had better not be drivel. Julia described Judith's editorial approach as "an iron fist in a kid glove," and indeed, Judith could not have been gentler as she encouraged me to write and praised my progress, but I still constantly feared that iron fist crushing my meager manuscript into hundreds of tiny shreds. (Years later, when I worked on my second book with Judith, I came to realize that the kid glove goes pretty deep. She no longer scared me; she simply overwhelmed me with her capabilities.)

When I was certain the amount of blood pouring from my head would cause my demise, it was Julia who mopped my brow and convinced me I wasn't going to die. It helped that she was also struggling with the book she was writing, *The Way to Cook*. She intended for it to be a comprehensive, instructional cookbook, but it was becoming massive and she knew she had to rope it back into a manageable shape—not a simple task when you consider that this was the same woman who in her *Mastering the Art of French Cooking* books devoted eight pages to describing how to make an omelet and eighteen to French bread. "Oh, my book!" she wrote to me. "It is getting so large—I have no idea how many pages but I've now done only two chapters, Poultry and Vegetables, and they seem immense, and it takes so long. How are you doing on yours?" And later in the letter, she admitted that she was "taking the day off as a reward for finishing my vegetable chapter. And I'm not going to take any work at all on this European trip—for the first time ever!" I'll bet she didn't write that last part to Judith.

"Blue-pencil" is the term used for what an editor does in editing a manuscript. Originally, all editors wrote in blue so their notes would stand out against white paper and black writing. Judith doesn't blue-pencil, she green-pencils. And she writes in small, finely formed cursive. When she returned my manuscript with her first edits, I sat down and page by page read her clear notes. What was that in the margin outside that paragraph? The writing was much smaller than the rest, infinitesimal, and I had to get out a magnifying glass. It was one word, *nice*, with an exclamation point after it. I stopped going through page by page and began flipping the pages over rapidly to find more *nice*s. There were three. Three Pulitzer prizes on the first read alone.

Julia called me shortly after I received the edit and wanted to know how it went. I told her that Judith must have liked what I wrote about such-and such because she'd written "nice" next to it with an exclamation point.

The elevated level of excitement in her tone was unmistakable. "How many *nice*s did you get?" she asked.

"Three."

"Why, that's wonderful! I always look for them first. Never get too many, but I love it when I do." From that point on, Julia and I shared the number of *nice*s as soon as we received our edits from Judith.

So, though our problems were quite different—Julia wondering what she could cut without jeopardizing her intent and I struggling with what to put in—we formed a writers' bond that replayed some years later when she asked me to write two books with her. Julia was much too gracious a person to suggest even remotely that she had as much to do with my book as she did, but I know she felt a connection to it. When eventually she gave the majority of her cookbooks to the Schlesinger Library, she told me, "But I still have yours. Always will."

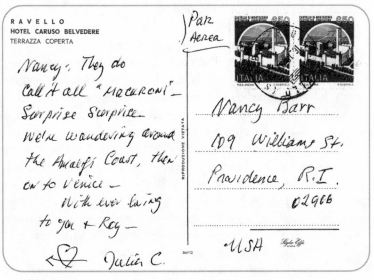

RAVELLO
HOTEL CARUSO BELVEDERE
TERRAZZA COPERTA

Par
Aerea

Nancy: They do call it all "MACARONI". Surprise Surprise. We're wandering around the Amalfi Coast, then on to Venice —
with ever loving to you + Roy —
Julia C.

Nancy Barr
109 Williams St.
Providence, R.I.
02906

USA

Julia's postcard from Italy, where she was delighted to discover that Italians do call pasta "macaroni."

I cannot separate Julia from my professional career. I don't know if I ever would have written cookbooks or even magazine articles were it not for her. It is doubtful that I would have had the opportunity to work in television. She was all that a mentor should be, and when my personal life needed guidance, she provided that as well.

When I originally enrolled in Madeleine Kamman's Modern Gourmet culinary school, my intention was to follow my nonprofessional degree with a teacher's diploma. Two pregnancies interrupted that goal, and it was seven years before I applied to Madeleine for a student-teacher position. By that time, she had moved the school to Annecy, France, which meant I would have to fulfill my two-week apprenticeship there. It was a difficult decision because I had never left my family for such a long stretch. No less difficult was my awareness that I was entering enemy camp, so to speak.

Sometime long before I applied to the program, Julia explained to me why she didn't trust "that woman from Newton." When Madeleine first moved to Boston to teach cooking classes, Julia invited her to her home and introduced her to the local culinary community. Julia thought she had a great new ally in her goal of introducing good French food to Americans since she and Madeleine shared not only a passion for classic French cuisine but also an unwavering goal of teaching its principles and techniques. But then, for reasons only she could know, Madeleine wrote a critical letter to WGBH, Julia's public broadcasting station in Boston, stating not only that Julia was neither French nor a chef but that perhaps she had other issues that made her unfit for the show. Liz told me that it was a "vicious" letter. Then, during a newspaper interview, Madeleine told the press that she had taken classes with Julia's *Mastering the Art of French Cooking* co-authors Simone Beck and Louisette Bertholle at Ecole des Trois Gourmandes, the cooking school the three had started in France, but had not learned a thing. She said she actually taught them a thing or two. Julia was at first stung and then angry. From that point on, even as I watched Madeleine try to assume a kinship over the years, Julia's comment was always, "Don't turn your back on her."

I'm not quite sure why Madeleine accepted me into the apprenticeship program, because from the very first class she was relentless in her quips about my work with Julia. "I suppose you learned that from *Julia!*" she'd say, and "Is that the way *Julia* does it?"—always out loud in the middle of a class I was teaching. At one point, in an attempt to relax a young student who was near-spasmodically trying to bone squab, I put my hand on her shoulder and said, "Relax. Cooking is fun."

"Fun!" Madeleine erupted from the other side of the kitchen. "You think this is fun? It's hard work and don't forget it." I tried to

Me having fun cooking in Julia's kitchen at La Pitchoune.

Lunch outside at La Pitchoune with Paul, Julia, and Simca.

convince myself that it wasn't me, that Madeleine was just being her ornery self, but a fellow student teacher told me that she was appalled at the hostility vented my way. After less than a week, I found the constant animosity unbearable, and I thought longingly of Julia, who was at her home in Provence. Philip and I had spent four perfect days there with her and Paul before he returned home and I left for Annecy. I wished desperately I could return to the warm environment of her home.

So I called her. For years after, when Julia and I recounted the story of my experience, we always said I called "sobbing." We liked to tell it that way because Julia liked to parody me by making the most despondent sobbing sounds and it made the story all the more funny and dramatic. I don't recall if I actually sobbed when I called, but I have no problem remembering how wretched I felt. "This was a big mistake. I'm so miserable," I said. "I think I'm going to leave. I was thinking that I could come back to La Pitchoune until it's time for me to return home."

"Don't you dare!" she said firmly instead of cooing the you-come-right-back-here-dearie words I expected to hear. "You bull it through and don't let *that woman* know she's getting to you."

"But—"

"No buts. Just do it!" Had she no heart? I needed rescuing, but she would have none of it. She acknowledged that "that woman" was most likely taking it out on me because I was "consorting with the enemy," but she insisted I tough it out.

I stayed in Annecy and did not let on to Madeleine how miserable she was making me, and for no reason I can comprehend, by the time I left, her attitude had completely changed. She saw me off at the train station, where she presented me with a lovely blue and white faience serving plate as a gift. Go figure.

It wasn't until we were both back home that Julia, with unmistakable compassion, told me how distressed she had been I was having such a hard time. "I wanted to run right up there and snatch you out of her clutches." It was, of course, exactly what I'd wanted her to do at the time. Instead, she allowed me to have the satisfaction of having bulled it through a tough situation, which is what she would have done, and it felt damned good.

6

Each friend represents a world in us, a world possibly not born until they arrive, and it is only by this meeting that a new world is born.

—Anaïs Nin, *The Diary of Anaïs Nin*

"*L*et's get a hot dog," Julia said. We were driving south from Cambridge on Route 128. It was about ten in the morning, and I was surprised, not by the hot dog but because Julia almost never ate between meals. She believed that snacking was a regrettable American habit brought about by a lack of enjoying good, satisfying food at mealtimes. I love hot dogs, but they were not on my mind at that particular time and place.

"Where should we go?" I asked.

"There's a highway stop just up ahead." Okay, it was going to be a fast-food hot dog.

The dog wasn't half bad, but the real feast was seeing other travelers poke each other and point our way, most likely asking if that really was Julia Child pushing a plastic cafeteria tray along the counter and ordering "one with everything."

Before I knew her, I would have been as amazed or amused as they were at the sight of not just any celebrity but a gourmet celebrity ordering a hot dog at a quick roadside stop. But I wasn't with a celebrity; I was with a friend.

In his *Life of Johnson*, James Boswell wrote, "We cannot tell the precise moment when friendship is formed. As in filling a vessel drop by drop, there is at last a drop which makes it run over." In a profession dominated by the pleasures of the table, the lines between collegial and social are often blurred, since so much of our work involves sharing good food and fine wine at a table surrounded by people who are jovial and friendly just because they are eating. Julia had good friends and it was obvious who they were, but she also had a most splendid way of making many people around her *feel* like friends. I don't know at what point I began to think of her as a friend or she me, but I remember the first time she said it.

We were working alone in her kitchen. It was late morning, three or maybe more years after we met. "Let's go out for lunch," she said.

"Great idea. Let's do it."

Two other people were working in the upstairs office, and I asked if I should invite them to join us.

"No," she said, and then, perhaps to clarify her quick response, she added, "They work for me. We're friends." I remember feeling glad that she'd said it. *I* felt that we were friends, and it was good to know she did as well.

From the get-go Julia made it easy to be her friend, and it could have been otherwise. After all, to culinary zealots, she was the food goddess, the high priestess of cuisine. Many devotees admit that dining with her for the first time involved a lot of self-pinching and silent repetition of *I am sitting at the table with Julia Child!* In less time than it takes to scramble an egg, she cleared idolatry from the table by being so regular, so utterly unpretentious. Those who couldn't make a quick transition from hero worship to "Let's go get a hot dog" missed out on the fun; Julia did not warm to constant fawners at all.

I think the foundation of our friendship formed as soon as I went on the road with her for those early demonstrations in Memphis and New Haven. We traveled well together—a deal breaker for friendship if ever there was one. Can you be flexible? Can you meet, smiling and chatty, for breakfast at 6:00 A.M., even though you were operating on less than five hours of sleep? Will you forgo the aisle seat—without grumbling that an inside one makes you claustrophobic—because there was only one left on the plane and Julia's long legs made any other seat impossibly uncomfortable for her? Is the focus of your day where your next meal will be? And, above all, will you have a good time, and never mention the T-word even when the days are long and the workload staggering?

That all worked for me. The early mornings and the long days were never an issue, since all my life I never seemed to require more than five hours of sleep; I was thrilled to have someone else awake and ready to talk at five-thirty in the morning. Seating was irrelevant. As Julia liked to note about my short stature, whether referring to an airplane seat or the middle spot in the back of a car, "Nancy can sit there. She has no legs." I was as guilty as the next passionate foodie of swooning over one meal while at the same time planning what and where I would eat the next. And, after 1984, I was happy to send for room service on Sunday nights so Julia wouldn't miss her favorite TV show, Angela Lansbury's *Murder, She Wrote*.

The have-a-good-time part was easy. We all loved what we were doing. And we had Liz, who made us all laugh with her quick, irreverent Boston Irish humor. Ten years older than I, Liz had been with Julia for some twenty years, and she gave me my Berlitz class in Julia-ese. She told me about the T-word and warned me, "We never mention the name of that other spread on the table," the one that's not real butter. I learned from her which people we never mentioned by name but only with sobriquets such as "that woman from Schenectady" or a sarcastically toned "*your friend* from Ohio."

But more than a language lesson, Liz showed me through her own candid relationship with Julia that Julia did not expect docile veneration from her friends. One day in Cambridge, we were testing Julia's recipe for a free-form meat loaf, which had to look particularly appetizing since it was destined for the cover of *Parade*. Brown food, such as meat loaf, is always a challenge for stylists and photographers, but that particular meatloaf really pushed the envelope. It was a long way from looking good, and worse, its texture was unpleasant and its flavor just so-so. Julia asked for our opinions, and we made polite comments: "Perhaps more eggs," "It seems a little tight," "Maybe a red sauce of some type on the top," and of course, "Cover it with parsley."

Then Liz piped up, "It looks like dog food."

"You're right," Julia said, and scrapped the recipe.

Liz did not restrict her candor with Julia to the privacy of Julia's home. She needled her in public, and Julia loved it. In addition to working for Julia, Liz consulted for a Boston wine shop. She had an appreciation for and knew much about wines from many countries, and eventually taught wine classes at my cooking school. Frequently in restaurants, waiters would hand Julia the wine list with an announcement from the chef or owner, "The wine is on us. Please choose whatever you would like." No question what he meant. The sky was the limit, and for a moment Liz would get a wistful look glancing at the possibilities. But she knew what Julia was going to order, and she mimicked Julia by mouthing the exact words at the same time Julia told the waiter, "A nice little Beaujolais would be lovely. Thank you." That's when Julia's eyes would twinkle, and she would poke Liz in the arm.

On nights like that, when our team dined alone, our conversations covered a wide range of topics. We weren't strictly colleagues discussing the latest culinary trends. We were friends talking about current affairs, gossiping, ribbing one another—and occasionally squabbling. My first experience with a family spat was in Memphis, and it was between Paul and Julia. It was also the first time I saw Julia dig in her heels in a way that just told you there was no sense in trying to talk her out of whatever bone she was gnawing.

And Paul was just as obstinate. On that evening, they locked horns in an unselfconscious, open argument at the table, and it felt just like family. Liz, Marian, Paul, Julia, and I had finished dinner, and although Julia usually enjoyed a nibble of something sweet after a meal, that night the chef had sent so many complimentary appetizers that none of us had room except Paul, who could always be counted on to eat a small dish of ice cream. When the waiter brought his ice cream, he also set a three-tiered tray of small sweets on the table.

"Who ordered those?" Paul asked.

"No one," Julia responded. "The chef sent them."

"I don't think he should send something that no one ordered."

"It's something chefs like to do."

"I don't think they should. If no one ordered them, then no one will eat them and they will go to waste."

"That's not the point, Paul. It's a nice thing to do and someone may want eat one." I had been eyeing the pieces of candied orange peel, but at that point, it was no longer dessert; it was a gauntlet that had been thrown down, and I wasn't about to take sides.

"If someone wanted to eat one, they would have ordered one," Paul insisted, and so it went, long after we signed the check, all during our departure from the restaurant, and in the elevator ride upstairs. It was not a heated, acrimonious argument, just a test of who would get in the last word. I don't know who did or how long into the night they argued, but they were their usual agreeable selves at breakfast.

With Julia making it obvious that she was just like everyone else and wanted to be treated that way, and Liz driving the point home by doing so, my rapport with Julia was equally open and unguarded. We liked each other, and the first of Boswell's imaginary drops of friendship began to fill the vessel.

Our closeness grew as I began to spend more time with her at home. "Come for dinner and spend the night," she said for the first time when we were working on *Parade*. "I have plenty of room, and you can have your own bathroom," she added, expressing a shared preference we established when we were on the road together—our own bedrooms and our own bathrooms. The bathroom was a draw, but not as much as the fact that sleeping over meant I would not have to deal with daily round trips in the horrid commuter traffic back and forth between Cambridge and Providence.

To Julia, "come for dinner" meant "we'll cook dinner together first, then we'll eat." Cooking with her for no reason other than eating was different from cooking for work. We didn't have to hurry for the cameras, take notes, or retest. Our meals were simple; we didn't look in cookbooks for fancy new dishes. Still, Julia applied the same careful preparation to everything we cooked, no matter how basic, as she did to her "audience" food. And because teaching and learning were such a part of who she was, cooking dinner was always an opportunity to learn something new.

The first cooking lesson Julia asked me to give her was how to make risotto. I was slightly surprised that she wanted me to give her an Italian cooking lesson. Overall, she wasn't a great fan of Italian food, nor did she think it involved the discipline and technique of French cuisine. But she loved risotto and was aware that a good one required know-how. The classic Italian rice dish was popping up around the country in restaurants of all ethnicities, in culinary magazines, and at catered events. A well-prepared risotto is ethereal; badly cooked, it's a blob of glue on the plate. Julia wanted me to show her how to make it exactly the way Marcella Hazan had taught me in Bologna.

"Can you bring the rice, dearie?" she asked when she called me at home. Rice variety is key to a good risotto. The grain must be able to dissolve enough to create the creamy texture yet remain firm enough at the center to deliver the characteristic bite of the dish.

I had a cupboard full of Italian rice—Arborio, Vialone Nano, Carnaroli. I chose the Carnaroli because, of the three, it produces the creamiest texture. I also brought my own meat broth from my freezer, since one of the most important lessons I learned from Marcella is that Italian *brodo* and French stock are not interchangeable. French stock is richer and its flavor is distractingly strong in a delicate risotto.

Julia stood next to me, observed, questioned, and commented on every step as I made the dish—how long did I sauté the rice before adding the wine, at what pace did I add the hot broth, how much broth and when should we stir in the final butter and cheese. Thank you, Marcella—our risotto was perfect, and Julia and I made it together often. When a grower sent Julia a bag of special California-grown rice, touted to be as good as the Italian Arborio for risotto, we couldn't wait to try it. I didn't think it was quite as good, but that might have been my heritage talking. Julia thought it was—undoubtedly her California roots speaking.

Usually what we cooked did not involve standing over each other and observing step-by-step preparations, and mostly I remember the easy way Julia applied her culinary training to just cooking. The first time I saw her make her "small chicken stock," I wondered why I had never even considered it. We were roasting a chicken, and Julia said we should make a "nice little velouté" to go with it. Velouté is one of the French "mother sauces" and a first lesson in culinary school. It's made by adding white stock to a flour-and-butter roux and then whatever flavorings or enrichments one chooses. I knew how to do that.

"Do you have chicken stock?" I asked, walking to the freezer.

"Yes. But we can make a small chicken stock. We don't need much."

I didn't know "small chicken stock." I only knew four-hour, twelve-quart-pot stock. Julia cut the wing tips from the bird and browned them in a one-quart saucepan with the neck and gizzards. She then added large pieces of onion (with the skin for color), unsalted canned chicken broth (sometimes just water), a tomato half for a bit of acid, and an herb bouquet, and by the time the chicken was cooked, we had a fine, rich stock for our sauce. Julia's "small stock" was a departure from traditional culinary school techniques and perhaps one of my first understandings of what she meant when she said, "You have to be a fearless cook." If you know what something is supposed to taste like and can get there a new way, "go whole hog and do it."

Our fearless-cook triumph together was polenta, the age-old, classic Italian cornmeal staple that had become as popular as risotto in American restaurants.

"Do you know how to make it?" Julia asked me. What kind of a question is that to ask an Italian? Before I learned how from Marcella, I learned how from my grandmother. Their methods were the same: drizzle cornmeal slowly through your fingers—*come neve* (like snow), Nonna said—into boiling water and stir well to prevent lumps from forming. Nothing to learn there, or so I thought. Julia wondered if we couldn't apply a trick she had learned, I think it was in making grits, that called for mixing the grain first with cold water until it is smooth and then adding boiling water to it and finishing the cooking. Blasphemy! But it worked. There was no loss of texture or flavor and absolutely no chance for lumps to form. Traditionally, as soon as polenta is fully cooked, it is immediately poured out on a plate or board and eaten, or shaped into a cylinder and cooled for later use. Excited with our cold-water success, Julia then wondered how long we could keep the cooked polenta in the pan before pouring it out. So we left the pot on the stove, and as water evaporated we added more boiling water to the pot. It kept perfectly for hours. Julia was so pleased with our results that she decided to use our recipe for an issue of *Parade,* and then some years later, when she asked me to teach a class with her at Mondavi Vineyards, she suggested I demonstrate our modern polenta. We always thought of the recipe as "our polenta."

Sometimes for dinner at Julia's there were just the three of us, Paul, Julia, and me, but often friends and colleagues joined us. Either way, we ate dinner in the kitchen, where the Childs preferred to entertain unless a sizeable guest list required the dining room table, which could seat twenty if necessary. The size of the guest list, not its pedigree, determined which room they used. The simple wood table in the center of the kitchen was permanently clothed in one or another of three colorful, Marimekko-style padded vinyl tablecloths that the Childs had purchased several years before. "We can just wipe them down. Whoosh!" Julia told me as she made a quick swiping motion with her arm. She used a round raffia mat, chosen from a large multicolored assortment, to cover each person's place at the table. Oversized light wood chairs with sweeping half-circle backs surrounded the table. Julia and Paul had purchased them in the 1950s when Paul was stationed in Norway with the diplomatic corps, and they made for good, comfortable lounging long after dinner.

There were two pantries lined up in tandem off the kitchen. The first, closest to the kitchen, was the "baking room," where a slab of marble sat atop the under-counter freezer used primarily for butter, nuts, and sundries used for desserts, clearly marked in the attached Post-it note. Sitting atop the marble top, several French wire baskets and American crockery pots held bouquets of wooden rolling pins in all sizes and shapes. The pegboard attached to the wall next to the top was covered with copper egg-white bowls, balloon whisks, an assortment of baker's tools and a variety of Norwegian pastry molds strange to me.

The second pantry had glass-front cupboards that stretched from a waist-high counter to the top of the very high ceilings, and wide, deep drawers from the counter to the floor. It held a visual history of Julia's travels with Paul and especially her television career in the form of the dishes, glassware, and colorful napkins she had used for her early shows. From the time I first began sharing those casual dinners at her house, she asked if I would set the table, and I loved choosing from this nostalgic collection.

"Which dishes would you like me to use?" I asked the first time, thinking that some must indeed be too special for her to risk breakage on such a casual night.

"It doesn't matter. Whatever you like."

Next to cooking in that kitchen with Julia, nothing gave me more pleasure than standing on a stool—or on the counter itself when necessary to reach to the very top of those cupboards—and choosing dinnerware. "Maybe the slightly chipped, deep green Provençal dishes with gently scalloped edges," I'd mutter to myself. "Or the pink-flowered faience." That pantry also held the liquor and wine, and Julia might well have thought I was in there nipping, I took so long to choose.

It never took me any time to decide on the breakfast setting: definitely the Scandinavian china coffee cups called "breakfast bowls." Decorated with a graceful pattern of blue and white flowers, each held the equivalent of at least two cups of coffee, and both the look and feel of the delicate china were lovely. When I watched Julia pour milk into her coffee from a small sterling-silver creamer in the shape of a cow, I regretted drinking mine black. I loved that cow. The tail curled saucily back onto itself to form a handle, and the milk poured from its mouth. I'm not sure why that cow enchanted me so, but even today I can picture every sculpted line of its miniature bovine body.

On the nights when Julia asked others to come to dinner, everyone cooked or at least helped some way in the kitchen. We delegated simple tasks such as trimming beans and washing salad greens to non-cooks. Philip mixed drinks, and Paul was responsible for selecting and opening the wine. When the need arose, Paul was the official knife sharpener. He would stand at the table expertly and patiently honing Julia's massive collection of knives on a whetstone. I've never known anyone who could bring the sharp edge back to a knife as Paul could. Going to dinner at Julia's was exactly as she described it—"cooking together is such fun."

Julia's casual manner of having her guests cook with her took the headiness out of the stature of her guests. I met Jacques Pépin and his wife, Gloria, at one of Julia's cook-along meals. They arrived with a pâté, and after setting it out on a platter with all the appropriate garnishes, Jacques jumped right in to cook with us. One of my idols, the late British cookbook author Jane Grigson, came to dinner once, and after chopping vegetables next to each other, we decided to continue our relationship with future correspondence. I met the very tall, very brilliant economist John Kenneth "Ken" Galbraith, President Kennedy's ambassador to India, numerous department chairs from Harvard, people with titles and Pulitzers and enough published books to start a library. They were all just cooks in the kitchen.

With or without company, Julia's meals were unpretentious. The only hors d'oeuvres were Pepperidge Farm Goldfish unless someone arrived with an appetizer or the ingredients to make one. Dessert was often store-bought vanilla ice cream with very good bourbon drizzled on top.

The meals were simple, but the conversations never were. Julia loved to stir up heated discussions with subjects that would top Emily Post's taboo list—legalization of drugs, abortion, animal rights, and (a Julia favorite) politics. She was a passionate, liberal Democrat who believed that her party was the true champion of the people, the one that could save the world. And, etiquette books be damned, she didn't hesitate to ask those around her where their loyalties lay. She asked me about my politics when a small group of us was enjoying a casual supper in her kitchen.

"Are you a Democrat or a Republican?"

"I'm an independent voter," I replied, confident that my independent stance was a highly discerning one. "I vote for the man."

Her index finger shot up. "No!" she responded emphatically, letting me know my answer was neither discerning nor acceptable. "You have to be one or the other. How are you registered?"

"W-Well," I stammered, "I'm registered as a Republican, but that's only because I did volunteer work for Senator John Chafee. I vote for as many Democrats."

"Chafee's a Republican?" The R-word came out as though it tasted bad.

"A very moderate Republican and a remarkable man. The best Rhode Island has ever had to offer." I went on to extol Chafee's many "Democratic" points of view, but Julia would have none of it. She was what my parents' generation called "a yellow-dog Democrat," that is, someone so staunchly loyal to the party that a vote for a yellow dog on the Democratic ticket was preferable to a vote outside party lines. Our friend Sally Jackson defended my position by declaring that I had a liberal heart in spite of my party registration. Nonetheless, for years Julia never missed an opportunity, when politics was the subject, to announce to a tableful of people, "Nancy's a Republican," always with a teasing glance in my direction.

Conversation was no less stimulating when there were just the three of us at dinner, although I have to admit that I often brought our talk around to the subject of espionage. I was relentless in questioning Paul about his experiences with the OSS during World War II. Julia already knew that I was certain that she had been a spy, or maybe I just wanted her to have been. I was even more suspicious of Paul. After all, he held a black belt in jujitsu, spoke French like a

Frenchman, and could ski down the steepest mountains on barrel slats. How much more James Bond can you be? He'd worked in the secret, strategic map room of the OSS, and when the war ended, the French awarded him the Legion of Honor, the highest civilian medal, for his wartime efforts. When I begged Paul to tell me if he had been a spy, he always denied it, but I watched for signs of dissimulation, such as furtive eye movements and shifts in body position. All to no avail, so I worked on Julia. "Was Paul a spy?"

"No. He drew maps," she'd say.

That sounded like hedging to me. "But they were strategic maps. And that sounds like a great cover for a spy."

"Well, if he was, I didn't know about it," she'd respond to my litany of reasons why he just had to be.

It was during the company dinners that Julia and I met many of each other's friends and families. She invited hers and told me to include mine. Julia's good friends and neighbors, Pat and Herb Pratt, were regulars at those dinners. The Childs and the Pratts were good friends and had connections to each other that predated their friendship. Herb's twin brother had been a student of Paul's at Avon Old Farms School, and Pat had graduated from Smith College seventeen years after Julia. But even without those connections, I'm sure they would have been friends. Pat could have been Julia's sister, raised in the same family. She has that same down-to-earth, unguarded way of greeting life, the same intense interest in people and things around her, the same sense of fun and whimsy that Julia had.

A landscape designer by profession, Pat was also a cooking assistant and recipe tester for Julia's PBS television series, for *Parade* issues, and for several of her cookbooks. Wearing her landscaping hat, Pat designed the enchanting garden that surrounded Julia's house. The yard was not large, but it seemed so by the way Pat created spaces and movement with her plantings. When Julia complained that she couldn't enjoy sitting out in her lovely new backyard because the yellow jackets were so bothersome, Pat designed a screen-wrapped, wrought-iron gazebo that sported two whimsical wire sculptures of oversized, nervy yellow jackets on top. Julia and Pat called it "the folly," and sixteen or more of us could sit comfortably at tables for an al fresco meal. Appropriately, Pat often showed up at dinner with a newly discovered variety of vegetable for us to cook.

Paul and Julia had no children of their own, but they both had siblings and an army of nieces, nephews, grandnieces, and grand-nephews between them. I met many of them around Julia's table. It took me a while to learn which hailed from the Child side of the family and which from the McWilliams side; they all seemed like one big clan. Whenever a niece or nephew arrived with a new off-spring, Julia referred to the offspring as "our baby."

I met Charlie Child, Paul's identical twin brother, in Julia's kitchen one morning at breakfast. I was alone in the kitchen making coffee. He looked and sounded so much like Paul that at first I thought it was. We introduced ourselves, I poured coffee into our breakfast bowls, and we sat down at the table and talked. He was a delightful man. Strong, confident, and self-reliant, Charlie was in his late seventies at the time and on his way to the Maine cabin that he and Paul had built years before with their own hands. There was no heat or running water in the cabin, so he would be up there chopping wood and hauling water all alone. Not only did I like him immensely, I was extremely impressed. Were there no slackers in that family? A biography of Julia says that Paul nicknamed me "Sparkle Plenty," but it was actually Charlie. Paul and Julia thought it fit, so they began to use it.

I shared meals at that kitchen table with Julia's sister, Dorothy (or Dort the Wort when she was a kid), but I met her first in New York, and I am unlikely ever to forget that meeting. It was about a year after I began working with Julia, and Dort, who lived in California, was visiting the city when we were there for *GMA*. We were staying at the Dorset Hotel, and Julia arranged for us to meet her sister for drinks in the hotel bar, then go out to dinner afterward. "We'll meet Dort at the entrance to the bar at seven," she told me as I left the elevator to go to my room.

I entered the lobby a few minutes before seven and stretched up so I could see over the heads of the convention-size crowd that was milling about between the bar and me. I saw someone I thought was Julia at the entrance to the bar and began to weave my way through the crowd. Several feet into the crowd, I heard an unmistakable *boop-boop* coming from near the elevators. I turned around and saw the real Julia several people behind me. She had her arm raised well above her head and her hand was making a castanet-like motion as she continued to *boop-boop*.

I looked back toward the bar just in time to hear counterfeit Julia return the *boop-boop* in the exact same voice. Her arm was raised and her hand was playing the same imaginary castanets. The lobby crowd was as amused as I was, their heads turning back and forth to follow the sound, and probably wondering along with me if we were seeing double. Julia and Dort seemed to be the only two in the room who were oblivious to the attention their *boop-boop*ing generated.

Dorothy is slightly taller than Julia was, but if you didn't see them standing together it was easy to mistake one for the other. Some years later when Julia, Dort, and I were traveling in California, we were waiting in line outside a popular breakfast spot when Dort and I decided to go inside to the ladies' room. Two or three customers greeted her and said, "I love your shows," "Love your books," Keep cooking." Dort smiled and thanked them in that same Julia warble.

Julia and Paul also came to dinner at our house, and although I don't recall what I cooked, I know I was long past thinking I had to cut paper booties for a rack of lamb in order to impress anyone. Something else, however, did concern me. The Childs were going to spend the night, since the next day they were driving to Connecticut and Providence was halfway to their destination. It was a sensible plan. I knew how Julia felt about sharing a bathroom, and although our master bedroom had its own, the guest room shared the one across the hall with the boys. Our house had been built before indoor plumbing even existed, and the bathroom had been converted from a former small bedroom, so it was a large room with two doors a distance from each other. Neither door had a lock, purposely. When I was about ten, I watched in fright as a firefighter mounted a two-story ladder next door to rescue a shrieking three-year-old girl who had locked herself in the bathroom and couldn't unlock her way out. I recalled the drama of that event when my sons were born, so no locks.

As I prepared for my guests, I thought about the likelihood of Brad chasing Andrew through one bathroom door and out the next—a rather common occurrence, but not one either Paul or Julia would expect. Philip and I decided to give them our room.

"I don't want to put you out," Julia said with obvious sincerity.

I explained about the unlocked bathroom, and she immediately responded, "Thank you. We'll sleep in your bedroom."

I do remember what I cooked when Paul and Julia first visited us at our summer home in 1984—lobster, local sweet corn, and local tomatoes. Sakonnet summers don't get any better than that. It was the perfect meal, but more than the food, I remember Julia's fascination with Philip's new toy. When she arrived, she was captivated by the sight of Brad and Andrew tooling around the grounds on a four-wheel, all-terrain vehicle—an ATV. She had never seen one in action and wanted a ride. Since Andrew was prone to frequent unscheduled wheelies and Brad was intent on testing the limits of what "all-terrain" meant, we decided it would be better if Philip gave her the ride.

"Be careful," I called after Philip as he took off with Julia's arms wrapped tightly around him. "That's precious cargo riding with you."

Brad and Andrew hoping for takers on their ATV demolition ride.

"Go faster," the seventy-two-year-old precious cargo instructed.

Who knows at what precise moment in those first few years Julia and I went from being colleagues to friends? I don't, and I doubt that she did. But I loved that she was my friend. Prone to foolishness, craving a laugh and a good time, she was a hoot. Forget her age; Julia Child never parted company with the spunky, outrageous Julia McWilliams who'd led her siblings and childhood friends through one mischievous neighborhood caper after another. She was always the slightly naughty Julia who'd piled her college friends into a 1929 Ford convertible and hauled them off to a nearby speakeasy; the adventurous Julia who, in the midst of World War II, joined the Office of Strategic Services and fearlessly ventured to far-off Ceylon (now Sri Lanka) aboard a ship with a handful of women and three thousand men; the same Julia who relished a hot dog with everything at ten in the morning.

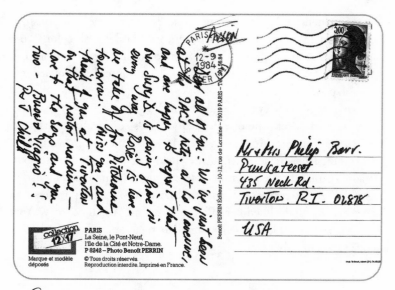

Julia never could seem to remember the name ATV, so forever after she referred to it as "that motor machine."

Undoubtedly, Julia was her most delightful when she was with a group of female friends, especially at culinary conferences. She reminded me of being at girls' camp or in college, when we played foolish pranks on each other, tried to sneak in after curfew, and rummaged through our roommates' closets for something to borrow. Julia and I couldn't exactly share clothes, given the difference in our sizes, but if I arrived unprepared for a turn in the weather, she'd dig up one of her cardigan sweaters for me and insist that the below-the-knee look was in. We shared scarves, and she was forever loaning me a dressy bag since I never seemed to remember to pack one. And notions, always notions, as well as cosmetics with the exception of mascara and nail polish. "I have the kind of eyes that can't wear it," she said when I asked to borrow mascara. As for the nail polish, I wore bright red and she always wore a pale fleshy pink color. "You don't notice it so much if it chips," she noted practically, and since I was always trying to cover unsightly nicks in mine, I acknowledged that she had a point.

Julia was so well prepared for everything that she always had the exact item that someone else needed and was so organized that she could always find it. However, we all drew the line at borrowing one of her rain hats. Julia's purse always held a few of those useful but dreadfully unattractive accordion-pleated plastic rain bonnets, "just in case." When "just in case" began to drizzle down, she'd put hers on, and when we all declined her offer, she'd tell us, "You'll be sorry." You have to be tremendously self-assured to wear one of those pleated shower caps in public.

Andrew G. Barr
Tabor Academy
Marion, Massachusetts 02738

and my mother even gave it a try in Florida.

Anyway, I hope that you are having a great time, and as soon as you get home we should all try to go out to dinner - I'm free for the next two months. Have a great summer -

Maneje Bueno, (I just took up Spanish)

Andrew Barr

Andrew G. Barr
Tabor Academy
Marion, Massachusetts 02738

Dear Julia,

How are you? I got out of school on the third, and am extatic that summer is finally here. My mother told me that you were in France - Oh what memories that brings back. Have you seen much of Mr. Fishbacher, or my favorite little Feline, Minou-Minou?

I hope the weather is as nice over there as it has been here. Have you spent any time on any of the wonderfull beaches, or better yet, have you attempted to parasail? In case you're not familiar w/ the wonderfull sport of parasailing, I'll describe it. One puts a parachute on their back, and attaches it to the back of a speed boat. When the boat takes off, up you go - and what a magnificent flight it is. You should give it a try, Brad and I did it in France,

Andrew was so impressed with Julia's ATV skills that he thought nothing of later suggesting parasailing to her.

A characteristic description of a culinary conference could well be "a series of mad dashes from one event to another." Evening affairs were the most hectic, since they usually involved a change of clothes and some makeup repair. One conference night, *Gourmet* magazine's food editor, Zanne Stewart, Julia, Susy Davidson, and I were scrambling to catch the last shuttle bus to an evening event. Harried and disheveled, we scampered onto the bus and took stock of our conditions.

"Does anyone have a comb or brush?" I asked.

"I do," said Julia, reaching into her purse and coming up with a slim plastic thingamajig that looked like a large key holder.

"What's this?" I asked.

"Unfold it," she said, obviously amused. And sure enough, when I bent it back on itself, plastic bristles popped out. I had never seen one before, and I'm not sure which one of us was more delighted—me at the discovery or Julia at having surprised me so.

Meanwhile, Susy was rummaging in vain through her purse. "I need lipstick," she said.

"Wait, I have some," Julia said as she reached back into her purse and produced a utilitarian-looking black plastic tube that was obviously not from her favorite Elizabeth Arden counter. Susy twisted the tube and up twirled a stick of brilliant apple-green lipstick.

"Excuse me?" Susy exclaimed, and Zanne and I looked at the green stick and immediately checked out Julia's lips. Had we missed green lips in our frenzied run for the bus? No. Her lips were a very pretty shade of pink and they were smiling impishly.

"Try it," she said. "It changes from green to pink when you put it on. It has something to do with your body chemistry."

None of us had seen or heard of green lipstick that turns to pink, so we all put it on, unaware of exactly how much chemistry had to do with the color. Instead of Julia's pretty pink, Susy's were a horrifying bright blue-pink; Zanne's and mine were a hideous orange that Zanne forever after referred to as "pumpkin lips." Nevertheless, we all got tubes of Magic Lips for Christmas. I also got a collapsible plastic hairbrush.

Sustaining the flexibility and spontaneity that made her so open to fun and adventure as a kid, she was, as an adult, always game for a party, a late-night dinner, or a spur-of-the-moment adventure. Mention zipping down to New York for someone's birthday, crashing a party in Santa Barbara, or even taking an excursion to Timbuktu by camel train, and her response would be, "Why not?"

In 1983, Philip and I had plans to visit Venice with our friends Dagmar de Pins and Walter Sullivan and Nan McEvoy, whom we'd met in Bologna during Marcella's classes. The Sullivans were bringing a good friend of theirs, Ron Schwartz from San Francisco. When I told Julia about our trip, she said, "That sounds like great fun."

"Why don't you come with us?" I said.

"Why not?" she said, immediately.

You can't always be certain that your friends are going to like your other friends, but I had a good feeling about Julia liking these

Me with Zanne Stewart showing off our pumpkin lips.

Nan McEvoy, me, and Dagmar de Pins Sullivan in Bologna taking notes at Marcella's classes.

friends and vice versa. Dagmar, Nan, and I had bonded from day one of cooking school. Philip and Walter, who, sadly has since passed away, were in Bologna as non-cooking participants, so as we three women—or, as Walter called us, "the three tamales"—learned to pound veal, hand-roll pasta, and palm little balls of bread dough into pencil-thin *grissini,* Walter and Philip hung out in Bologna and did their bonding in local restaurants.

Dagmar de Pins Sullivan is the ultimate food fanatic. In class and in restaurants, she wrote down every detail of what she ate. She purchased untold numbers of cookbooks written in English, Italian, and French. She was raised in France and still divided her time between there and California, so she was able to read the French and English books. Her Italian was limited, but she was a good guesser and an excellent cook, so she could assume her way through the Italian ones. She grew up surrounded by good food and wine; her grandfather was Georges de Latour, founder of Napa Valley's Beaulieu Vineyards. Her French-born parents, the Marquis and Marquise de Pins, insisted upon eating well.

Nan, whose grandfather Michael de Young founded the *San Francisco Chronicle* in 1865—the original parent company of Chronicle Books, now owned by her son Nion—claimed to be only "somewhat interested" in food and cooking. So years later, she surprised us all by starting a Tuscan-style olive grove in California and producing McEvoy Ranch oil. As Nan tells the story, she didn't intend to do it. She was merely looking for a "wonderful place in the country" where she could have her grandchildren visit and experience the great outdoors. After she fell in love with a 550-acre former dairy ranch in Petaluma, she learned that it was strictly zoned for agriculture, which meant she couldn't build so much as a tool shed without an agricultural purpose. So she went to Tuscany, bought a hundred tiny olive sprigs, and hired an Italian expert in olive oil production. The local agriculturists said it couldn't be done. In fact, Julia and I visited Nan shortly after the trees arrived and we weren't so sure it could be done. Today there are eighteen thousand trees in the grove and a very fine product on the market. Nan, much like Julia, is one of those people for whom the words "You can't do that" are fuel for determination and not water on the fire.

It was more than a mutual passion for food that made me think that Julia would like Nan, Dagmar, and Walter. They all shared deep California roots—roots that foster a can-do spirit common in many people who trace their heritage to a pioneering spirit. Throughout the trip, whenever a change of plans or spontaneous suggestion came up, it was impossible to tell whether it was Nan, the Sullivans, or Julia who first said, "Why not?"

Walter, who had a way of making such things happen, arranged for us to have balconied rooms at the posh Hotel Danieli directly on the Venice lagoon. Philip and I stayed in a room next to Paul and Julia's, and on our first evening, before we left to go out for dinner, Philip and Julia stood side by side on adjoining balconies to absorb the glorious sites of Venice. It was dusk, and they were standing there just as the multitude of glittering lights came awake along the length of the canal.

"Isn't that magical," Philip said to Julia. "We're so lucky to be here."

"It has nothing to do with luck," she responded. "We work very hard and we've earned this."

As I suspected, the Sullivans, their friend Ron, Nan, and the Childs took to each other like pasta and *ragù*. One night at dinner, the subject of "crunchily undercooked vegetables," as Julia called them, came up. Italians cook their vegetables until they are cooked—completely, through to the center. American chefs, on the other hand, were in the throes of the notion that a quick dip in boiling water or a flash in a hot sauté pan was sufficient cooking. The color stayed bright, but the vegetables were crunchy. "I like my vegetables raw or cooked," Julia said, "but that in-between ridiculousness is inedible. I won't eat them." Dagmar was just as disdainful as Julia was about improperly cooked food, and our discussion of certain chefs' lack of classic technique inspired Dagmar to give a most amusing example. Many years earlier, her father had ordered dinner in the elegant dining room of San Francisco's Huntington Hotel. He chose lamb, and the waiter asked him how he would like it cooked.

The Marquis de Pins directed his very regal visage at him and replied, "As it should be."

Julia loved the story, and at every opportunity she saw for the phrase, she pounded the table lightly with her fist and said, "As it should be," and immediately made that expression a common phrase in the trip's vernacular. At one of Venice's better restaurants, the waiter kept our bottle of white wine off to the side of the dining room and was supposedly keeping an eye on our glasses so he could refill them when necessary. But we were consuming the wine faster than he was keeping watch, and finally Julia said to Walter, "Walter, the wine is pouring like glue." Walter broke into his charming, infectious grin and left the table. Within minutes, waiters placed two bottles of wine in ice-filled buckets by our table, and Julia planted her fist on the table, grinned at Walter, and said, "As it should be!"

At every turn of that trip, Walter was our hero. He was just one of those fun-loving men who delighted in surprising those around him. One night we ate dinner at a small but popular trattoria, Da Ivo. The food was traditional Tuscan, not Venetian, but we were all ready

Paul and Julia, me, Ron Schwartz, Dagmar and Walter Sullivan, and Philip Barr in Venice. Nan McEvoy took the photo.

for a change of menu. It was situated directly on the canal, and we sat by a window where we could watch the occasional gondola glide by.

"You know," Julia said, gesturing toward the boat, "that's something we haven't done. We should, though." We all agreed and went back to our meal. With the check paid, we rose and headed to exit at the front of the restaurant. But Walter stopped us.

"This way," he said, leading us instead toward the back. At that point in our trip, we were all ready to follow him anywhere. "Anywhere" in that case was into the kitchen, and one by one—firmly supported by a chef or dishwasher on each side—we stepped out the floor-length window next to the sink, down a few narrow stone steps, and into two waiting gondolas that glided us back to the hotel. It was

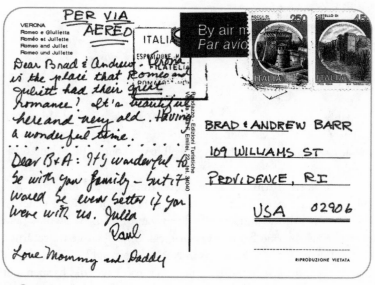

Julia and Paul's note to Brad and Andrew on our postcard from Venice.

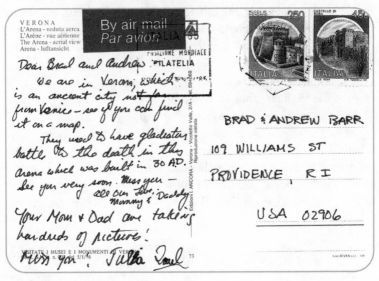

Julia and Paul's note to Brad and Andrew on our postcard from Venice.

probably one of the only times Julia was able to walk through a restaurant kitchen without having to stop and sign autographs. No one knew who she was. They may well have thought that Walter was the star, and for us he was.

Our Venice trip was such a good time that the following year Julia suggested we join her, Paul, and the Pratts for another Venetian holiday. This time, Philip, the Sullivans, and I said, "Why not?" and that trip, as the one before, was magical. Shortly after we returned home, Julia visited the Sullivans in Napa Valley, and Julia and Walter decided on our next trip—to China. That trip never did happen, but they had a good time planning it.

No question, Julia had a sense of wanderlust. But more than that, she liked traveling abroad because it allowed her to move

Second trip to Venice with Paul and Julia Child, the Sullivans, and Pat and Herb Pratt.

around out of the celebrity spotlight and just be the wife, friend, and tourist she could never be at home. I can't imagine what a weird feeling it must be to walk around knowing that practically everyone recognizes you. It gives a decidedly literal meaning to Shakespeare's "all the world's a stage." In a play that lasted almost four decades, Julia was always onstage, and she played her part with the understanding that fame is a two-way street. "I fell in love with the public, the public fell in love with me, and I tried to keep it that way," she said in an interview for the *New York Times*. Keeping it that way meant never eating an uninterrupted meal in a restaurant, never shopping for food or bathroom towels or underwear without being asked for her autograph, never having a private moment in a public place.

But in Europe she could be anonymous. Of course, occasionally American tourists recognized her, but so infrequently that it often

Julia's postcard from California after visiting the Sullivans and planning a trip to China.

came as a surprise. On our first trip to Venice, we were sitting at a table upstairs at Harry's Bar, looking over our menus.

"I wonder how the risotto is here," Julia asked.

Before any of us could comment, a voice from the next table said, "It's delicious. Do you want to try it, Julia?" Julia actually looked startled to hear her name come from somewhere other than our table. She turned around to see a young man holding out his own plate of risotto for her to try. She hesitated for a moment, and then she chose to be the Julia that audiences loved. She picked up her fork and dug right in.

Occasionally Julia disregarded her vow to love and be loved. When an American tourist followed her around in a Venice museum, trailed her out of the museum, then finally yelled at her back, "Is that you, Julia?" Julia flatly responded, "No," without stopping or turning.

She ignored a fan at London's Heathrow Airport early in the morning after we flew in overnight from Boston and were standing at the end of a very long customs line. A most unattractive, large man was standing at the beginning of the line, and when he looked beyond the many curves in the queue and spotted Julia, he began to shout in an irritating voice, "Julia! Julia! Over here."

Julia looked at her feet and pretended not to hear, but he was relentless and continued to call her name. All up and down the line, heads were turning in our direction. I was used to strangers approaching her, but I realized that morning how absolutely grating it is to have someone call your name repeatedly across a crowded room. It was like being the object of a hazing.

"Stand in front of me so he can't see me," she said.

Was she kidding? Given the difference in our heights, it was impossible to block her, but I hoisted my carry-on onto my shoulder and did my best. It accomplished her goal: the man got the message and stopped yelling her name. If he ceased being a fan, I'm sure Julia couldn't have cared less. There *are* limits, and shouting across a crowded hall is one of them.

Those trips to Venice and the times we shared with family and friends, out of the spotlight, made me realize how very much Julia enjoyed being just one of the gang. That's not to say that she craved anonymity. She enjoyed her fame. Far from being one of those celebrities who only dare to appear on the streets concealed by wigs, strange hats, and oversized sunglasses, she strode about her world undisguised. Somehow, she maintained a balance in her life. No matter how many people recognized her, how many awards she received, or how many books she sold, she remained centered on her true self, not her celebrity persona. At culinary conferences, she always insisted on wearing a name tag, although the people at the registration desks told her she wouldn't need one. "I want one, just like everyone else," she'd say. In reality, of course, she was not like everyone else; she was famous. But

Susy, Jasper, Julia, Andrew, and Fern after enjoying a hot dog at Jasper's.

she chose not to allow her fame to define who she was—one of the reasons that Julia herself was more special than her fame ever was.

Recently, I was talking to my son Andrew about Julia and told him that I couldn't remember when he last saw her.

"It was at the Summer Shack in Cambridge," he said, being young enough for instant recall. Jasper White, the popular Boston chef, cookbook author, and good friend of Julia's, had recently opened that branch of his seafood restaurant, so we were there sometime around 2000.

"We were with Susy Davidson and another friend of yours," Andrew added. He had known Susy since he was four years old, so he had no problem remembering her name. It sparked my memory of the day. Our other friend was Fern Berman, who runs her own Manhattan-based culinary public relations firm. Fern and Susy had come to Cambridge the day before, and the three of us cooked dinner with Julia and then had a regular old-fashioned girls' overnight.

"Oh, yes. That lunch was fun. Do you remember what we ate?" I asked him.

"Well, I remember we had clam chowder and sweet corn. And we shared a large bowl of steamers. And Julia ordered a hot dog." Of course she did.

I shall not die of a cold. I shall die of having lived.

—Willa Cather, novelist

At the age of seventy-two, when so many of her contemporaries were exchanging work schedules for cruise itineraries and office spaces for lake houses, Julia embraced no such wishes. In many ways, she was just hitting her stride. She had a new PBS series on the air *(Dinner at Julia's)*, a set of instructional videotapes on the market *(The Way to Cook)*, and a book of the same name in the works. She was writing a monthly feature for *Parade*, appearing regularly on *Good Morning America*, and traveling around the country in her crusade to build state chapters of the burgeoning American Institute of Wine and Food. Those are just the high points. The fact is that after nearly a quarter of a century in the public eye, she was as active and productive as ever.

"When you rest, you rust," she said, and "When you stop, you drop." I don't know if she would have felt the same had she been in another field of work. "It would be a shame to be caught up in something that doesn't make you tremble with joy," she often mused. For Julia, there was no waning culinary passion, no disillusionment, and definitely no retiring.

Some of what kept her going was her abhorrence of being bored or, worse, being boring. "Retired people are boring," she once remarked to a reporter. Hyperbole, perhaps, but it was her typical pithy response to retirement questions, which irritated her like lumps in cake batter. Interviewers who asked such questions overlooked a fundamental facet of Julia's personality: she had an extraordinary inner drive to accomplish things. It's hard to say what created that drive, but my money's on a gene from that pioneering grandfather who pushed west for the California gold. The culinary frontier of the early 1980s was expanding, and Julia intended to participate in that expansion. In 1983, she updated *Mastering the Art of French Cooking* to include the use of equipment that was unavailable when she first wrote the book—food processors, handheld electric whisks, electric mixer attachments. She ventured into the world of media technology with videos and DVDs. I have no doubt that were she alive today, she would have her own interactive Web site with animated recipe demonstrations.

Fortunately, Julia sustained the energy she needed to support her unflagging passion and drive. In her seventies, she began to bolster her stamina with catnaps. Once or twice a day, for eight minutes—not seven, not nine, but eight—she'd put her head down and fall soundly asleep. If possible, she'd find a spot where she could stretch out unobserved. "Wake me in eight minutes," she'd say, but it was hardly ever necessary because she had an internal alarm clock that woke her. She'd reappear fully awake and ready to resume whatever activity required her attention. When there was not an available place to which she could steal away, she napped wherever she was—in her seat at the movies, in lectures, on airplanes. That's nothing unusual or noteworthy, but Julia snored. It was a gentle snore, but audible within a considerable radius. I knew she was sensitive about it, because I snore too—although not so gently, according to my family—and she and I chided ourselves ashamedly for being victims of such an unfeminine trait. She wanted me to wake her if she was snoring, so whenever I noticed heads turning in her direction, I would nudge her gently, and she'd wake and raise her eyebrows questioningly at me. I'd nod, she'd mouth, "Thank you," and then she'd doze off again and snore. I hated disturbing her, so I began to just let her sleep and snore her gentle snore. After eight minutes, she'd wake up secure in the belief that she had snuck in her eight minutes without a sound because I hadn't jostled her awake.

I let her sleep and snore one time on an airplane but missed that she had nodded off with her finger pressing the *D* key on her laptop. When she woke up, there were pages and pages of *D*'s.

"Why, that's amazing," Julia said, and started to count them.

"Please, Julia! Go to the top and copy the material we wrote and paste it into a new document."

"You're right," she said. I'm kind of sorry now that we didn't count them and I keep meaning to sit down one day, rest my finger on the *D* key, and leave it there for eight minutes.

In 1985, the seventy-three-year-old French Chef set out to conquer Italy, or at least lend her spin on Italian food. "Julia Child in Italy" was a weeklong sequence of episodes that *Good Morning America* taped in five Italian cities. When the trip first came up, I didn't expect to be included, since ABC usually hired production assistants even the film crew on location for such projects.

One morning at the studio, Julia was upstairs in makeup and I was doing my thing with masking tape and cafeteria trays in the prep kitchen. Sonya walked in looking quite pleased with herself. Producing live television is a demanding—most would say stressful—job, and Sonya usually did not smile like that until the show was off the air.

"How's your Italian coming along?" she asked me. She knew that I'd signed up for language classes after my last trip to Italy, when I'd concluded that in order to travel easily in any foreign country, it is obligatory to know exactly how to use the telephones, where to find a bathroom, and, above all, precisely what is said after the train station loudspeaker demands that we pay immediate *attenzione.*

"My kitchen Italian's pretty good and the classes are helping with the basics. I think I can move around without getting lost, anyway."

"Good, because you're coming with us."

Sonya was never much of a hugger, but I had her in a big one when Julia walked in. "I guess you've told her," she said.

Our Italian itinerary included shoots in Parma, Bologna, Florence, Siena, the wine region of Chianti, and the Adriatic city of Ravenna—in other words, delicate pink Parma prosciutto, nutty Parmigiano-Reggiano cheese, plump *tortelli,* rich *panforte, bistecca alla fiorentina, ragù alla bolognese, brodetto, biscotti di Prato,* and *Vin Santo.* What made the trip especially appealing was the fact that we were not just going to tour Italy, we were going to "work" Italy, going behind the scenes into the kitchens to "see how it's *really* done," as Julia put it.

Sonya had more than food in her production plan. She wanted to portray the history and traditions of Italy as well as the cuisine, and ABC's staff of researchers pored over facts about *la bella Italia,* leaving no morsel of food or cultural tidbit unturned. They provided us with reams of information that included tales of Verdi in Parma, education and medical firsts in Bologna, horse races in Siena, Dante, and eels in Ravenna.

Leaving the cultural investigations in the hands of the researchers, Sonya arranged for the culinary talent who would appear on camera with Julia. She chose two already familiar to American audiences—Marcella

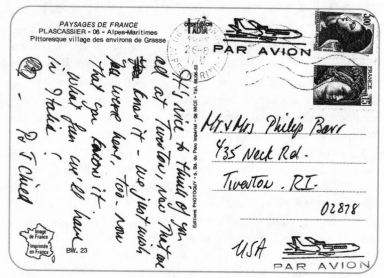

Postcard from Julia saying we would have fun with GMA in Italy—and we did!

Hazan, whom Julia called "my mentor in all things Italian," and cookbook author and teacher Giuliano Bugialli. The others were known in Italy for their expertise in preparing dishes typical of their regions. Food itself was the primary talent, and Sonya "booked" a seafood *brodetto* in a tiny restaurant by the Adriatic Sea; a classic meat sauce, *ragù alla bolognese*, in Bologna, its birthplace; and *bistecca alla fiorentina* in a Florentine restaurant. Julia, who boasted at every opportunity that she was "a card-carrying carnivore," was most excited about the *bistecca*, a plate-sized porterhouse steak that can weigh as much as two pounds and is the product of the rare, porcelain-white Tuscan Chianina cattle. The itinerary was shaping up into a gastronomic dream. Then Sonya ran into a snag.

The trip was to include a cooking segment in the Chianti region of Tuscany at what was purported to be the oldest winery in existence, the tenth-century renovated fortress of Baron Ricasoli. About a month before our departure, Sonya discovered that Seagram's of Canada owned the winery and she wanted every place we visited to be truly Italian. We had to regroup. (Since then, the Ricasoli family has bought back the winery and it is once again as it should be, Italian.)

As serendipity would have it, less than a week after this disheartening discovery, I was at Julia's when the phone rang and the call was for me. A soft-spoken woman with a heavy Italian accent introduced herself as Lorenza de' Medici of the Badia a Coltibuono winery. She explained that she was in Rhode Island promoting her wines at a local banquet room and wished to meet with me about a cooking school she was planning to start the following year at her vineyard.

"How long will you be in Rhode Island?" I asked.

"I leave in the morning." There was something about her graciousness and her earnest but unassuming tone that made me want to meet her. I looked at my watch. "I can be back in Rhode Island by six. How long will you be where you are?"

"I'll stay until you get here," she said.

With the exception of a few waiters clearing used glasses and removing tablecloths, Lorenza was alone in the banquet room. She was sitting at a table with two clean glasses and a bottle of her Badia a Coltibuono wine. She poured me a glass and then told me about her home near Gaiole in Chianti. "Home" was a converted ninth-century Benedictine abbey with vineyards that yielded the elegant Chianti we were drinking and olive groves that kept her kitchen well stocked with peppery Tuscan extra-virgin olive oil. The extensive gardens on the property provided vegetables and fruit for the classes she wanted to teach in her kitchen. It sounded incredible, but I knew about monks' lives and wondered if she could entice American students to endure a cell-like existence in order to learn to cook. Then she showed me a brochure of her Abbey of the Good Harvest, which she called a "farmhouse villa." The warmly decorated bedrooms, spacious and efficient kitchen with workspace sufficient to accommodate at least twelve students, gracious dining room that could seat five times as many, and reception room with a fireplace that appeared larger than the room we were occupying at the moment were hardly monastic.

I called Julia to tell her that Badia a Coltibuono had everything Sonya was looking for—the respected Chianti label, the magnificent estate, even the chef to cook with Julia (Lorenza wrote cooking *and* gardening articles for Italy's premier culinary magazine, *La Cucina Italiana*).

"Call Sonya immediately!" Julia urged. "It sounds just like the sort of place we want."

Sonya agreed, we put Badia a Coltibuono on the itinerary, and for a number of years after that I brought groups of students to Lorenza's classes. Not one of the happy, satisfied students ever referred to their experience at Badia a Coltibuono as "monastic."

We left for Italy in September 1985, and for the first time since I began working with Julia, Paul was not with us. His health had been failing, and Julia thought the hectic pace of the trip would be too much for her eighty-three-year-old husband. So he remained at home with a relative. It was the right decision, but I missed my Italian tutor and Julia missed her partner. She telephoned him daily, sometimes twice.

My job in Italy was to work with the chefs in the kitchens setting up the food for the camera. In some cases, Julia cooked with a chef on camera and I had to prepare swaps and backups just as I did in the *GMA* studios. For other segments, the cameras only shot footage of Julia tasting the food, so all I needed was a finished dish that looked appetizing. Sonya worked out the schedule: we met the film crew each morning to shoot Julia in a scene that established our location, and then Sonya, Julia, and the crew left to tape segments on the culinary specialties of the area while I left for the restaurant to oversee the food preparation.

We began shooting "Julia Child in Italy" with a cultural segment in Parma. Framed by the historic nineteenth-century opera house Teatro Regio, treasured especially for performances by Verdi and Toscanini, Julia walked across the old stone-paved street toward the camera while the melodic strains of a Verdi opera played in the background. As in the ABC studios at home, neither she nor anyone else ever definitely scripted what she was to say. Sonya could always count on her to come up with whatever fit the moment. I don't recall what pertinent comment she made about the city or opera, but I do distinctly remember that she warned any would-be divas to beware: Italian audiences in Verdi's times critiqued unsatisfying concerts by hurling rotten tomatoes.

Julia, Sonya, and the crew then left the scene with a representative from the Parma del Consorzio—the association that oversees the production and controls the quality of the Parmesan foods. Their schedule included footage of Julia learning the two-thousand-year-old art of making Parmigiano-Reggiano—"the crown king of all cheeses," as the local Parmigiani call it—and then the patting of the great fat pigs that ate the whey from the same cow's milk whose curds went into the cheese. The shooting continued in the air-drying rooms, where the breezes from the nearby Po River converted plain old ham into exquisite prosciutto di Parma and another type of ham called culatello. I visited both on previous trips to Italy and learned that the exceptional flavor of the products was a result of the unique air from the nearby Po River and that the flavor was not only irreproducible but also unrivaled anywhere else in the world. Who's going to argue with an Italian? Anyway, the flavor of the pork products was far superior to any other we had tasted.

Meanwhile, fortified with my rudimentary new second language, I ventured into my first restaurant kitchen in Parma. It wasn't really a restaurant, not even the small one that the Italians call a *trattoria*. In fact, when a local Parma newspaper published an article about Julia and American television being in their city, they referred to Al Vecchio Molinetto as our stop for "fast food." Sonya didn't plan to show any cooking in the restaurant, just Julia enjoying a local specialty, *torta fritta*. So I needed a finished dish as well as the recipe in case viewers wrote in for it. My small book of Italian foods told me *torta fritta* translates to "fried cake," and in other regions of Italy, with slight variations of ingredients, they were called *crescentine, gnocchi fritto,* or *chizze*. But my book did not explain exactly what they were. It wasn't until I walked into the kitchen and met the four women, all clad completely in white, that I realized what they were making was good old-fashioned fried dough. Every Italian American street festival in the United States has at least one stand selling deep-fried dough, usually dusted with sugar.

Three of the women were standing at a long wooden counter that held several towel-covered mounds of what I surmised was the resting dough. They were rolling ready dough into large thin sheets and swiftly cutting them into rough triangular shapes. Signora Ermina, apparently the executive woman in white, was standing at the stove and slipping two or three triangles at a time into a large pan of simmering fat. She nudged the frying pieces tenderly here and there and turned them over carefully until in no time at all they turned a golden brown and floated to the top, revealing that they were now delicate pockets. She transferred the pockets to paper towels to drain, split one open in the middle, filled it with the prized products of Parma—wispy slices of Parma ham and slivers of Parmigiano-Reggiano cheese—and handed it to me. I had eaten more than my share of street-festival fried dough, but never had I tasted the ethereal likes of the fried heaven those women were making.

I wanted the recipe, not just for viewers but for myself. Since all the dough we needed for the shoot was already made and resting under those towels, I had to ask them to start from the beginning. It was no easy task. None of the women spoke any English, and when I addressed them in my elementary Italian, they didn't seem to understand that either. Turns out they spoke not standard Italian but a local dialect, unfamiliar to me. I was clueless as to what they were telling me.

Undaunted and on a mission, I resorted to my most fluent form of Italian—gesturing, shrugging, and raising my eyebrows. I made them understand that I wanted to see them make the dough from the start. Signora Ermina understood when I removed a towel from a mound of dough, pointed at it, then lifted my shoulders and said, "*Come fa?*"—close enough to "How is it made?" She put flour on the counter and added salt and lard. Several times I said, "*Aspeta*" (wait) with my hand held up and "*Quanto?*" (how much) with raised shoulders. She understood. She pointed to the flour and then to the 500-gram mark on a nearby scale. She held up the other ingredients for me to see and said something in dialect that could have been a measurement but most likely was my nonna's standard reply: "This much." Ermina was on to me by then, and before she dissolved the yeast in water, she motioned for me to put my finger in the water to feel that it was warm. By the time she added the yeasty water to the flour, we were conversing like old friends. She pointed to the liquid, raised her shoulders, and tilted her head back and forth, which I understood perfectly: sometimes you need more, sometimes less. We gestured our way through kneading, and when she set the dough aside under a kitchen towel, I pointed at my watch and asked, "*Per quanto tempo?*" She raised one finger, lifted her shoulders, and wrinkled her forehead into a questioning expression. Easy translation: about an hour, maybe more, maybe less. I looked at the dough we made and those ready to roll and wrote down, "Let rest one hour or until doubled in size." I had my recipe.

The crew arrived, and before the cameras were finished setting up, Julia had devoured at least three *torta fritta* along with a glass of local Lambrusco wine. "These are absolutely delicious," she said. "How do they make them, Nancy?"

I told her exactly how, and she said, "I'm so glad you've learned to speak Italian." Indeed!

I made out better linguistically at our next restaurant stop, Ai Tigli in nearby Pilastro, where Carla Cantoni spoke the Italian I knew as she walked me through the secrets of *tortelli alla parmigiani*, elongated ravioli filled with ricotta and herbs. At first, she hesitated to allow me to help her with the several pieces of *tortelli* we needed for the setup. But I knew I could do it her way. She did not use ravioli trays but formed them by hand, just as my nonna did. And she rolled the dough with a hand-cranked pasta machine, not the four-foot-long pasta pin Marcella had taught us to use in Bologna. Hand-rolling pasta is an art not easily mastered. Italian women who are able to transform a pound of flour and eggs into a perfect, thin pasta circle as large as a hula hoop are called *sfogliarine,* from the Italian word for "sheet of pastry," *sfoglia*. The legend is that you can recognize *sfoglarine* by their wide hips since the process of rolling requires a constant back-and-forth rocking motion. I bought a pasta pin when I was in Marcella's class, but the hip thing discouraged me from using it very much.

Carla and I were still making *tortelli* when Julia and the crew arrived. Now, here is the tell-all part of this book. Julia Child had a checkered past—with pasta. She didn't really love it. She never quite understood its pervasive appeal , especially to American restaurateurs whose only association with Italy was a couple of waiters named Angelo and Giovanni. She made an occasional concession to its popularity in her work, but when she created Lasagne à la Française for one of her early TV programs, she claims she was "almost lynched by the Italian anti-defamation league." Although children showed no such hostility when she made her Spaghetti Marco Polo on the *Mister Rogers' Neighborhood* TV show, horrified pasta chauvinists wrote angry letters after seeing her eat the spaghetti with chopsticks. She defended her method by saying she'd chosen it in tribute to Marco Polo's journeys in China. "It's more fun with chopsticks, and they truly eat spaghetti that way in China; I've seen them do it," she wrote in *From Julia Child's Kitchen*. But, with all that talk of lynching, Julia remained a bit gun-shy—or I guess in this case rope-shy—about making pasta for her audiences. When for a Christmas issue of *Parade* Rosie suggested that we make green and red lasagna, Julia asked me to develop the recipe. I created a nontraditional spinach and roasted red pepper lasagna for the issue, and Julia clearly stated in print that it was my recipe and included my photo so there would be no question of its Italian authorship—or perhaps, if there was to be a lynching, it would be my head in the noose.

So on that *tortelli* day in Parma, Julia stood back for a while and watched as Carla and I made pasta. But she never could resist trying her hand at kitchen machinery, so she hijacked the pasta machine and rolled out the dough. The mechanics of the machine intrigued her more than the sheets of pasta she produced. In the end, she did not experience the epiphany my Italian passions hoped she would. She continued to think that too much hoopla surrounded our fascination with pasta, and I don't recall her ever making it again, although she did enthusiastically consume Carla's *tortelli*, which were swimming in butter and Parmesan cheese.

In Bologna, we shot footage of Julia and Marcella Hazan enjoying an al fresco lunch of a veal chop pounded until it was the size of a small plate, then breaded and fried until golden. Marcella explained that this was the traditional Milanese manner of preparing a perfect *cotoletta*. Julia agreed with the "perfect"; not only was it a beautifully simple preparation, but as Julia said, "the meat was real baby veal and not small cow."

Julia and I with Marcella Hazan, our mentor in all things Italian.

Julia cooked on camera in Bologna with a local cookbook author who demonstrated the long-cooking, classic method of making a Bolognese sauce using finely chopped beef and not hamburger, as so many recipes specify. Julia thought the sauce was delicious but had a less positive reaction to the talent. In his preproduction letters to Sonya, he claimed he was fluent in English. He neglected to mention that his pronunciation was so bad that he might as well have been speaking Chinese. Julia had so such difficulty understanding him that she took to a lot of atypical nodding instead of her usual pertinent comments or playful bantering.

My prep area for readying the veal and the sauce was the kitchen of a local restaurant where the language barrier was the least of my problems. The entire staff was male and had never had a woman work in the kitchen with them. They could think of only one reason for a woman to be in their midst, and it had nothing to do with cooking. In most ways, they were simply playful. They made the large amount of Bolognese sauce we needed in a very tall pot, so tall that I could not see into it or reach the bottom with a spoon to stir it. So they provided me with a chair to stand on—was I forever going to have to cook standing on a stool?—and then hovered suggestively in a grinning group around me. At worst, they would not let me cook. I was by no means a militant feminist—I liked men to open doors for me, enjoyed flirting, and chuckled at wolf whistles—but their antics were interfering with my work.

I took a cup of espresso outside to the patio and told Julia that I thought my honor was in jeopardy in there. She told me that was how it was in French kitchens and obviously Italian ones as well. She spoke from her own experience, since she'd studied in a male-dominated arena when she was the only woman in a class of male ex-GIs at the Cordon Bleu. She held her own in Paris, but of course, six feet two inches of Julia Child was a lot more imposing than five feet two inches of Nancy Barr. Besides, she spoke enough French to declare her seriousness of purpose and to discourage unwelcome advances in two languages.

"But it's so archaic," I complained to Julia. "Haven't they heard of women's liberation?"

"It will be a long time coming to the European kitchen, so just tough it out in there." Despite the fact that her career had so much to do with opening restaurant kitchens to female chefs, Julia did not consider herself a feminist at all. She believed in equal kitchen rights for all but did not zero in on women. In fact, she disliked being labeled a women's rights activist. It was just not her cause, so she was not about to race into the kitchen wielding a cleaver in order to threaten the men into behaving and treating me as a culinary equal. Assuming my most authoritative (but still diminutive) stance, I returned to the kitchen and got the job done.

Our cultural feature in Bologna was the seventeenth-century wooden surgery amphitheater, Teatro Anatomico (Anatomical Theater), located in the Palazzo dell'Archiginnasio in the old University of Bologna. The original structure had collapsed in 1944, a casualty of World War II air raids, and was then painstakingly salvaged and restored to its original beauty, with its pine paneling, professor's chair, statues, and models. The focal point is the white-linen-clothed operating table that sits in the center of the room so that students and doctors could watch the dissections. Of course, there would be no dissection the day of our visit, but Julia loved the idea—no doubt she envisioned the table laden with a large steer ready to become chops and roasts.

Just as our transportation arrived at the hotel, Sonya realized that she'd left papers she needed in her room. We were on a tight schedule and there was no time for her to retrieve them. "Will you get them, Nancy, and take a taxi over?" Since there was no food at the shoot and nothing for me to do but imagine some poor body stretched out on the table as exhibit A, I didn't have to be there when they were.

"No problem. I'll see you there."

"Here, I'll take your tote bag with me. And hurry, because the shoot is a quick one and we won't be there long."

I got the papers and hopped right into an available taxi.

"*Dove?*" the driver asked. I told him where I wanted to go, in English. He didn't speak English. Sonya had my tote bag with my itinerary and I couldn't remember the Italian name of where I was supposed to be. But I knew the concept of the place, so how hard could it be to explain? I figured *vecchio università da Bologna* (old university of Bologna) was a good place to begin. The University of Bologna, old and new, covers a lot of city territory, and so my comment helped him not at all.

"*Non capisco,*" he replied. I comprehended that completely; he didn't understand. So I began tossing out all the Italian words I knew that had anything remotely to do with my image of where I was supposed to be. Museum, that was easy, *museo*, but there are hundreds of museums in Bologna. He pulled over to the side and turned to look at me, fortunately with amusement and not annoyance. Good—I could pantomime. I stiffened my fingers to look like what I thought was a cutting implement, and feigning a look of painful agony, I said *hospital* in English and *historico*, what I thought must be the Italian word for "historical." *Hospital* was pretty close to the Italian word, *ospedale*, but obviously *historico* sounded more like the Italian for "hysterical" than the proper word, *storico*.

"Allora," he said, his eyes shooting open in recognition. *"Si, signorina. Subito."* And he took off at a considerable speed, which he maintained until he came to a screeching halt in front of the emergency room entrance of the local hospital.

I might well still be there had Sonya not sent out an all-points bulletin for me. As the taxi driver and I sat in the hospital parking lot once again trying to communicate where it was I wanted to be, I heard his two-way radio sputter out some Italian followed by the words "Signora Barr."

"That's me! *È mio! È mio!"* I cried, pointing to the radio and then to myself.

I arrived at the Teatro Anatomico just as the crew was getting ready to leave. "What happened to you?" Julia and Sonya asked.

"I had to stop off for a little surgery," I said.

"I hope they didn't remove anything you needed," Julia responded without asking for more of an explanation.

With all my body parts intact, we left Bologna behind and headed south to Tuscany. The crew left in a van, and Sonya, Julia, and I took the long, peaceful drive together, sharing the backseat of a comfortable Mercedes-Benz behind a driver who spoke a smattering of English and could comprehend my Italian. At least he had no trouble understanding me when I conveyed Julia's several requests that we stop along the autostrada for something to eat—usually *panini*, little sandwiches, which in Italian sound so . . . well, little and uncaloric. Julia liked the ham and cheese best. Since snacking was not a Julia thing, her frequent suggestions that we stop had more to with her curiosity about what those roadside eateries offered than her hunger.

Although she would have thought it odd, I've always regretted that I didn't have a tape recorder running during that drive. I only recall bits and pieces of our conversation, but I do remember how richly colorful her stories were. In his wonderful book *The Italians,* Luigi Barzini, Jr. wrote that over centuries, artists credited sojourns in Italy for inspiring the color and light of their paintings. When a person *feels* and not just *sees* Italy, Barzini's observation about inspiration applies to many aspects of life. Our trip was all about food, and to Italians, food means so much more than eating. It is about the joys of gathering around the table with family and friends, about making fruit and vegetables grow, about tradition and memories. When our television family sat down for meals together, we felt Italy. Julia's conversation during that ride reflected that feeling because she spoke of food memories and of growing up in California. She told us how captivated her family had been when her father bought an avocado tree in Mexico and planted it in their backyard. "It was the first avocado anyone in our neighborhood had ever seen, and we all thought it was exotic." In those days, it was.

She told us about a trip her family had taken to Tijuana when she was not yet a teenager and how Caesar Cardini himself made them his latest creation, the Caesar salad, right next to their table. Years after her family's trip, she conversed at length with Caesar's daughter, Rosa Cardini, and then wrote the story and published the recipe for the authentic version of the salad in her book *From Julia Child's Kitchen.* But the written word could not compare with her description during our ride. With a storytelling performance worthy of Scheherazade, she told and pantomimed how the man himself carefully, systematically, and with deliberate drama seasoned the romaine with garlic, olive oil, lemon, salt, coddled eggs, Parmesan cheese, homemade croutons, six drops of Worcestershire sauce, and eight grinds from the peppermill. Slowly and gracefully, she demonstrated how Cardini had gently "scooped under the leaves to make them turn like a large wave breaking toward him" to prevent the tender lettuce from bruising.

"What about the anchovies?" I asked, breaking the spell.

"No," she said emphatically with her index finger raised. "There were no anchovies in his recipe. Worcestershire has a little anchovy in it, and that's how anchovies crept into the salad."

Julia's memories of the family meals at home were more about the fun of being together than the creativity of the food. "My mother didn't cook," she told us. "All she knew how to make were baking powder biscuits, Welsh rarebit, and codfish balls with egg sauce." Otherwise, hired cooks prepared the food, and it was standard meat-and-potatoes fare—average but ample, which was what was important to Julia, who said that as a child she was "always hungry."

Other than relating her mother's limited kitchen skills, Julia spoke of her with great affection. Caro died when Julia was only twenty-five. She was a fun-loving, spirited nonconformist who was tall for her generation and had a high-pitched voice. Julia's mother, like Julia, graduated from Smith, where she excelled in sports and mischief. As Julia described her mother, I thought how similar she sounded to Julia. "She was a free spirit," Julia said, and I have no doubt she was.

Julia spoke about her father with less affection. John McWilliams, a well-to-do real estate investor and successful businessman, was an extremely conservative man, and he did not consider the artsy—I think he said "bohemian"—Paul Child a suitable match for his daughter. "I couldn't believe he would just dismiss the man I loved," she told us. She never really forgave him for that. I found it hard to forgive

Mr. McWilliams, never even knowing him, when Julia told us he'd said that she would probably never marry since she was so tall and unlikely to find a man who wanted such an ungainly woman.

I already knew the story of Julia's culinary awakening, but Sonya asked and Julia told us how Paul had introduced her to the art and finesse of fine cooking in China, shortly after they met. "I thought Paul and his friends were terribly worldly and sophisticated, and when they suggested going out to real Chinese restaurants, I was happy to go along. The food was just delicious—like nothing I ever tasted. And everyone at the table talked about the food. What was in the dishes. How they were cooked. That's when I became interested in food."

Then she told the story of that day in November 1948 when, as a thirty-seven-year-old newlywed, on her first day in France, she had the culinary experience that she said was "an opening up of the soul and spirit for me." As many times as I heard and would hear her tell the story of the life-altering lunch she and Paul ate at the restaurant La Couronne in Rouen, I never tired of hearing it. Her face would take on a lover's glow, her eyes glistened with a wistful look, and her speech slowed so she could tenderly illustrate how she savored each dish. "We began with oysters *portugaises* and a bottle of Pouilly-Fuissé," she cooed, describing how the wine was chilled perfectly and how the briny, craggy-shelled oysters tasted like none she had known growing up. She told us how each Christmas her father ordered oysters from Massachusetts. "They arrived packed in straw in a large wooden barrel. We ate them for months, and I did not particularly like them." Those oysters *portugaises* were life-altering not just because they began the meal that made Julia vow to learn to cook but because they converted Julia into an oyster fanatic. At the countless restaurant meals I shared with her, she *always* suggested we begin by sharing a large order of oysters on the half shell when they were on the menu. When a restaurant offered multiple varieties, she asked for a few of each. The Oyster Bar at Grand Central Station was one of her first choices when we left the *GMA* studios and wanted lunch before returning to Boston. I didn't like raw oysters much when I met Julia; I love them now.

At that meal in Rouen, Paul and Julia followed the oysters with sole meunière. "It was Dover sole," she said, and neither British-born Sonya nor I needed to hear more to understand that it was the sole prized above all others for its flavor and texture. "He brought it to the table whole." She pantomimed and described how he flawlessly lifted the delicate fish from the bones with a knife and a large fork and presented them each with a perfectly browned fillet, then spooned over the fish "a delicious, simple sauce of browned Normandy butter, lemon, and parsley." To hear and see Julia describe that meal at La Couronne was to listen to a love story.

Barzini's inspirational Italy had wielded its influence on Julia's memories, and I was disappointed when our driver pulled up to our hotel in Florence.

The upside of being in Florence was that we would be staying in the same hotel for three consecutive nights and not moving each day to a new location. Instead of waking early and packing our bags for transport to places south, east, or north, we ate a leisurely breakfast while attempting to translate the Italian newspaper over coffee and Italian croissant wanna-bes. In the evening, before dinner, we lingered over cocktails sitting in cushy, tapestry-upholstered chairs in a lounge just off the lobby, enjoying the occasional melodies that wafted in from the piano bar behind us.

One evening, Julia and I sat in the lounge awaiting a visit from one of her international admirers. Faith Willinger had introduced herself to Julia years before in a letter describing her own insatiable passion for cooking and asking Julia for advice on how to turn her passion into a career. Julia wrote back, telling her to "go to France and eat!" It was her version of Horace Greeley's recipe for success: "Go West, young man." As it turns out, Faith took Julia's advice but substituted Italy for France. She ate, learned, married an Italian, and opened a promising culinary tour business. Faith chronicled her experiences in letters to Julia, and when she read in the Italian newspaper that her mentor-by-post was in Florence, she sent a note to the hotel asking Julia if they could meet. Encouraging young colleagues was one of Julia's career-long commitments, and she sent Faith a return message inviting her to meet us at the hotel for drinks the following evening.

Julia and I settled into chairs facing the lobby so that Faith would see us as soon as she entered the hotel. Julia ordered her regular drink, an upside-down gin martini, and I ordered a glass of wine. My order was easy; Julia was exacting about how she wanted her favorite libation prepared, and it was always a bit confusing to waiters, but more so in Italy, where she had to deal with the language discrepancies.

"It should be in a tall wineglass," she said, gracefully air-sketching the shape of the glass with her hands. "Lots of ice, and then fill it to here with Noilly Pratt vermouth," she said, cupping the imaginary glass in her left hand and pointing to a spot near the top with her right index finger. "Noilly Pratt," she repeated. It was the only vermouth Julia drank or used for cooking. Still holding the phantom glass, she waved two fingers pinched close together over the top and scrunched her eyes. "And ju-u-u-st a splash of gin," she said, drawing it out to emphasize that she really wanted about as much as one could spray from a small atomizer.

We watched people come and go through the lobby, scanning faces for anyone who looked as though they might be someone named Faith Willinger, although neither one of us had a clue what that look was. Then a woman strolled into the lobby, looked at Julia, smiled, and gave a little wave. Julia smiled back and signaled to her to come join us. She selected the chair next to mine, across the coffee table from Julia. We exchanged simple pleasantries, and then for several moments the situation was awkward. Uncharacteristic of ingénue food professionals, Faith wasn't offering much information on exactly what she did, and Julia didn't really remember enough about her to pose pertinent questions. Not a problem. Years as a wife in the diplomatic corps had trained Julia well to handle the most uncomfortable of social situations.

"Now, tell Nancy all about yourself. She is a fine Italian cook and would love to hear about what you do," she said with genuine enthusiasm.

The woman turned her attention to me but didn't seem to know where to begin, so, taking a clue from Julia, I helped her out.

"I understand you are very involved with food." It seemed a wide-open area for her to run with.

"Well, I don't do much cooking, but my roommate does. She loves to cook." To say the least, her answer surprised me, but if I looked perplexed, it wasn't only because of her response. I realized that I recognized this woman but couldn't quite place her. I could even picture her in a different dress, with a big smile and dangling earrings. And then it came to me. Her face was on the small cardboard billboard sitting on an easel in the lobby. She was the piano bar entertainer. Julia and I had read about her the day we arrived. Obviously she'd been walking by us on her way to perform, recognized Julia, and, as fans all over the world did, smiled and waved. I hated that she might think Julia had invited her over only because we thought she was someone else, so I quickly devised a ploy to ease us all out of an embarrassing situation.

"I'm sorry," I said, "I didn't get your name." I hoped that Julia would hear that her name was not Faith Willinger, make the connection with the billboard, and then diplomatically switch topics from food to song.

Julia did hear her reply and immediately boomed, "Well, you're not who you're supposed to be at all!" So much for diplomacy. But after explaining the mix-up, Julia moved right into asking her all about herself—what had brought her from America to Italy, what she sang—which made the performer feel quite comfortable, especially, I suppose, since she didn't have to talk about food. The real Faith showed up soon after, and I don't remember if we told Faith what had preceded her arrival, but I do remember making a mental note that directness has a place in diplomacy.

Our first shoot in Florence was the one Julia most anticipated—*bistecca alla fiorentina.* The amount of setup was insignificant, so we descended as a group on the restaurant in the center of Florence. The restaurant was known not just for the essential authenticity of the Chianina beef but also for cooking the meat in large, wood-fired brick ovens. With the cameras rolling, the chef salted the huge steak, drizzled it with olive oil, and transferred it to a footed Tuscan grill that sat over hot coals. In less time than we could say "*Mamma mia,* that's a steak," he turned it over, cooked it briefly on the other side, and transferred it to a plate. The steak was so large that it hung over the sides. Julia was already seated at a table, and as soon as the director said, "Action," she picked up her fork and knife and cut into the beef. Other than the thin seared layer on the outside, the meat was blood-red, practically raw. Julia looked at it for a minute before saying anything, and I thought she might be questioning her carnivore loyalties. But hers had been a pause of appreciation. "Now that's a steak!" she said enthusiastically. Had it not been so early in the morning, I think she might have come close to eating the whole thing.

The next day our car and van drove through the winding hills of Chianti to Badia a Coltibuono, and we saw for ourselves that it was the idyllic place promised by the brochures. Julia met Lorenza de' Medici, and the mutual admiration and affection were immediate. Lorenza has a gentle, captivating graciousness as well as an astute sense of business. Those qualities did not go unnoticed by Julia, who within a short time was encouraging Lorenza to join the International Association of Cooking Schools so she could "get known." Lorenza did join and rallied other Italian culinary professionals to do the same; each year at meetings, Julia would ask me if our "Italian ladies" had arrived yet.

On camera, Julia and Lorenza displayed the easy, friendly demeanor of two friends cooking their way through traditional Tuscan recipes—a pork roast laced with rosemary and garlic, and white beans cooked with tomatoes and sage. For the closing shot, the two new friends sat outside at a simple round country table set on a stepped terrace and prepared to toast the audience *arrivederci* with the house-label *Vin Santo*. You know those movie outtakes in which the actors just cannot stop laughing? That's what that parting shot became. Julia could not remember the name of where she was. She'd begin, "This is Julia Child with Lorenza de' Medici, wishing you bon appétit from . . . Bad . . ." Then she'd stop and ask Lorenza to say the name again for her. After three or four takes, both she and Lorenza would break into giggles as Julia tried to get the three words together in a row. When it became clear that Julia was not going to be able to say the name, Sonya suggested a new ending. Julia said, "This is Julia Child with Lorenza de' Medici, wishing you bon appétit," and then Lorenza added, "From Badia a Coltibuono."

The next day's talent was Giuliano Bugialli, who was supposed to give Julia a lesson in how to make two traditional Tuscan recipes that used leftover bread: a salad, *panzanella,* and tomato bread soup, *pappa al pomodoro.* Instead we were about to get a lesson in the Italian casual attitude about time. *Domani* is a favorite word of Italians, and it does not necessarily mean exactly "tomorrow." A better translation is "when I get around to it." Sonya called Giuliano early in the morning to confirm that day's shoot and discovered that the day was not convenient for him after all. "Perhaps tomorrow," he said. His excuses were legitimate; he kept and continues to keep a demanding schedule, but it put Sonya in an impossible scheduling dilemma, and she was upset when she reported the news to Julia and the waiting crew.

"Get him on the phone for me," Julia said with such authority that we all sat up at attention. Julia informed Giuliano that we would be at his school that afternoon exactly at the appointed time to shoot the spot as planned, and then, without waiting for his reply, she hung up the phone. We were, he did, and we left for Ravenna and eels.

The eels excited Julia more than they did me, but then she was the one who would have to hold up a live slithering beast, so I didn't mention my distaste for them. Christmas Eve dinners at my Italian grandmother's had fostered a dislike of the fish I could only think of as snake, but I had not yet sampled the delicate creatures of the Adriatic Sea, which were nothing like the ones I remembered. Besides, after Julia told me the fascinating story about eels, I thought they deserved to be on camera.

All the female eels in Europe and America, after lolling about for seven years in fresh water, swim downstream in search of their mates, express their affection, and then travel thousands of miles to the salty waters of the Sargasso Sea, between Bermuda and Puerto Rico, to deposit their eggs; then, for all their labors, they die. The wee hatchlings then make the long journey back to their familial waters and continue the cycle.

Sitting in front of Dante's tomb, Julia held a bottle of white wine in one hand and in the other, high above her head, a vigorously squiggling eel. After telling viewers that Dante wrote about the benefits of drinking wine flavored with eel, she dropped her eel into the wine bottle. Then she suggested that viewers try it and let her know how it tasted.

Our splendid week was over, and the next day Julia and I left Italy. It was late when we returned to Boston, and I spent the night at her house.

"Buona notte," she said, giving me a hug as we stood in the upstairs hall between our rooms. "It was a good trip."

"It certainly was," I agreed, and then a childhood memory of my own came out of nowhere into my head. *"Sogni d'oro,"* I said.

"What does that mean?" Julia asked.

"Golden dreams. It's how my grandmother always said goodnight to us."

"Sogni d'oro," she said smiling. And forever after, that was how Julia and I said goodnight to each other.

Chapter

8

Life is just one damn thing after another.

—Elbert Hubbard, writer and publisher

*J*ulia was never one to sigh, but on the few occasions she did, the sigh usually came before or after her saying, *"Immer etwas."*

"What does that mean?" I asked the first time I heard her say it.

"It's always something," Julia translated. It was a phrase she'd learned in Germany in the mid-1950s, when the State Department transferred Paul there from France. Julia wasn't thrilled about the move, but she was quite fond of the expression and the huge German-made potato ricer she bought. It was a solid, well-made instrument that Julia used with enthusiasm. "You see, the potato goes in and you go *schoooom* and out she comes!"

Her KitchenAid K5A stand mixer eventually replaced the ricer, but *"immer etwas"* stuck, and from 1985 to 1991 Julia had several occasions to use it. So did I.

Julia's primary concern was Paul. His mental health was declining, and he grew more and more confused about where he was and what was happening around him. Through all the years since his heart attack and strokes, Julia dealt with his condition as a minor alteration in the way they went about their lives. She took more charge of their activities and daily routines, but her work and Paul's participation in it never came to a halt. He traveled with her, attended every conference, and joined her for dinners, whether they were social or work-related. The only times I remember him not being with us were the days or nights that Julia and I took Boston-area cooking classes. He stayed at home, alone, for those few hours, writing the letters he loved to write or reading. Then, several months before our trip to Italy, Paul took his regular morning walk to the corner of the street for a newspaper. Within minutes, he returned and said that he couldn't remember where he was going. Julia was visibly shaken. She realized that it was no longer safe to leave Paul by himself. Her decision not to have Paul travel with us in Italy was based on her fear that he would become disoriented, since the long on-camera hours would keep her from his side. Feeling that he would benefit from less household confusion around him, she asked *Parade* to move the shoots from her house to Jim Sherer's photographic studios, and gave Rosie and me more control over the sessions. Then in 1986 she resigned from *Parade* altogether. Sheila Lukins and Julee Rosso, authors of *The Silver Palate Cookbook* and subsequently *The New Basics Cookbook,* took over her position. Through it all, Julia demonstrated a remarkable ability to balance the two most important aspects of her life—her work and her love for her husband.

Paul's health was not the only *"immer etwas"* on the table. Julia learned that the illness plaguing her lawyer, Bob Johnson, was AIDS. He had been in and out of the hospital with what he said was a strange disease he'd contracted during a Caribbean vacation. Then his behavior became erratic, and Sonya said he often called her late at night in a frenzied state—about what, she couldn't quite determine. But no one suspected AIDS, least of all Julia. It was too new a disease to be the first thing to come to mind when someone exhibited what are now recognized as characteristic symptoms. Besides, Julia never knew Bob was gay, so she probably wouldn't have made a connection between his symptoms and what was at the time considered a gay disease.

Julia was both stunned and greatly saddened by the news. Bob was not only her lawyer, he was her friend. As her lawyer of almost twenty years, he was a tough negotiator on her behalf, making demands that Julia herself never would have. He saw ways in which Julia could increase her visibility as well as her income, and he made them happen. Bob was aggressive with Julia's career and she liked that about him, though not everyone else around her did.

I didn't know Bob all that well, but when Julia told me, I was sad for him, sad for her, and sad to know how close to home that insidious disease could strike. I thought of a conversation Julia, Paul, Philip, and I had in Verona during our 1984 trip to Italy, when the awareness of AIDS first crept up in the United States.

Julia was close to what I would call obsessed over what we didn't know about this threat to our health. "What if the chef in the kitchen has AIDS and sneezes into our food?" was the type of question she continually asked. Although at that time little was known by anyone about how AIDS was transmitted, as a member of the medical community, Philip knew enough to tell her that a sneeze was not going to do it. But, as she did with all that was newsworthy, Julia read all the information that was available, and she determined that there were no definitive scientific facts about what caused AIDS, so she continued to speculate on the possibilities of transmission.

When she received the devastating news about Bob, he was in the hospital with no hope of recovering. Knowing her paranoia about contracting the illness, I was surprised when she told me she'd visited him.

"How is he?" I asked.

"He's not going to make it."

I couldn't help wondering how she'd dealt with the visit. "Did you go into the room?" I asked.

"Oh, yes. I gave him a hug and told him how sad I was."

Bob died in September 1986, and I still think about Julia's courage in walking into that room without knowing for sure whether she was putting herself in danger. Paul had said that he loved that his wife had guts, and she did. She cared about Bob, and she was willing and able to table her own fears to show him that she did. Julia verbally expressed her feelings for Bob by dedicating *The Way to Cook* to him: "To the memory of Robert H. Johnson, dear friend and mentor who brought so much of this to pass."

In 1987 and 1988, Julia spent more time in Santa Barbara, where she and Paul could take long walks together on the beach and she could keep closer watch over him in the smaller home. "He's like a clock, slowly winding down," she told me, and when Philip, the boys, and I visited with her in 1987, I saw that indeed he was. He was quieter than usual. He constantly fell asleep during meals, and simple tasks confused him. Probably most difficult for Julia was Paul's need to have her always with him. She had obligations to fulfill and a book to write. When she traveled to conferences, gave demonstrations, or made appearances at signings and interviews, she brought a friend or member of the family with her so that Paul would not be alone.

I don't suppose there is any convenient time for surgery, but if there were, that time in Julia's life would not qualify. Convenient or not, one of Julia's knees simply gave out. The many years of "standing behind a stove," as she put it, took its toll on what was already in tough shape from the basketball and skiing injury. Medication could no longer relieve her pain, and she underwent a total knee replacement. Following surgery, Julia faced a rigorous regimen of physical therapy; typical of the way she did things, she threw herself into it "whole hog." She was back on her feet in a remarkably short time and back on the road. But it wasn't long before "always something" struck, and that something was a broken hip. According to Julia, she was "plunging around" in her office, did not see the computer cord in her way, tripped over it, and broke her hip. More surgery, then more physical therapy. She called me from the hospital after the surgery and, as I expected she would, said, "*Immer etwas*," but there was no sigh that time. She was as mad as a wet hen at herself for doing it. "How could I be so stupid?" she said, and I could picture her slamming her fist down on her hospital tray.

Meanwhile, back East, my life wasn't going along much better. My friend Dagmar de Pins Sullivan says the French have an axiom for it: "It only rains on wet people." Once it starts to rain on you, it never does seem to let up. I've always traced the start of my drenching to 1986, when Philip and I renovated our summer home. I think old houses have ghosts and ours was a historic house. Built in the seventeenth century, with a "new" addition dating to the 1800s, the house had not been modified since then. Our ghosts had roamed undisturbed for a long time and were decidedly unhappy about the chaos of construction. I blame them for the troubles.

Because it was an extensive renovation, we completely emptied every room and locked the contents in the carriage house. Then thieves completely emptied the carriage house into their truck, leaving us with a few sand shovels and a warped wooden tennis racket. As the saying goes, once bitten, twice shy, so before we moved into our newly renovated, nearly empty house we asked the builders to install a sophisticated alarm system that not only would alert us to break-ins but also would warn us if the interior temperature dropped so low as to freeze the pipes. When the system signaled the alarm company of an attempted break-in in February, they called us and said the police had checked all doors and windows and saw no signs of a robbery. They reset the alarm. It went off twice more, and the company said there must be a short in the wiring. They shut the system down and I agreed to meet them there the next afternoon so they could fix it. Sure enough, the house was secure and our possessions in place—and all soaking wet. The company had installed the wiring backward, so the alarm was yelling, *Burglar, burglar, burglar,* when it should have said, *Help! Get down here immediately because the pipes are frozen and about to burst and water will gush through the ceilings and . . . gulp . . . too late.* The repairs were finished by summer, but it hardly mattered. By then Philip's father was hospitalized with congestive heart failure, and between squiring the boys to their summer activities and dashing to the city to be with my father-in-law, I only saw enough of the house to know I missed being there. The following summer was worse. My mother had a stroke, and it stopped me in my tracks. I closed my cooking schools, stopped writing articles, said no when the IACP asked me to be conference chair, and told Sonya I could no longer work at *GMA* for anyone other than Julia. I concentrated my attention on family and my book, which somehow was still on track to meet the deadline. I told myself that next year would be better. It wasn't. After twenty-two years of being like the proverbial contented team of oxen pulling along the same path, Philip and I began to tug in opposite directions. We tried to work it out, but in the end we decided to separate, and a few years later to divorce. It was an amicable divorce; Philip is still today a very dear, close friend. I refer to him not as my ex but as my "starter husband." It is so much less hostile-sounding. But any divorce is hard, and the couple of years that led to it were stressful.

Ironically, Julia, with no children of her own, was the friend who advised me that the most crucial aspect of dealing with the divorce was to concentrate on our sons. "Divorce is like having the rug pulled out from under them. You have to make them feel secure." When I told her I could not be at the fall taping for *Good Morning America,* she told me I was making the right decision. "Stay close to home," she told me.

Next to the boys, she was most concerned about what I saw as the one upside of what I was going through: I weighed less than I ever had.

"You're so thin, dearie. I'm worried about you," she said when I next saw her.

"Please don't be," I replied, tightening the belt on my size 2 slacks.

In the summer of 1989, I had as much cause to worry about her as she did about me. She made what she said was one of the most difficult decisions of her life: she put Paul in a nursing home. Fairlawn Nursing Home in Lexington is a beautiful facility and close to their Cambridge home, so she could visit him, often two or three times a day. But it grieved her not to have him with her, and more so when he repeatedly asked her to bring him home. The first time I visited Paul with her, I sensed why it had been such a painful decision.

When we walked into his room, he was sitting in a chair by the window, baseball cap firmly set on his head, patiently waiting for his Julie and their ritual walk around the grounds. I bent over his chair to kiss his cheek. His still bright blue eyes smiled directly into mine and he said, "Forgive me for not leaping to my feet." All that charm still there in spite of his infirmities. He was still her Paul. I wanted to bring him home myself.

When we returned to the room after our walk around the grounds, Paul stretched out on the bed. Julia climbed up next to him, leaned back against the headboard, and rubbed the top of his head. "How's my Paulsky doing?" she said, using her pet name for him.

Sensing the personal nature of the moment, I said, "I'll wait outside."

"No, stay with us," Julia said.

I sat in Paul's chair and for fifteen minutes or more witnessed that tender side of Julia, so rarely if ever seen by her public. Indeed, some people who knew her well said they never saw that side of her.

Her public image was always that of a strong woman. "She's sensible, no-nonsense, straightforward," columnists would write, and fans would echo it. But Julia had a romantic, sensitive side that was extremely endearing. A Puccini aria, a sad movie, even a beautifully cooked meal that reminded her of Paris could make her tear up.

As I sat quietly observing the tenderness of their relationship, I thought back to the time when Julia was choosing the music that would accompany her series *Dinner at Julia's*. We were in her Cambridge kitchen cooking dinner. Paul was upstairs napping. The doorbell rang, and Julia collected a small package from the delivery service. It was the completed audiotape of the piano piece that had been specially arranged and recorded for the show.

"We should listen," she said.

I agreed, but I was at that moment broiling an entire oven rack of vegetables and couldn't leave them, so Julia said she'd bring the portable tape recorder into the kitchen.

A few minutes later, still occupied with the broiler, I heard the pleasant, familiar sounds of "These Foolish Things," coming from the recorder sitting on the nearby counter. Julia was watching the recorder; her back was to me.

"That's lovely," I said when the tape ended.

"Isn't it?" she replied, and when she turned to me I realized that she was crying—not just tearing up but crying.

"Are you all right, Julia?" I said, walking over and putting my hand on her arm.

"It's a favorite song of Paul's and mine," she said.

I couldn't know which foolish things had aroused the memories that made her cry that day, or which ones were going through her head as we sat in silence at Fairlawn. But I felt the bond shared by those two very special people and I saw their heartache at being separated.

There's a sad, poignant lyric in a Tom Waits song, "Grapefruit Moon": "Every time I hear that melody, something breaks inside."

But that wasn't Julia. Things might bend inside her, but they didn't break. She didn't wallow in self-pity or allow her sadness to govern her life. Along with guts, Paul had said that Julia "was tough, worked like mad, and never gave up on things." In spite of her concern for Paul, she did indeed work like mad.

In October 1989, her truly wondrous *The Way to Cook* was released, and she began an intense, two-month promotional tour in San Francisco two days after the earthquake that shook that city. "Do you really think you should go there now?" I asked her.

"Why not?" she said.

In city after city, the crowds were enormous and the pace heroic, especially since she insisted on returning to Cambridge at least once a week to visit Paul.

Undaunted by earthquakes, the frenzied pace, or long hours, seventy-seven-year-old Julia Child hawked her book with the same intensity of purpose that she'd had when she was fifty and promoting *Mastering the Art of French Cooking*. "It's my job," she responded when anyone questioned her how she could maintain such a pace. She took her job of selling books seriously, right down to the last one. But there was one that got away, and I loved to tease her about it.

Julia stayed with me in Providence in November 1989 when she was in town to promote her book at a local Cooks and Books event. Several of my friends left books at my house for her to sign, and there was a large pile waiting for her on the kitchen table. Six of the books belonged to my friend Mary Higgins, who wanted one autographed to her cousin Geraldine. Julia and I had a lot of catching up to do, so we were talking nonstop as I shuffled open books to her waiting pen. While asking or answering questions, she'd glance at the list of names I wrote out for her, sign a book, and push it to the side. Inadvertently she signed two books in a row to Geraldine.

"That's okay, Julia," I said. "I'm sure we can get another one from the committee."

"That would be a waste of this one," she said with her hand guarding the book as though it were the last one in existence.

"Well, maybe I can cut that page out with a razor and you can sign on the next page," I suggested.

"No. I'll sign one of my own and keep this one."

"What will you do with it?" I asked.

"I'll take it with me on the book tour until I find a Geraldine."

I knew she would hate lugging that book around with her. More than once she had mentioned that it weighed an appalling five pounds plus. "I don't think Geraldine is on any list of the most popular girls' names, Julia. It's not like Susan or Jane. I don't think you're going to come across one."

"I'm sure I will," she stubbornly insisted. She carried that book back and forth across the country, certain that at some bookstore, demonstration, or culinary event someone would ask her to write, "Bon appétit to Geraldine." We spoke often on the phone during her travels, and I couldn't help asking each time, "Find a Geraldine yet?"

"No, but I will."

When she returned, she still had the book. "No Geraldine?" I asked.

"I can't believe I didn't meet a one. I was thinking I'd send it to Geraldine Ferraro as a gift."

Julia worked liked mad, down to the last book, not only because that was her character but also because she never took her success or her audience's acceptance of her work for granted. I saw this so clearly when we were in London before *The Way to Cook* was released there.

"Look at all these cookbooks," she said as we wandered through the downstairs cookbook section of Hatchards bookstore. "I wonder if anyone really wants another book from me." To me it was a no-brainer; anything she published was sure to be a success. But she wasn't looking for quick platitudes from me, and I asked her what made her think they wouldn't. She said it was because she didn't have a regular television program at the time and you have to be out there for people to know you. I remember wishing I had the right words to encourage her, but when we got upstairs, I saw that Julia was not one to rely on words alone anyway.

She pulled me aside and whispered, "Dearie, will you go back downstairs and turn my books cover out?" Hatchards had several of her books, but they were positioned on the shelves with their spines facing out. Cookbook authors resolutely believe that if the cover is showing, the book is more apt to sell, so she sent me back downstairs to turn her covers out.

The official finish of Julia's book tour by no means signaled an end to her full and active schedule. In fact, somehow it seemed to become even more hectic. Fortunately, that's when Stephanie Hersh applied for a job. "I'm going to try her out," Julia told me. "I haven't promised her she can stay."

With degrees from both Katherine Gibbs and the Culinary Institute of America, Stephanie had the organizational skills to whip the chaos of Julia's schedule into shape and the culinary expertise to see and understand the whole picture of Julia's work. The "tryout" lasted for all the years to come, and "Thank God for Stephanie" became a common Julia refrain.

By spring 1990, the chaos in my personal life had dissipated, my manuscript was at the printer, and I was back in action—Julia action, which meant we were off on new adventures, not ever getting T, and having fun again. Occasionally we were also getting lost.

In addition to the phrase *"immer etwas"* and the potato ricer, Julia had acquired a proficiency for reading maps when she and Paul explored Germany by taking long road trips.

"Paul would drive and I was the navigator," she told me during a road trip we were taking from southern Massachusetts to Cambridge. We were in her car, I was driving, and she decided to give me a demonstration of her skill. "Let's pull off the highway at the next exit and find our way on the back roads. I have a good map."

So I left the sure route and, following Julia's commands, jigged and jagged along deserted country roads. We seemed to be moving in the right direction, but then a sprawling, fenced-in facility of some sort blocked our way.

"Well, that's not supposed to be there at all," Julia said, looking back at the map. "This road should go straight through."

"How old is that map?" I asked.

"We bought it when we moved to Cambridge." That was some thirty years before! I suggested we turn around and try to find our way back to the highway, but Julia said we had to "stay the course." She scrutinized her map, directed me to turn this way and that, and we maneuvered our way around the facility. It was getting dark, and there were no streetlights and no major roads in sight. I checked the gas tank. I wondered if we had any food in the car. I thought about the newspaper headlines: "Culinary Giant Found Starved to Death with Clueless Driver." Julia's frequent comments that "this seems right" gave me no comfort, especially when what "seemed right" brought us to a halt in front of a mountain of a rock. "Must have been a meteor," Julia said. "It's not on the map either." Somehow she navigated us out of the wilderness, onto a street with lights, and, to my great relief, onto Memorial Drive in Cambridge. I have no idea how she did it, and I suspect she didn't either. I just know she loved every minute of the off-road adventure.

In 1990, we took on Colorado. The *Food & Wine* Classic is a four-day-long foodie lollapalooza that *Food & Wine* magazine sponsors each June in Aspen. Julia wanted to go not just for the event itself but because it was an opportunity to spend time with a favorite niece, Phila, who lives in nearby Golden, Colorado. As soon as we arrived in Aspen, Julia experienced the unpleasant, sapping effects of the high altitude. She walked more slowly and had to stop and rest often. At times she seemed to struggle for air. I was concerned, but she assured me she was fine.

Less fine were the preparations for her demonstrations. She planned to make the quick puff pastry recipe that she had done hundreds of times, and we needed several batches of the dough ready to use. But her recipe didn't work in the high altitude. The very low humidity and low air pressure had disastrous results for the dough, robbing the water we kept adding well beyond the amount the recipe called for. We were having a desperate time getting the proportions right, and several times I tried to get Julia to go to her room, assuring her that I would let her know as soon as we were close to working it out. "I'd rather stay," she said emphatically. Friends around the kitchen left their own prep stations to offer advice, and it was the elfin dynamo Barbara Tropp who saved the day. Barbara was a lovely lady who until her unfair and untimely death was the chef-owner of the truly outstanding China Moon restaurant in San Francisco. In Aspen, she introduced us to the secrets of pastry making in the mountains. We needed to add more of the high-protein all-purpose flour and less of the softer cake flour and increase the water by so many tablespoons per thousand feet of altitude in order to offset the high rate of evaporation.

We got it right, but the multiple testings and then making all the dough we needed for the demonstration took a long time, and the altitude took its toll on Julia. With several neatly wrapped packages of perfect puff pastry tucked into the refrigerator and clearly marked with Julia's name, we returned to the hotel. I thought it was enough of a day for her and suggested that perhaps she should rest that evening instead of attending any of the planned events. I should have known better; I did but I forgot. Julia refused to stay put, and after a quick change of clothes we headed out for a dinner that lasted well past midnight.

Me, Paula Lambert, Julia, Nancy Harris, and Barbara Pool Fenzl each losing ten pounds by doing "the stance."

The next day she was ready to play with her friends. Cookbook author Pat Wells arrived in Aspen with a new trick: "the stance." In France she'd learned from some model types that if you stand with one shoulder to the camera, extend your arms slightly forward, and turn only your head toward the camera, you miraculously look pounds thinner. We thought this was the best thing since American foie gras, and like silly schoolgirls we would chant "the stance, the stance" whenever someone asked to take a picture. It may not have made us look any thinner, but it sure did make us smile broadly.

That summer we also found ourselves playing outside the food world. The Boston Pops invited Julia to conduct a musical piece during its annual concert at its Cape Cod esplanade. It was not Julia's first concert performance—in the 1960s she'd done an incomparable reading of *Tubby the Tuba* at Boston Symphony Hall with Arthur

Fiedler. Julia invited Susy Davidson and me to go along with her for the Pops weekend, and we arrived in Hyannis the night before the concert, dined out with Charlie Gibson and his wife, who have a summer home on the Cape, and said goodnight with promises to resume eating at breakfast.

"Knock me up at eight," Julia said, using her favorite expression for a wake-up call. She knew it was slang for getting pregnant and thought it was a hoot to use it as she did.

As promised, Susy and I stood knocking on her door at eight the next morning. There was no answer.

"Maybe she's still sleeping," Susy offered, but I raised my eyebrows at her and we dismissed it as an improbable explanation.

"Although she could be in the shower," I suggested. "There are phones in the rooms' bathrooms. Let's call her from the lobby."

The phone rang and rang, and after checking the dining room to see if she was already breakfasting, we began to worry.

"Wait!" I said, remembering. "I have a key to her room." We let ourselves in, quietly announcing our arrival lest hell had frozen over and she was still sleeping. She was sitting at her desk with a set of headphones securely on her head and the cord attached to a Sony Walkman. She was waving a pencil in the air with a great deal of liveliness.

"Good morning," she said when we moved into her line of vision. She slid the headphones from her ears to her neck. "I'm practicing. It's a demanding piece." During the performance, John Williams was to call her up onstage, where he would pass her his baton and she would conduct the orchestra in "The Stars and Stripes Forever." "Lots of booming," she said. "I want to make sure I'm ready for them."

"How are you doing with it?" we asked.

"I think I need a lot more practice," she said. "I'm going to stay here for the morning." She returned to the Sony and her pencil and spent hours practicing her upbeats, downbeats, and flourishes.

Susy, me, and Julia singing and keeping time.

On a beautiful, clear summer evening, Susy, Julia, and I sat in the audience singing along with the music when asked to. Just as planned, partway through the show, John Williams called her to the stage and passed her his baton—or tried to. When he held it out to her, she waved her hand and shook her head. Before I could even think that she was chickening out, she walked over to the horn section, where an obvious conspirator reached down and pulled something from under a coat on the stage floor. It was a four-foot-long wooden spoon, and Julia accepted it with exaggerated conductor's pomp before returning to a delighted John Williams. With every note perfectly beat by the spoon's vigorous waving, she conducted "The Stars and Stripes Forever," accented by her piece of orchestrated hamming.

Julia conducting with her wooden spoon.

It's lovely never to lose the delight of surprising people, and Julia didn't. She got me, yet again, during a demonstration at which she made a cake that called for six beaten egg whites. When we were setting up for the show, she asked for both a K5A stand mixer and a copper bowl for the whites.

"Which one are you going to use?" I asked.

"I haven't decided," she said, so I had both ready.

When it came time to beat the whites, she explained to the audience the difference between beating egg whites in the copper bowl and doing it in the mixer.

"Let's see which is faster, shall we?" she said to the audience. For a moment I thought she would start the K5A and then begin whisking by hand, but she turned to me. "Nancy, you use the bowl, and I'll use the machine."

Notice where my waist is compared to Julia's as we stand side by side at a counter constructed to accommodate her six feet plus.

As was the case in Providence when I met Julia, the demonstration counter was at least four inches higher than normal height, and I immediately thought of how fatiguing it is to whisk with one's arms raised, so I cradled the bowl low against my stomach.

"I think you'd better put it on the counter so everyone can see," Julia said. I could tell by the devilish look in her eyes that she was creating a skit and I was the straight man, so I went with it and made an exaggerated gesture of lifting the bowl onto the counter. The audience snickered.

"Want a box to stand on?" she said, and the audience roared.

I declined and readied myself for the workout.

"On three," she said, taking hold of the machine's on-off handle. We began, and I whisked with all my might. Julia made a show of casually looking in her bowl and then over into mine. I was far behind.

She leaned her arm on her machine, rested her chin in her palm, and pretended to be daydreaming. I sweated. "I think mine are ready," she said, turning off the machine and holding up the beaters to show the peaked egg whites. "How are you doing?"

"Not quite there," I said, changing arms.

"Maybe you should have taken the box."

Demonstrations, signings, concerts—they were all Julia as usual, but with an added twist. "I am under attack" is how Julia described the not so usual. "I suddenly have to defend myself, and everything I have done and worked for." She was referring to the frequent assaults on her use of butter and cream—or, as she defined it, "nutrition rearing its ugly head." Julia aggressively defended her way of cooking because she believed adamantly that a fear of food would be the death of gastronomy. Moderation, she insisted, was the key, and looking back now, from a time when food scientists tell us "the other spread" is more harmful than butter and invalidate so many erstwhile culinary taboos, Julia's approach makes more sense than ever.

If having to defend herself was new to Julia, then the incident in the elevator was revolutionary. In November, the publishing company Alfred A. Knopf threw a party for its authors. It was a grand affair held, appropriately, at the New York Public Library. My Knopf book, *We Called It Macaroni*, was about to be released, and that qualified me for an invitation, but with a guest list that included the likes of John Updike and Toni Morrison, not to mention Julia with her multiple Knopf publications, I admit that I felt like a poser. That feeling was accentuated by the realization that Julia and I were going to share a car to the event with Anne Rice, whose vampire books were swarming bookstore windows all over the city.

"I'll no doubt be the least recognized person at the party," I told Julia.

"Doesn't matter. Just go up to people and tell them who you are."

Sound advice, and typical Julia, but not part of my DNA. I clutched my invitation, mustered a feeble sense of entitlement to it, and stepped into the ornately mirrored elevator of the posh Park Avenue hotel where we were staying. Two floors down, the doors opened and an elegantly dressed woman got in. She took one look at Julia, pointed an impressively bejeweled finger at her, and asked in a somewhat imperious tone, "Are you who I think you are?" People often asked that when taken aback by an unexpected Julia sighting, and she responded with one of her typical, self-effacing retorts.

"Just that old cook."

The woman looked disappointed—or maybe it was annoyed, because she quickly turned her back on us with a clipped explanation. "I'm sorry. You're not who I thought you were at all."

Julia actually looked startled. With the exception of her sister, Dorothy, no one looked or sounded like Julia. No one. We stared at each other wide-eyed but remained speechless until we were in the lobby and all we saw of the woman was the back of her sable coat slipping into the revolving door.

"I don't feel quite so inadequate anymore," I said, causing Julia to smile and poke me in the arm. For years afterward, I could make her smile by pointing to her and asking, "Are you who I think you are?" I've always regretted that Julia and I were too surprised to ask the woman who she thought Julia was.

Nineteen ninety was a good year, a year without "something," until December. That's when Sonya died. She made it through surgery for cancer, and the doctors expected her to make a full recovery. Our joy at that news was shattered when, after returning home, she died in the night of a pulmonary embolism. She was fifty-four years old. When the *New York Times* asked Julia for a statement, she said, "Her talents for creating a kitchen drama in two and a half minutes were awesome. I am indeed indebted to her." Sonya was more than Julia's producer and my boss; she was our friend, and her death hurt. The pain was even sharper when our new producer, Jane Bollinger, told me that Sonya had planned a surprise for me but never had a chance to tell me. "She planned to schedule you for an appearance on the show with your book. I intend to honor her wishes." It was a bittersweet moment. Sonya had taught me so much about what made a good television food spot, and I wished that she could be there to see if I got it right. But Sonya had taught Jane as well, and she produced a good segment for me. So good, in fact, that ABC affiliates around the country asked me to appear on their shows. My own busy book tour put a temporary end to my frolicking days with Julia.

That May, Julia and I did our first book signing together, and I was excited at the prospect of sharing that time with the person who was so responsible for my writing the book in the first place. It was in Vancouver at the annual conference of the International Association of Culinary Professionals. Each year, the organization holds an afternoon-long book fair at which a throng of hopeful authors sit at tables that wind around and through a large meeting room and attempt to sell and then sign their books. IACP headquarters seats the authors around the tables alphabetically by their last names. When Julia and I located our places, we saw that they were far apart. Julia poked me in the arm and, with a voice and demeanor worthy of any undercover operative, said to me, "Switch the names so we can sit next to each other."

Of course, she could have just asked headquarters to switch our places and they would have, but that would have eliminated her fun of standing guard while I crept up to the table and switched my place card with that of whoever was right next to her. I regretted it the minute the doors opened and the crowds came in.

Julia wanted to sit next to a friend so she would have someone to gab with when there was a lull. But for Julia there never *was* a lull. People swarmed to our table and stood in long lines waiting to meet her. She generously introduced me to her hordes of fans as "a good Italian cook, with a good Italian book." People would politely if vaguely acknowledge me, perhaps glance at my book, and then put their coffee cups, wineglasses, purses, and small shopping bags down in front of me, hand me a camera, and ask me to take a picture of them with Julia. It is very hard to sell books with that kind of competition seated next to you. I decided that the following year I would sit where the alphabet said I should, but when the fair mercifully ended, Julia said what a long afternoon it had been and added, "It's a good thing we had each other," and I decided it had been a very fruitful time after all.

That summer, I took the boys to France and we spent part of our time at her house in Provence. Julia was in Oslo with Russ and Marian Morash shooting an hour-long piece for WGBH, *A Taste of Norway with Julia Child*. I couldn't wait for her to return to Cambridge

Brad and Andrew staged this photo to send to Julia from her home in France.

so I could call her and let her know that Simca's brother-in-law, Herr Fischbacher, whom Julia had warned us could be gruff and unfriendly, was generously squiring us around the beaches along the Riviera and joining us for cocktails.

But she called me before I called her. The phone rang, and the minute she said, "Nancy," I knew something was wrong. Her voice was loud and shaky.

"What's happened, Julia?" I asked.

"Liz died."

Liz? Liz Bishop, a good, good friend who for so many years was there with her quick wit, who was always expertly running interference for Julia through a crowd, always managing the schedule to balance work and fun? "Oh, my God. How?"

Julia told me that Liz and her husband, Jack, had been out on their boat. Liz had a headache; she lay down in her cabin and died in her sleep of a brain aneurysm. Of all the setbacks that Julia had faced in the past years, I think Liz's death was one of the most difficult for her to grasp. It was too sudden. There was no slow winding down, no previous illness to warn that it might come. It just happened. Sometimes "always something" just does.

*In spite of illness, in spite even of the archenemy sorrow,
one can remain alive long past the usual date of disintegration
if one is unafraid of change, insatiable in intellectual curiosity,
interested in big things, and happy in small ways.*

—Edith Wharton, A Backward Glance

*J*ulia gave me only two pieces of advice about getting older: be prepared to wear shoes with straps that hold them on your feet, and have your chin waxed at least twice a year. Shoes with straps and chin waxing. That was it.

She told me the first while we were shopping and I was trying on shoes.

"You're always looking for a pair of little black shoes," she correctly observed.

"And never finding the perfect ones that are both comfortable and good-looking."

"Just you wait until you're in your seventies," she said, and that's when she told me about the straps. I looked down at her size 12 black

Julia in her comfortable Mary Janes and me in stylish shoes that were most likely killing my feet.

leather Mary Jane pumps and wondered how long it would be before I reluctantly purchased the same strapped pump I had incessantly begged my mother to buy me at an age she said was too young for heels.

Julia gave me the cosmetic advice one morning at her house as she was sheepishly ducking out of the work we were doing.

"I'm going out. I won't be long," she said, adding that her friend Pat Pratt was picking her up.

"Where are you going?" I asked, a bit miffed to be left at the house while she and Pat tootled off to have fun somewhere.

She smirked as though she had the best joke but wasn't going to tell. Then she owned up to where she was going. "After a certain age, a woman has to keep an eye on her chin." She admitted that she never found more than a couple of unwelcome strands, and since I had been waxing for years, that bit of advice did not bother me nearly as much as the straps.

Other than shoes that would suddenly start falling off my feet and hair that would rudely sprout in unwelcome places, she did not suggest that I would have to make any concessions to age. Lord knows she didn't! Not even in 1992, the year she turned eighty. Despite the fading ink on her birth certificate, she did not consider herself to be in her twilight years. Nor could she identify with her contemporaries who did. When she returned from her sixtieth reunion at Smith College, I asked her if she'd had a good time.

"No!" she bellowed disgustedly. "I'm never going to another one."

"Why not?" I asked, foolishly thinking that the two-hour road trip from Cambridge to Northampton had been too much for her.

"They're all old people!" she said.

When Julia said "old," it had nothing to do with years and everything to do with attitude. Many of her contemporaries had settled into complacent, sedentary lifestyles and she simply could not relate to them. So she gravitated to younger friends who were as active as she was—or perhaps we gravitated to her because she was as youthful as any of us and a heck of a lot more fun than most. When I look at over twenty years of favorite photos taken at parties, on trips, or at spontaneous get-togethers, there's Julia in the midst of our cozy group of friends, all of whom were much younger. And she always fit in. We never truncated our plans because lunch, then dinner, then a late-night party might be too much for an octogenarian. We didn't temper our words, withhold racy stories, or refrain from telling dirty jokes because they might be offensive to someone born into a less permissive generation. Actually, as I think about it, Julia told more of those stories and jokes than we did.

On the few occasions when something reminded us that Julia was indeed so much older than the rest of us, it actually took us aback.

Julia with her "contemporaries" at Susy Davidson's bridal shower.

Just before Julia's eightieth birthday, Susy Davidson traveled with her to France. Their day began with a predawn wake-up call and a live appearance on *Good Morning America*. After taping some additional shows, Julia and Susy spent the better part of the afternoon at a veal-tasting lunch arranged by *Food & Wine* magazine and representatives from the veal board. Then Julia and Susy left for the airport. Susy wrote me an account of their travels.

"We took an overnight flight to Paris, then a taxi to the Gare de Lyon. We were on our way to visit Pat and Walter Wells and Walter had offered to meet us at the station so he could drive us the hour or so to their house. Julia insisted that wouldn't be necessary. *We'd* be fine. But when we arrived at the station, we searched futilely for a porter and had no choice but to lug our suitcases up a huge staircase to the train platforms and then onto the train. Once we heaved everything on the train and got it all stowed, Julia sank down in her seat and sighed, 'I just can't believe there was no one to help us with our bags. What would old people do?' To illustrate, she then pointed to a gray-haired lady sitting in front of us. 'Just look at her. What would she do?'"

Susy told me that it was only when she observed that, except for the color of her hair, the gray-haired woman didn't look so much older than Julia, did it occur to her that Julia had probably been coloring her hair for over forty years.

I had a similar awakening in London when Julia and I were there for a long weekend. A revival of Noël Coward's 1930 play *Private Lives* was in the theater and Julia wanted to see it, mostly because the British-born, flamboyantly risqué American actress Joan Collins was starring. Somehow Susy Davidson rooted up two front-row seats for us to the standing-room-only performance, and Julia was thrilled.

When the lights went up at intermission, I turned to her and asked, "How do you like it?"

"It's good. But I liked the original better. I saw Noël Coward and Gertrude Lawrence in it and they were *very* good."

It took me a minute to wrap my mind around that piece of information. Julia was old enough to have attended a play that starred people who, in my frame of reference, were historical figures. That realization did nothing to alter my sense of Julia's youthfulness, but it heightened my awareness of just how long she had been living.

Even as I write about Julia and age, I can feel her index finger firmly poking into my upper arm and her telling me to drop it, it's not significant. It wasn't to her, and it wasn't to us, but now, looking back, I have to ask myself what it was that kept her so young. Oliver Wendell Holmes wrote, "Men do not quit playing because they grow old; they grow old because they quit playing." Julia simply never stopped playing. Throughout her life, she maintained an unflagging passion for her work, a relentless curiosity about everything and everyone, and a constant drive to try new things. "Life itself is the proper binge," she told *Time* magazine when she was in her sixties, and in her eighties, she was as she always had been, insatiable. There were still places she wanted to go, things she needed to do, and, as it turns out, people she wanted to meet.

In the years since my divorce and Paul's placement in the nursing home, Julia and I talked a lot about how sad it was to be alone. She said that we had to keep busy, so we made a pact to be each other's Saturday night date when we had nothing else to do. But this plan was only semisatisfactory to Julia. "I don't think it's good for us to always be seen out with women," she said. "I think we need to find some nice men to go out with." Julia's emotional attachment and daily attention to Paul were as fervent and unambiguous as they ever were, but she wanted to walk into the plethora of events she attended with a man, not a woman, taking her arm.

"I agree, but nice men aren't all that easy to find."

"Well, let's work at it."

She called me less than a week after the "nice men" conversation.

"I won't be available this Saturday night. I found a man." Who knew she meant we should find men right away? I hadn't even made a list of prospects and she already had a date.

John McJennett was an old friend of the Childs. John's late wife, Toni, had met Paul in 1928 when he crashed her twenty-first-birthday party at her Paris apartment on the Left Bank. Paul, cradling two bottles of claret, knocked on Toni's door and introduced himself by saying, "You're having a party. I think I'd like to come." They kept in touch and renewed the friendship after Toni married John, Julia married Paul, and the two men served in the State Department. John was a few years older than Julia and at least an inch taller. A Harvard graduate, he was smart; a marine who had survived two Iwo Jima landings, he knew well how to tough things out; a former semiprofessional baseball player, he was agile. He was also interesting, dashingly handsome, and

Me with John in Julia's kitchen for my fiftieth-birthday party.

one of the nicest men I've ever known. The only thing John was missing was a knowledge of who was who and what was what in the culinary world. One night at dinner, a large group of us was discussing Martha Stewart's latest projects, and for quite a while we shared information about Martha doing this and Martha doing that. John listened patiently and then after several minutes asked, "Who is this Martha chick anyway?"

Having John in her life was good for Julia. There was a renewed spark in her desire to entertain at home. She held more dinner parties and reestablished her annual Christmas cocktail party. As any good friend would be, I was downright jealous, and told Julia so. So she offered to fix me up with another old friend. "We'll have to dust him off a bit," she said. "But he's quite presentable." I declined her offer and instead feigned her can-do attitude and began to find dates on

John had a great sense of humor and made us all laugh — obviously!

my own, thanks mostly to our friend Sally Jackson, who kept a Rolodex of old boyfriends. But it would be five years and three boyfriends before I met my perfect "nice man."

During the seven months that led to her August 15 eightieth birthday, from New Orleans to San Diego, San Francisco, Napa and Sonoma, Las Vegas, Miami, France, Chicago, and Texas, Julia went at a pace that defied her age, and she entirely ignored what had become the B-word. She considered the milestone irrelevant. The culinary world, on the other hand, was obsessed with it. Beginning weeks before her actual birthday and continuing well into the following year, more than three hundred Julia parties were celebrated, and she appeared at them all. All! As reticent as she was to celebrate her age, the outpouring of affection touched her.

Most of the parties were lavishly produced, extravagantly orchestrated, jolly affairs that were also fund-raisers for causes dear to Julia, so with swelled coffers as an incentive she agreed to take part in them. The Boston television station that had launched Julia's career, WGBH, hosted a party in November at the Copley Plaza in Boston. Luminaries from the worlds of gastronomy, arts, and politics filled the room or appeared on the large portable screen to pay tribute. The Boston Pops paraded into the room playing a piece especially composed for her, "Fanfare with Pots and Pots," with pots, pans, whisks, and wooden spoons. They continued to serenade Julia from the stage, and it was truly amazing how melodious the music was. I guess if the metaphor holds that Julia made music in the kitchen, it follows that the Pops made kitchen in their music. The actress Diana Rigg took

Me with Julia's Johnny-on-the-spot, Stephanie Hersh, at the Boston birthday party.

Me with John McJennet at the Boston birthday party.

the stage and read "Cook and Nifty Wench," a poem Paul had written for Julia's forty-ninth birthday; it was a bittersweet moment. I know Julia wished he were there.

Fourteen chefs prepared a delicious meal the following January at the Rainbow Room in New York. It was a good time, but perhaps it went on too long because she abandoned me. She stayed to cheer the parade of waiters carrying sparkler-lit, individual baked Alaskas around the darkened room, and to hear Jean Stapleton read a poem. But after Julia accepted a giant whisk garnished with flowers and pearls and marched around the room with it on her shoulder, she gave me a subtle poke and said, "Let's go. I'll call for the car."

I was more than ready; it wasn't my only party with her that week. "I'm going to the ladies' room first," I said.

"Okay. I'll get our coats."

Ladies' room accomplished, I went to the coat check area, but there was no Julia. I waited for a while, knowing how long it can take Julia to walk through a crowd. Then I decided to get our coats to be ready for her. I had to describe them to the girl at the coat check because, at Julia's suggestion, I had hidden my small purse with my money and claim check in the sleeve of my coat so I wouldn't have to carry it around.

"Mrs. Child picked them up already," the girl told me.

"Did she leave?" I asked. She didn't know. I looked back into the dining room and went back to the ladies' room; no Julia. I decided to wait in the car, hoping that she would assume that's where I was. I stepped out onto the street just in time to see the car pulling away from the curb with Julia sitting in the backseat. I had to run half a block in heels too high for walking to catch them at the corner and beat on the window.

"What are you doing?" I asked, truly incredulous that she was leaving without me.

"I thought you were having a good time and would find your way back when you were ready."

"But you have my coat and my purse and my money!" I wailed at her like a petulant child as I slid onto the seat next to her. "What were you *thinking*?"

She just grinned at me like a party girl who'd eaten the whole baked Alaska and split the scene with someone else's cash and fur coat. She thought it was terribly funny, but I told her I was not amused at the thought of traipsing coatless and penniless through the late-night streets of New York, where untold dangers would most likely deprive my sons of a mother. In truth, I was really only pretending to be miffed at her. I knew she would have sent the car back for me, with my coat and purse, but I wanted to be able to needle her for a couple of days. I

We began Julia's New York party the night before with dinner at the Rainbow Room. John, Julia, Michael Whiting, me, Will Lashley, Susy Davidson, and Rozanne Gold.

guess I was just addicted to that devilish grin and the twinkle in her eyes that needling wrought.

For the February party at the Ritz-Carlton in Marina del Rey, California, the hosts flew in a gaggle of nine French chefs to join forces in the kitchen with some sixty American chefs who held sway over French-inspired restaurants. The spirited, good-natured Gallic kitchen bantering was projected onto screens in the dining room for the entertainment of the five hundred guests, who enjoyed an incredible five-hour meal preceded by about sixty different kinds of hors d'oeuvres. At the end of dinner, the chefs rolled out a cart with a birthday cake carved, molded, and decorated as a replica of her kitchen,

Me and Sally Jackson expressing our affection with a cardboard cutout doll of Julia at her party in Marina del Rey.

complete with a marzipan Julia standing by a chocolate stove. The French chefs then performed a quite admirable can-can.

The public parties were, as Julia noted, embarrassingly prolific. The private ones were special. A small group of us gathered at her friend Jasper White's Cambridge restaurant. For dessert, he prepared chocolate bars with "Happy Birthday Julia" written in icing so she could take a bite out of the hoopla of her birthday. She did so with great relish. Pam Fiore, who was then the editor of *Travel & Leisure* magazine, held a beautiful dinner party in Julia's honor at her New York apartment, where a group of us including Susy, Victor and Marcella Hazan, *Food & Wine* editor Mary Simons, and *Good Morning America* producer Jane Bollinger, did our best to sing on key the lyrics of songs Pam wrote for Julia.

Julia, Russ Morash, Jasper White, me, and Sally Jackson celebrating Julia at Jasper's restaurant.

Julia taking a bite out of her birthday at Jasper's restaurant party.

Pam Fiore passing the song round off to Mary Simons, then editor of Food & Wine magazine.

Pam Fiore encouraging John and me to sing on key. It was hopeless!

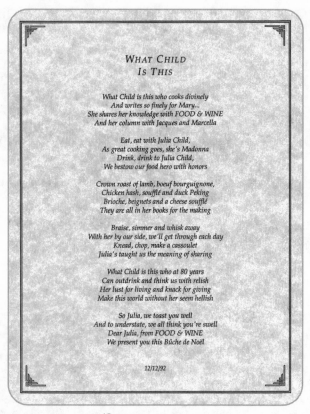

WHAT CHILD IS THIS

What Child is this who cooks divinely
And writes so finely for Mary...
She shares her knowledge with FOOD & WINE
And her column with Jacques and Marcella

Eat, eat with Julia Child,
As great cooking goes, she's Madonna
Drink, drink to Julia Child,
We bestow our food hero with honors

Crown roast of lamb, boeuf bourguignone,
Chicken hash, soufflé and duck Peking
Brioche, beignets and a cheese soufflé
They are all in her books for the making

Braise, simmer and whisk away
With her by our side, we'll get through each day
Knead, chop, make a cassoulet
Julia's taught us the meaning of sharing

What Child is this who at 80 years
Can outdrink and think us with relish
Her lust for living and knack for giving
Make this world without her seem hellish

So Julia, we toast you well
And to understate, we all think you're swell
Dear Julia, from FOOD & WINE
We present you this Bûche de Noël

12/12/92

Pam Fiore's song lyrics.

Susy Davidson planned the perfect Julia party at Julia's home. Close friends gathered in the Cambridge kitchen to cook dinner together. Before congregating in her backyard to sip cocktails and devour Jonah crab claws and an assortment of her favorite oysters, we gossiped and gabbed in her kitchen while trimming, peeling, and roasting. We didn't want Julia to have to do any of the work, but she

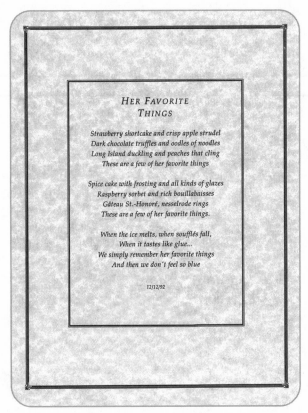

HER FAVORITE THINGS

Strawberry shortcake and crisp apple strudel
Dark chocolate truffles and oodles of noodles
Long Island duckling and peaches that cling
These are a few of her favorite things

Spice cake with frosting and all kinds of glazes
Raspberry sorbet and rich bouillabaisses
Gâteau St.-Honoré, nesselrode rings
These are a few of her favorite things.

When the ice melts, when soufflés fall,
When it tastes like glue...
We simply remember her favorite things
And then we don't feel so blue

12/12/92

Pam Fiore's song lyrics.

couldn't keep out of the kitchen. She found a space by a cutting board, looked around at us all clad in specially made aprons stenciled with "Happy Birthday Julia," and beamed. "Isn't cooking together fun?"

The toasts we gave that evening, unlike those at the public gatherings, didn't tout Julia's many accomplishments or extol her generous contributions to the field of gastronomy. We poked fun at

The Twelve Days of Christmas

On the first day of Christmas, Miss Julia made for me
A ROBUST ALSATIAN CHOUCROUTE.

On the second day of Christmas, Miss Julia made for me
TWO TURTLE SOUPS and a robust Alsatian choucroute.

On the third day of Christmas, Miss Julia made for me
THREE FRENCH FRIES, two turtle soups and a robust Alsatian choucroute.

On the fourth day of Christmas, Miss Julia made for me
FOUR GRILLING BIRDS, three French fries, two turtle soups and a robust Alsatian choucroute.

On the fifth day of Christmas, Miss Julia made for me
FIVE CRÈME BRÛLÉES...four grilling birds, three French fries and a robust Alsatian choucroute.

On the sixth day of Christmas, Miss Julia made for me
SIX GEESE PÂTÉ-ING...five crème brûlées...four grilling birds, three French fries, two turtle soups and
a robust Alsatian choucroute.

On the seventh day of Christmas, Miss Julia made for me
SEVEN DUCKS L'ORANGE-ING, six geese pâté-ing...five crème brûlées...four grilling birds, three French
fries, two turtle soups and a robust Alsatian choucroute.

On the eighth day of Christmas, Miss Julia made for me
EIGHT LAMBS A-STEWING, seven ducks l'Orange-ing, six geese pâté-ing...five crème brûlées...four grilling
birds, three French fries, two turtle soups and a robust Alsatian choucroute.

On the ninth day of Christmas, Miss Julia made for me,
NINE VEAUS BLANQUETTE-ING, eight lambs a-stewing, seven ducks l'Orange-ing, six geese pâté-ing...
five crème brûlées...four grilling birds, three French fries, two turtle soups and a robust Alsatian choucroute.

On the tenth day of Christmas, Miss Julia made for me,
TEN TARTES TATIN-ING, nine veaus blanquette-ing, eight lambs a-stewing, seven ducks l'Orange-ing,
six geese pâté-ing...five crème brûlées...four grilling birds, three French fries, two turtle soups and a
robust Alsatian choucroute.

On the eleventh day of Christmas, Miss Julia made for me,
ELEVEN POIRES HELENE-ING, ten tartes tatin-ing, nine veaus blanquette-ing, eight lambs a-
stewing, seven ducks l'Orange-ing, six geese pâté-ing...five crème brûlées...four grilling birds,
three French fries, two turtle soups and a robust Alsatian choucroute.

On the twelfth day of Christmas, Miss Julia made for me,
TWELVE CHOCOLATES MOUSSE-ING, eleven poires Helene-ing, ten tartes tatin-ing,
nine veaus blanquette-ing, eight lambs a-stewing, seven ducks l'Orange-ing, six geese
pâté-ing...five crème brûlées...four grilling birds, three French fries, two turtle soups
and a robust Alsatian choucroute.

12/12/92

Pam Fiore's song lyrics.

her. In my toast, I accused her of being a real pain. "You just never let up. You told me to write magazine articles. I did. Then you said write more and I did. Then you said to write a book. I did. You just never know when to stop pushing."

Before my bottom hit the chair, Julia shot back, "When are you going to write another book?"

Me in Julia's kitchen trimming the meat for her party.

Susy Davidson, Paula Lambert, and me in our "Happy Birthday Julia" aprons in Julia's dining room.

Julia and Evan Jones in their birthday aprons admiring her cake.

Julia on her way to a lecture at the Oxford Symposium.

So at eighty, with her energy, passion, and quick wit still intact, she kept going and doing as she always had, or perhaps more so. She seemed determined to pack as much living into her life as was humanly possible.

In September 1992, Julia and I had plans to attend the Oxford Symposium on Food. About a month before we were to leave, Julia learned that Sarah Nops, a director of London's Cordon Bleu cooking school, was planning a reception to introduce the local community to the American Institute of Wine and Food. "Well, we have to go," Julia told me, and we changed our travel dates to include a stay in London. Then about two weeks before we left for London, I received an invitation from Anna Tasca Lanza to visit her in Sicily. The contessa

Some of our esteemed classmates from the Oxford Symposium: Paul Levy, author of The Official Foodie Handbook, Jeffrey Steingarten, Vogue food critic, and British author and scholar Alan Davidson.

would be conducting cooking classes at her grand, twelve-hundred-acre country estate, Regaleali, which is both a vineyard and a working farm that produces all the food for the estate. It was an opportunity to experience Sicilian cuisine at its best, but the classes began two days after the end of the Oxford Symposium, and as much as I wanted to go, it just didn't seem possible.

"It would be fun," I said to Julia. "But I don't think we can do it."

"Why not?" she retorted.

"Well, I don't know. Seems like a lot of juggling; we'd have to change our tickets again and we'd have to pack for the weather in both places." In spite of the thousands of miles we'd traveled together, her art of fitting everything into one small suitcase had

Oxford attendees just like to have fun. Raymond Sokolov, editor of the Wall Street Journal's Leisure and Arts page, and Jeffrey Steingarten shocking me!

never rubbed off on me, and I imagined the several suitcases I would be forced to schlep in order to accommodate both climates.

"My travel agent can take care of the tickets, and I always pack the same clothes," she said. That usually meant a couple of pairs of slacks, one dark skirt, several colorful blouses, one pair of black pumps, and her New Balance sneakers. It all fit into one manageable suitcase. "I think we should do it," she said. "Why not?" I had no good reason why not, especially since my sons were by then in boarding school and I didn't have to be home for them or a manuscript.

"No reason—let's do it," I said.

"Good. I'll take care of the plane reservations."

Partying at Paul Levy's after the Oxford Symposium.

"Okay. I'll find a place in London for us to stay." I already had in mind to ask Dagmar and Walter Sullivan if we could stay in their London flat. They were in California, and I knew they wouldn't be using it. When I told Julia the Sullivans said it was fine for us to stay at the flat, she decided to fill our already full schedule with more activities—and, as it turned out, some classic Julia fun.

That trip to the Oxford Symposium was our second or third, and in previous years British friends had generously entertained us at parties in their homes and treated us to meals at restaurants and private eating clubs. Julia decided that since we were going to be in a private flat, we should host a thank-you party.

A friend of mine from Rhode Island, Hope Hudner, had plans to stay with us in London, and the three of us organized a lovely,

Julia and Hope Hudner getting ready to greet our guests at a very respectable cocktail party.

rather sophisticated cocktail party and sent invitations to a host of English friends and foodies. Following the party, a group of us went to dinner, and when Julia, Hope, and I returned to the flat, we changed into our nightclothes and regrouped in the living room for girl talk. Ever-courteous person that she is, Hope began to plan what kind of thank-you would be fitting for the Sullivans. Julia thought we should take photos of us in the flat and attach them to notes. Hope had a Polaroid camera with her that could be set to take automatic pictures, and we began to say "souf-*flé*" for the camera. Then Julia McWilliams took over and convinced us that simple photos were a bore. The Sullivans' flat held numerous pieces of valuable, irreplaceable porcelain that had been in the family since who knows when. Julia decided that we should take pictures that looked as though we were smashing all that china and send them to the Sullivans. Ever so gingerly, we held the porcelain in precarious poses and took our photos. I can't even begin to imagine what Dagmar must have thought when she opened our thank-you notes.

The next day, Julia went to the hospital to visit her good friend Elizabeth David, the British cookbook author, who was very ill. I asked Julia if she wanted me to go with her, but she said it was probably best if she went alone. When she returned, I asked with appropriate gravity, "How did it go?"

"We had a good time," Julia said. Turns out that when Elizabeth saw Julia, she told her to bring her some decent food or she would expire on the spot. Julia went shopping and returned to Elizabeth's room with pâté de foie gras, caviar, and champagne or

Smashing the sullivan's porcelain in our bathrobes. Not really.

Julia and students from Regaleali enjoying a boat trip around the small islands of Sicily.

vodka—I don't recall which. I only remember Julia saying that they spread the contraband on the bed and had a picnic that was hardly medically sanctioned.

"Weren't you afraid you'd get caught?" I asked her.

"No," she said. I was traveling with an octogenarian delinquent!

Julia was unstoppable in her determination to binge on life. After receptions, parties, and "sick visits" in London, and lectures and more parties in Oxford, we arrived in Sicily for more parties, trips around the island in an old wooden boat, and lessons in Italian sign language.

For Julia, binging on life required a healthy appetite of curiosity, and she was, as she said she had been as a kid, always hungry. What made her curiosity so richly rewarding was that she noticed what went on around her, which gave her an extraordinary number of things to examine. People, things, and activities that might pass unnoticed to others caught her attention. On a trip to Napa Valley, John, Julia, my latest boyfriend and I stood in the parking lot after a tour of the Napa Valley Wine Train wondering where to go next. A truck pulled up near us, the driver went inside one of the buildings, and Julia noticed that the vehicle was shaking slightly. She asked me what I thought might be causing it. I had no idea. In truth, I had paid no attention at all to the truck. Julia was curious, so she walked up to the back and peeked in. To her delight, she found a cargo of lambs. When the driver returned, she engaged him in conversation and not only learned about the methods of raising of lambs in California but also found, upon her return to Cambridge, a neatly trimmed leg of lamb waiting in the freezer for her. Julia didn't stop there. She was

Fred Plotkin in Palermo, Sicily, teaching Julia the Italian sign language for squisito, "delicious."

Julia discovering the lamb cargo.

curious about the effects of agriculture and climate on the flavor and texture of lamb, and before long, we were oven-deep in an exhaustive tasting of lamb from different parts of the country. And all because she noticed a truck shaking!

As always, her curiosity extended far beyond the culinary. In 1993, Susy Davidson arranged for us all, including Julia's niece Phila and her family, to spend the week following the Aspen Classic at a ranch tucked away in the middle of nowhere in southern Colorado. The ranch offered lessons in fly-fishing, which appealed to Julia since she was a passionate aficionado, and horseback riding in the high aspens, which Susy, Phila, and I planned to do. Brochures showed western-style bunkhouses lined up outside a main dining room watched over by several stuffed animal heads, and we all agreed that it was the perfect spot to relax and pursue pleasures not necessarily

Julia in her fly-fishing outfit, me ready to ride horseback, the owners of the ranch, and John.

food-related. John was at that time having respiratory problems, and there was some discussion as to whether the trip would be safe for him. Trouper that he was, he asked the doctor for an oxygen tank and joined us.

It was a long, eight-hour-plus drive from Aspen to the ranch, and we decided to make a stop in Denver at the Tattered Cover Bookstore and buy a book on tape for the trip. We wanted something suspenseful and mysterious, and Julia and I stood looking at the possibilities. I spotted Anne Rice's name on a box of tapes entitled *Exit to Eden* and I picked it up.

"I just read her *Interview with the Vampire* and I really couldn't put it down."

Our happy, rested group at the Colorado ranch.

"I've wanted to read her vampire story, but since you already have, let's get this," she said, taking the box to the register without examining it.

We climbed back in the car with me in the driver's seat, Julia riding shotgun, and John and Susy in back, with Susy diagonally behind me so I could see her gestured directions to turn left or right. We didn't want unnecessary talking to interrupt the storytelling.

I must have been concentrating especially hard on negotiating the streets out of Denver because I don't remember hearing the beginning of the tape. My first clue that it was not about anything as pedestrian as vampires was when I looked in the mirror at Susy for instructions on which way to turn. Her eyebrows were arched high in her forehead and she darted her startled eyes from me to the tape. I tuned in just in time to hear something about black leather and chains.

"What's this?" I asked, fumbling for and then ejecting the tape. "There must be a mistake. Do the tapes all say Anne Rice?"

It turns out that Rice writes explicitly erotic and wickedly pornographic stories that in book form appear under a pseudonym. On tape, they carry her name. At the time, we only knew we had something that seemed highly inappropriate to everyone but Julia.

"Well, let's listen to it anyway," she said, pushing the tape back into play position. Susy looked aghast, and I'm sure I heard John pulling extra hard on his oxygen tank. Meanwhile on the CD, two characters named Lisa and Elliot were pushing the envelope on the limits of pleasure at the Club, an exclusive, hidden resort devoted to the fulfillment of forbidden fantasies.

"What's he doing to her?" Julia asked. Was that John gasping? Susy was giggling.

"Look, Julia, we—we can listen to it, but I'm not explaining it to you." It wasn't so much that I was embarrassed; I wasn't exactly sure what kind of forbidden fantasies Lisa and Elliot were engaged in, and I wasn't sure John ever wanted to know. But Julia wanted to figure it out, so Susy and I did our best to offer commentary. John rolled down his window.

Julia's desire to go at the pace she did when she was eighty was inspirational. She could do it, because overall she was blessed with remarkably good health and a stalwart constitution. "Sleep well?" I'd ask her mornings when we were together. "Always do," she'd say with a complacent lilt in her voice. And she always did, just as she always ate well, without a tinge of indigestion. Surgery, medicine, and sitting more all helped with her knee problems, and the rare times when something else did lay her low, her seeming supernatural recuperative powers put her back on her feet in no time. Her physical and mental resilience was remarkable.

"I think you must have some special chromosome makeup," I once suggested to her.

"Red meat and gin," she said, but I think it was DNA and mind-set. Whether it was the common cold or hip surgery, she was usually out the door for lunch long before the florist could rush the inevitable vanful of get-well bouquets to her bedside.

I used to love to look through Paul Child's photos, which occupied several storage areas of their house. Paul was a fine photographer and a gifted artist. His paintings, photographs, and several pieces of intricately carved wood furniture filled the house. Julia was justly proud of his work and was always pleased to show it to me. We were looking through photographs and I saw some from their wedding. I commented on how pretty she looked wearing a short-sleeved, two-piece, dotted dress that accented her slim figure and long legs. Yet I couldn't help but notice the large bandage on her head.

"Pimple?" I snickered.

"Head injury," she responded.

"Excuse me?"

"Paul and I were in an accident the day before our wedding. I hit the windshield, was thrown out of the car and knocked unconscious, and my shoes came off. We both had several lacerations, and Paul liked to joke that we were married in stitches."

I got my mouth to close just enough to ask, "And you got married anyway?"

"Why not?"

I didn't know why not other than that a person with a normal chromosome makeup would probably need more than a day to recover from an accident that knocked her out and required suturing.

More than once Julia's cavalier attitude about her health caused me alarm. On our Sicilian trip, we checked into a hotel in Taormina, went to our separate rooms, and agreed to "knock each other up" for

Julia and me touring in Taormina, Sicily, after her quick recovery from her fall.

dinner in an hour or so. At the appointed time, I knocked on her door, she opened it, and I was alarmed to see an egg-sized lump on her forehead.

"Lord, Julia! What happened?"

She gingerly touched the lump and said, "Oh, this. I tripped and fell down those foolish stairs." Her room had a small foyer and then two steps that led down into the bedroom. "The fall knocked me out, for I don't know how long. Then I took a short nap."

I was frantic thinking of what might have been the outcome of her going to sleep after a fall that left such an obvious injury. "Why didn't you call me right away when you woke up from the fall?"

"Well, I woke up, so I figured I was okay."

It was only at my adamant insistence that she agreed to see the local doctor, who confirmed that she was indeed okay, and I wondered what it would take for her to holler for help. I found out in 1994 during a trip to The Greenbrier.

The annual Symposium for Professional Food Writers at The Greenbrier in White Sulphur Springs, West Virginia, is something Julia and I loved to attend. It was always a small, congenial group of food writers watched over with efficient, attentive concern by its director, Antonia Allegra, and held in a resort teeming with the grace of past decades. One year I was scheduled to be a speaker at nine o'clock in the morning, and although public speaking does not make me nervous, going over what I am planning to say often keeps me tossing and turning all night. Hoping to avoid that, I took a sleeping pill and fell into a deep sleep. When the phone next to my bed startled me awake, I thought for a moment it was my wake-up call, but it was still dark outside and the clock said one. I anxiously grabbed for the receiver, certain that something had happened at home. It was Julia.

"I think I need your help, dearie. Can you come to my room?"

I threw on my bathrobe and let myself into her suite. She was sitting on the bed holding a towel to her mouth. There were two bloodied hand towels on the floor by her feet.

"My God. What happened?" I asked, walking over to stand in front of her.

She lifted the towel away from her face, and I could immediately see the source of all the blood. Her lip was split.

"I got up to go to the bathroom and tripped over that bench at the end of the bed. I fell into the dresser. So stupid."

I turned to look at the dresser and grimaced at the sight of all that brass hardware that had done battle with the full force of Julia's face as she went crashing down. My own face ached just to think of it. I sat down on the bed next to her and took a closer look at the damage. "I think I'd better call for a doctor," I said.

"I think you're right."

Fortunately, besides being a luxurious resort, The Greenbrier has a medically staffed clinic. A very young doctor took us immediately into an examining room and had Julia lie down on an examining table.

"You'll need stitches," he told her after assessing the damage.

"Fine," said Julia.

As he began to numb her lip with a needle that seemed the size of a crochet hook, Julia took hold of my hand. I was awfully glad she did, because I wasn't very good at watching needles going into someone else's body parts. Besides, the sleeping pill was still doing its thing, and I was fighting an overwhelming inclination to simply slide under the table and close my eyes. Her hand steadied me.

While we waited for the local anesthetic to take effect, I tried to comfort her, although she hardly seemed to need it as much as I did. I was in serious danger of passing out. I gripped the table with my free hand and told myself to focus on Julia—she must need something. The working side of her mouth was moving, and she was saying something to the doctor. Was she delirious? She was discussing meat.

"I don't think the meat is very good here," she mumbled. "Tonight they served us a slab of . . ."

Oh, God, I thought, *please don't talk about the meat.* I already felt queasy. Now not only was I going to slide under the table, but my stomach was going to rebel against that night's dinner.

The doctor looked perplexed; he had no answer for the meat dilemma. Julia continued to give her assessment of the problem, and I gripped her hand and the table harder. She squeezed back to let me know she was okay—or more likely because she saw the state I was in and wanted to save my life.

With a bit of prodding, Julia agreed to take a wheelchair back to the room, although God knows I needed it much more than she did. She accepted the painkillers the doctor gave her, and I tucked her into bed just seconds before I collapsed on her sofa. I bolted awake early the next morning and immediately checked on her; she was sleeping soundly. I nudged her gently to make sure she was . . . well, you know. I asked a mutual friend to stay with her while I gave my talk, and when I returned, she was still asleep. I began to worry. I nudged her again, and she responded but remained in deep sleep. She woke just after noon and said she felt tired but okay.

"Are you hungry? I asked.

"A little."

"Do you think you could eat some soup or soft-boiled eggs?"

"Ice cream. Vanilla."

I got the ice cream, but she ate only a few mouthfuls before going back to sleep. I really began to worry and called the doctor. He came down and checked all her vital signs and said she was fine, just understandably worn out and sleepy from the medication. After a few more mouthfuls of ice cream at dinnertime, she went back to sleep and I went back to the couch. I checked on her repeatedly during the night and wondered if I should try to get her back to Cambridge. But how? Ambulance? Stretched out on the backseat of a car? Private plane?

At five the next morning she was sitting up in bed. "I look a fright. I think I won't go to the lectures today."

"I'd hardly think so!"

"I think it would be nice, though, to ask Anne and Mark up for cocktails tonight," she said, referring to good friends Anne Willan and her husband, Mark Cherniavsky, who own the French culinary school La Varenne, which has a branch at The Greenbrier. "Let's see if the kitchen will send up some food and drinks." So although she opted not to attend any of the symposium programs because she "looked a fright," she partied in her room that night and the next, exhibiting not a smidgeon of infirm behavior.

Two days later, we decided it would be best to return to Cambridge. Her assistant, Stephanie, rightly convinced her that she should see her own doctor and perhaps a plastic surgeon, since the stitches were in such a conspicuous place. The Greenbrier provided a car to drive us to the airport in Washington, D.C. Since Julia was sensitive about being in public with a lip that was still quite swollen and discolored, she wrapped a long lavender chiffon scarf around the lower part of her face. At the airport, a woman approached her and began the usual litany of adorations, ending with the proffered piece of paper and request for an autograph. When she left, Julia turned to me with a look of surprise registering on the visible part of her face. I thought she was aghast that anyone would bother an obviously injured person, so her comment took me aback. "How do you think she recognized me?" she mumbled through the chiffon.

I think that in order to live life at eighty with gusto, you have to have a somewhat elevated degree of fearlessness. Never do I remember Julia refusing to do something because it might be dangerous. And if something such as being knocked out by a fall or splitting a lip wide open did occur, she didn't agonize about how much worse it could have been. When a hot-air balloon dumped her out of the basket upon landing, she told the story not with an emphasis on how it could have broken her legs or her back but with a dramatic swooshing of her arms and imaginative sound effects to describe "what a ride it was!"

During a trip to Miami, we got lost driving to a restaurant. Julia was in the backseat, my latest boyfriend was driving, and I was sitting in front without benefit of a map. Cell phones were a thing of the future, so we pulled into a gas station and I got out to call the restaurant for directions. My boyfriend got out to pump gas. A man sprang out of nowhere, opened the back door, grabbed Julia's purse, and disappeared in a flash. No one but Julia saw him, and when she calmly told us what happened, I was in a panic thinking that he could have had a knife and slashed her, or punched her, or hit her over the head with a heavy object. Julia was concerned only because her purse held her address book and she wondered how she would reconstruct the information he stole. It wasn't that she conquered her fears; she just didn't have them, and that gave her love of adventure a wide scope. I sometimes found that unnerving.

When Judith Jones turned seventy in 1994, a small group of friends arranged a surprise birthday party for her at Lutèce in New York. The owner, André Soltner, was a good friend of Judith's and such an excellent chef that it just sounded like the best time ever. Julia, Marian Morash, and I excitedly arranged to travel together, flying from Boston in the morning and back in the evening. But the day of the party it began to snow, and when Marian and I arrived to pick up Julia, it was really coming down. "Maybe it's not such a good idea to go," Marian and I suggested.

Julia promptly called the airport, learned that planes were flying, and said we were off. The weather got worse, however, and planes were delayed; Marian and I began to think that it was a very bad idea. Maybe we'd get down there, but we all needed to be back home that night, and could we make it? "Well, I'm going," Julia said, and we boarded the nearly empty plane. As we sat on the runway, takeoff on hold, snowfall getting heavier, Marian and I were white-knuckling our armrests and wondering if they'd let us off. Julia was reading *Newsweek*.

"Aren't you just a little nervous?" I asked her.

"About what?" she responded, turning the page.

Julia was right to think that her age in years was insignificant. Her spirit was ageless and that is how we thought of her—ageless. Those rare occasions that reminded us of how old she was were always a bit startling. I once lamented to Judith Jones how I wished I could conjure up the colorful language and expressions that Julia did so easily. "Don't forget," Judith told me, "Julia has eight decades of colloquialisms to choose from." Eight decades! Julia had been around eight decades! Somehow I'd missed that.

*Passion is energy. Feel the power that comes
from focusing on what excites you.*

—Oprah Winfrey

"Find something you're passionate about and keep tremendously interested in it," Julia once said, and in her eighties she was as passionate about food and cooking as she was the day she discovered oysters and Dover sole in Rouen. For thirty continuous years, her enthusiasm for her work, coupled with her unflagging energy, kept her on the move and in the public eye, and she wasn't about to slow down when she still had things to say and much to teach. Television was her favorite classroom and several new TV opportunities became available to her. In 1993, she accepted an offer to host a new PBS television show, *Cooking with Master Chefs*. It was a fifteen-program series that featured a different chef each week, taped on location in the featured chefs' kitchens.

Usually, for cooking shows of this type, the production crew tapes the chef cooking and the chef gives the written recipes to a recipe tester, who tests and edits the recipes for a book that will accompany the show. In fact, that is how the producers had planned to do the show when they asked Julia to narrate the series. They had not expected her actually to be on the road with them, but for her to watch the edited shows and tape her comments and enlightenments from a comfortable chair in her Cambridge home.

"Just like Alistair Cooke on *Masterpiece Theatre,*" Julia told me.

"Only she'll be Alistair Cookie," her assistant, Stephanie Hersh, added.

But then Julia agreed to allow the accompanying book to carry her name, and true to form, there was no way that she would lend her name to any material whose quality and trustworthiness she did not personally oversee. She wanted to be on the scene to taste, smell, and measure the food she would describe to her audiences.

So, with a great deal of enthusiasm, Julia left for California to capture the culinary secrets of Alice Waters, Jeremiah Tower, and Nancy Silverton on her laptop computer. Because the book had to be available for purchase by the time the show aired, Julia was in an *Iron Chef*-like race with the presses. She did not have the luxury of waiting to view the tapes at home but had to write most of the book on the road. It was an overwhelming job.

When she returned to Cambridge about a week later, she called immediately to ask if I could go up to her house for dinner and spend the night. "I need to talk to you," she said in an unfamiliar tone.

As we stood side by side—actually, the top of my shoulder to her side—at her kitchen counter preparing dinner, she said to me, "I don't think I can do it. It's just much more work than I thought." I was dumbfounded. It seemed as though nothing had ever been too much work for her, and if it ever had been, then, in her words, she bulled it through anyway. "Can you come with me and help write the rest of the book? I need you."

I was in the middle of ghostwriting a cookbook for another publisher and was up to my ears in work. How could I possibly say yes? How could I say no? "Of course. That will be great."

"Thank you. I am very grateful."

It's what friends do for friends, and I didn't think very much of it, so I was extremely touched by Julia's kind words in the acknowledgments of the book, *Cooking with Master Chefs*: "Deepest and special thanks go to my friend and colleague, Nancy Verde Barr, 'Without whom . . . We first met while I was doing a fund-raising cooking demonstration some years ago for Planned Parenthood in Providence, Rhode Island. She appeared as a young volunteer from that organization, to help us out with buying, arranging, cooking, and so forth. She was wonderful in every way and we all said, 'Let's hang on to her!' And we did, and we have all been together these many years—doing television series, book tours, demonstrations . . . When I found, while working on this book, that I'd never survive and get all the writing done on schedule by myself, I called for help, and Nancy came. We spent hours glued to the set, taking down every chefly word on our twin laptops, and she helped with the writing, and the chefs' biographies, and reediting, and the proofing. We work well together and my thanks are infinite."

I packed my bags, my half-finished ghosted manuscript, and my laptop and joined Julia for work in New York, Washington, D.C., and New Orleans. I immediately understood why she had asked me for help. She didn't lack the energy to do the work; it simply was not a one-person job, especially given the rushed time frame. We spent most days on the set, where we wrote down every detail of what the chefs did, and then we translated their actions into recipes that were doable for the home cook. Other days we were on airplanes flying to the next gig. We worked on the planes; we worked every morning in her hotel room before five; we never saw bed before eleven at night. It was a grueling schedule for anyone, let alone someone in her eighties, but Julia set the pace and kept to it with remarkable energy.

She also set the standard for the book. A stenographer could have recorded the words, but Julia needed more. She wanted to measure the exact length of André Soltner's bacon lardons, describe the placement of herbs in Charlie Palmer's potato maximes, and verbally capture the exact aroma of Emeril Lagasse's crab boil. She insisted that the recipes be of the type that was her stock in trade—detailed with explanations, suggestions on equipment, and elaborations on ingredients.

The recipes themselves were a problem, since few of the chefs gave us material that would make sense to the home cook. In some cases the recipes were little more than ideas, a dish that the chef prepared by the seat of his pants and then attempted to scratch out in writing on paper to fit what he did. Those that were written out in detail were often recalculated from a restaurant recipe designed to serve a large number of people. Dividing a recipe for two hundred into servings for six or eight leaves the reader with silly amounts such as 3½ cups plus ½ teaspoon of flour, or 16 tablespoons of oil instead of the equivalent but easier to measure 1 cup. One chef agreeably computed his restaurant recipe so that the meat served a nice tidy dinner for six; the sauce served a hundred and fifty!

Julia organized our work so that it was a lot like two people doing a crossword puzzle in tandem. We each recorded what the chefs did and then passed a disc back and forth to combine our notes, add missing directions, and correct ingredient amounts until we had one document that held workable recipes. She made me responsible for interviewing the chefs and writing their culinary biographies. It was a workable system, although Julia had a computer mishap that threatened to sidetrack it.

I was writing about Charlie Palmer's career when she handed me the disc with his recipes.

"Here's Palmer," she said.

"This should be fun," I said.

Two days before, she'd spilled coffee on her computer, destroying the *E* key, and there hadn't been time to have it repaired. After her initial annoyance with herself for her clumsiness—and subsequently a new rule, which she noted with several Post-it notes, that there should be "NO DRINKS NEAR COMPUTERS"—she decided to substitute #'s for the *E*'s. Sometimes she just forgot and punched the unworkable *E* key anyway, which produced nothing. I opened the file marked "P#ppr-Sar#d V#nison Staks with Pinot Noir and Sun-Dri#d Ch#rris" and was glad I'd been at the shoot and knew that those hieroglyphics translated to "Pepper-Seared Venison Steaks with Sun-Dried Cherries."

I've often wondered why it took the producers so long to realize that Julia did not belong in the back of a room pecking away at a computer. She belonged on camera, and eventually that's where she wound up. She still had to write the book, but she could also do what she loved most, perform for her audiences. And when she appeared on camera with Jacques Pépin, she was vintage Julia, sassy as ever. She joined Pépin in his kitchen while he made a lobster soufflé. With the cameras rolling, Julia asked Jacques how he removed the lobster meat from the claws. As he demonstrated his method, Julia picked up the lobster tail, removed the meat from the shell, and said, "Here, Jacques. I have a nice piece of tail for you." Everyone laughed, the cameras stopped, and the crew set up to reshoot the segment. She said it again.

Julia and Jacques together on camera were magic, and it was natural that the producers decided to pair them again for more TV shows. There were two *Cooking in Concert* specials and a PBS series, *Julia and Jacques Cooking at Home*. They were good friends who greatly respected each other's abilities even as they disagreed, often adamantly but always amusingly, about such things as the necessary amount of butter and cream in a recipe, or how thick a hamburger should be. The playful arguments never undermined what each was about, and that was the same thing. Jacques explained what that same thing was in his introduction to the book that accompanied the *Cooking at Home* series. "On the whole we agreed as to what is important: taste over appearance, simplicity in recipes, using the proper techniques, using the best-quality ingredients, following the seasons, keeping an open mind to new food preparations, and of course, sharing both wine and food with family and friends."

Julia adored being on television, but as Jacques pointed out, she never lost sight of her goal to promote the art of cooking. She drew the line when that goal was compromised. For a number of years, she made appearances on *Late Night with David Letterman.* David, whom she really liked, did a lot of crazy shtick with her food. She made crepes and David threw them like Frisbees out to the audience, but she kept teaching. On another show when she espoused the joys of real butter, David picked up a stick and bit off nearly half of it, yumming his agreement with her. She smiled and continued with her lesson. On the night she showed David how to make the perfect hamburger, the electricity, not David, messed her up. The electric cooktop was set in a rolling cart, which we kept backstage until she was ready to go on the set. The pan was hot and ready to cook, but when the stagehands moved the cart out front during a commercial break, they discovered that the electrical source on the stage did not work and the pan gradually began to cool until it could no longer cook anything. Undaunted by her inability to fry the hamburger, Julia walked David through beef tartare even as David made mayhem of the spot. Somehow, in spite of his foolishness, she always managed to keep her cooking professional. Then the producers asked her to appear on a show in which she would chop a bunch of watermelons up with an axe. She refused. "That's kiddy stuff," she said to me. "Not what we're about." She never did another of his shows.

The success of Julia and Jacques together on camera led to more programs that featured Julia with other successful television personalities. At a fund-raiser for the International Association of Culinary Professionals Foundation in San Antonio, Texas, we paired her up with Graham Kerr for the first of three television shows they would do together. In spite of all the years the two had been performing, they did not know each other very well. But when Graham walked into our San Antonio suite with that glorious smile and snappy tartan kilt, I think Julia fell in love. Their onstage presence was delightful. Like Julia, Graham is serious about his cooking, but he also knows that the name of the game is entertainment, so he was ready to give the audience what they wanted.

After much faxing back and forth, the two decided to make a bouillabaisse-style fish soup garnished with rouille, the traditional paste made with hot chilies, garlic, breadcrumbs, and olive oil. Since Graham concentrated on healthy cooking, he demonstrated his light version of a rouille using a food processor. Julia made hers with a mortar and pestle.

Graham's processor rouille went quickly, and he asked Julia to taste and sign off on it. She approved and then went back to her work, pounding away. When she considered her rouille done, she gave Graham a taste. His whole body reacted and he made small gasping sounds.

"Whoa!" he said with a little laugh. "What happened?"

"It's all that garlic," she said, challenging him to handle the enormous quantity of garlic that she had added.

Graham tucked one arm behind his back, lifted the other above his head, and did a few flamenco steps to demonstrate that such a sauce belonged in a very hot climate, or maybe it was to say that her rouille brought out the Latin lover in him.

Julia gave him a flirtatious smile.

"Darling," he said to her, "as an Englishman, I think I've just been violated." The audience roared.

Julia looked down appreciatively at her rouille. "I didn't know it would be that easy," she said, leaving Graham speechless and the audience in stitches.

With shows on PBS and her network spots on *Good Morning America*, what else could television offer her? Cable. In 1993, the Food Network was in its infancy on cable television, and they asked Julia if she would do a series of shows for them. Julia didn't want to do a cooking show, but she agreed to be a regular monthly guest on the network's program *Food News and Views*, appearing with one or the other of the show's two hosts, David Rosengarten and Donna Hanover. She also suggested to them that they should hire me as her producer.

The production crew and talent on the set of the Food Network's Food News and Views.

My job for each taping session of five shows was to come up with a number of timely culinary issues, run them by Julia to see which ones she liked, and then write up a number of suggested questions for the hosts. It didn't take me long to realize that I was no Barbara Walters. Unlike producing pieces where food is the star, producing news of any ilk demands journalism skills I just didn't have. Julia never thought the shows were as dreary as I did, but I would have given my new KitchenAid K5A stand mixer with copper egg white bowl for one hour with Barbara, Lesley Stahl, or Diane Sawyer, who could say, "These are the questions you want to have the host ask." The spots with David weren't so bad, since he was passionate and well informed about the topics and was able to bring his own knowledge and questions to the table. As professional as Donna was as a television news person, however, she wasn't as tuned into the food world as David was, and so she relied on my sappy questions.

Sample Topics from Julia's Appearances on the Food Network's Food News and Views

The Weighting of America

Americans are more overweight than ever. I think it's been estimated that one out of three adults is overweight. The Snack Food Association (who are they?) predicted that on Super Bowl Sunday Americans would consume 28 million pounds of potato chips, Doritos, and corn chips. Could this be the problem?

Where's Dr. Schwartz?

In —— Dr. Schwartz created a stir regarding MSG. Where is he and what's he doing today? What's happened to his studies? Have they been challenged in journals?

The Food Police in a Republican Congress

Will their hands-off government policies affect the "food police"? Will people start to take an attitude of being personally responsible for what they eat?

Politically Correct Food

Has the Clinton administration given us a new line of politically correct food? George H. W. Bush had his no-broccoli dinners and Ronald Reagan his jelly beans. Will Bill Clinton give us junk food or will we be more influenced by Hillary Clinton's light-food bent?

Food as Medicine

Have we come to the point of an "eat saffron pasta and call me in the morning" approach to food? Is it better to chew garlic pills than to include a healthy dose of garlic in your diet?

Bypassing Breakfast

In a recent survey, 55 percent of those polled said that they can't find time for breakfast even though 84 percent said that they think it is the most important meal of the day. Twenty-eight percent said it takes too long to prepare, but does it? Eggs are quick, but perhaps they are afraid of them. Breads and cereals are fortified and quick. Julia is busy; does she ever skip breakfast? Never.

Will Trendiness Kill the Mashed Potato?

It probably went out of vogue the first time because it was too ho-hum. Now it may disappear because it has become a fad food. In Chicago's Mashed Potato Club, spuds are the centerpiece, with offerings of forty-two garnishes to spice them up. Chocolate mashed potatoes, peanut butter mashed potatoes—what are we thinking of? Some things blend well with a spud, but others are ridiculous. The trendiness will probably kill the reemergence of this delicious vegetable.

For those shows, however, I was brilliant at reminding Julia not to slouch. Julia and I have the same bad habit of slouching when we sit, and for years we reminded each other often, "Sit up!" (We also shared a cowlick in the exact same spot on the back of our heads, so we alternated posture and hair alerts.) For the shows, Julia and the hosts sat in high-backed, narrow wing chairs that seemed to make Julia want to slump more than usual. So we worked out a system whereby she would always look at me just before the cameras rolled, and if I was making exaggerated circling motions with my shoulders, it meant she looked slouched.

When the producers of *Cooking with Master Chefs* asked Julia to do another series in 1994, she agreed primarily because they wisely decided to bring the chefs to Julia rather than have her traipse around the country to them. Once again, Julia and I were responsible for writing the book. The crew converted her kitchen into a set and her dining room into a control room, and Julia and I added an office area to "my bedroom" upstairs and one to the basement, aka, food prep area. Appropriately called *In Julia's Kitchen with Master Chefs*, the series, like the one before it, combined what Julia loved best: being on television and working with other chefs.

Not having to travel for the show was a plus, but because Julia not only had to write the book but also perform on camera, the workload was just as demanding for her. Passion and energy in hand, she rose to the occasion. During the week I lived at Julia's house, and although I was well used to her stamina, I still marveled at it. She thought nothing of getting up at five in the morning, doing twenty minutes of exercise on the stationary bike that stood in her bedroom, and arriving fully dressed ready to cook breakfast at six. We then put in a full day's work, and it was usually nine or later at night before she declared it was time to stop. I have to admit there were times when my thoughts would drift longingly to delivery pizza, but Julia would

JULIA'S ITALIAN-STYLE SWORDFISH

Serves 2

One of my favorite after-work meals was Julia's baked swordfish, which she called Italian-style. She always kept a jar of Italian seasoning in her cupboard, and although both of us championed the use of fresh herbs, the jar held mostly oregano and fennel, which in their dried state are decidedly Italian American flavors and far from objectionable.

Two 6-ounce swordfish steaks, each 3/4 inch thick
Salt and pepper
About 1/4 cup extra-virgin olive oil
A few tablespoons dried Italian seasoning

1. Preheat the oven to 400°F.

2. Season the fish on both sides with salt and pepper. Choose an oven-proof baking dish just large enough to hold both pieces of fish comfortably without their sides touching. Pour enough olive oil into the dish to coat the bottom completely and sprinkle the seasoning over the bottom.

3. Lay the fish in the dish and brush the tops with more olive oil. Bake for 4 minutes, then turn the fish over and continue to bake until done, 4 to 6 minutes.

insist on preparing a "proper" meal, which meant meat, chicken, or fish plus vegetables. It would be eleven o'clock before we finished eating and cleaning up. And up again at five the next morning.

We wrote the book in tandem as we had the first one, and as with the first one, the highlight of my day was reading her notes. I marveled at her carefree, unselfconscious style of writing. When the recipes were completed, Julia would ask me to take the first stab at the headnotes to the recipes, and I would stress and struggle to try to sound like her. She'd always tell me what I wrote was "*very* good,"

NANCY'S BUTTER MARINARA SAUCE

Serves 2

Regardless of the country's mania for pasta, which Julia pronounced with a short a like in past, she wasn't wild about it and was quick to tell people so. But she'd always add, perhaps truthfully, maybe diplomatically, "I like the way Nancy fixes it." My secret was butter. My family's traditional Neapolitan quick tomato sauce begins with olive oil, but when I was making it for Julia, I substituted butter because I knew it would be more appealing to her.

4 tablespoons unsalted butter
1 teaspoon extra-virgin olive oil
1 small onion, minced
Salt
One 28-ounce can Italian peeled plum tomatoes, lightly drained
1/4 cup fresh basil, torn into small pieces
1/2 pound pasta, freshly cooked

1. Melt the butter and oil in a heavy medium saucepan over medium-low heat, being careful not to let the butter color. Stir in the onion, season with salt, and cook gently until it has softened. Be very careful not to let the onion brown or it will become bitter.

2. Pour the tomatoes into a bowl and break them into small pieces with your hands, then add them to the pan when the onions are softened. Bring to a boil, then reduce the heat and add the basil and a bit more salt. Simmer for 15 minutes. Serve over 1/2 pound of cooked pasta.

then she'd change it. My "large roasting chicken" became her "ample chicken of a certain age." I wrote "classic apple pie" and she amended it to "everybody's favorite American-national-hero pie." All too rarely, I wrote something that must have sounded like her voice because she'd guffaw and leave it just as it was.

I loved reading Julia's notes on chefs' recipes

Charlie Trotter's List of Recipes

This is a list of proposed recipes from chef Charlie Trotter to make on the show. Julia's initial notes to me appear in italics.

Seared Diver Scallops with Mushrooms, Bacon, Curried Carrot Broth. Sauté mushrooms in rendered bacon fat. Sauté scallops in butter. Serve them over the mushrooms and surround with broth.

Curried Carrot Broth: Sweat onions, garlic then apple, add curry, paprika, etc. & cook, then purée and sieve and mix with 1 lb. butter. Add several tablespoons to 1 cup reduced carrot juice.

Sounds ok but not world shaking.

Quinoa with olive oil, poached tomatoes, etc.

Do we need another of these 3rd world grains?? The tomatoes are interesting.

Belgian Endive with Japanese Pear, Greens, Hazelnuts, Chèvre. A salad type of dish, julienned endive tied in upright bundles and surrounded with chèvre cream, hazelnuts, pear pieces, julienned apricots.

A rather fiercely nouvelle type of thing. Probably eats good.

Smoked Salmon with Potato, Avocado, Papaya, Herb Sauce. Recipes included for herb oil, parsley juice, pulped avocado, pickled papaya, potato tuiles. A kind of napoleon of smoked salmon squares in 3 layers.

The potato is like Gross's mashed potato wafers—he could think of something else. Sounds nice, if he would think of some alternative to the potato.

Almond Torte, Nectarines, Lavender Ice Cream. An almond cake baked in 2-inch ramekins surrounded on one side by slices of poached nectarines and on the other by the lavender ice cream.

Sounds nice, with recipes for each thing. (Would the torte be nicer if imbibed with nectarine syrup??)

Poached Beef Tenderloin with Lobster Potatoes, Mushroom–Foie Gras Sauce. Tenderloin slices fanned around one side of a plate, and mashed potatoes mixed with lobster meat, bacon, parsley on the other side. The sauce around all.

A rather typical young chef's reach for glory???

When the galleys for the book arrived, Julia was horrified to see that instead of being neatly secured with rubber bands and sent snug in a box, the loose pages had been shipped in an oversized mailer that allowed them to shift around so they were difficult to manage. She went to her office to deal with them and I worked in my bedroom office down the hallway within earshot. I heard her guffaw, so I trotted down to see what was amusing her.

"I've written a scathing letter to the head of Knopf complaining about the manner in which the galleys were sent."

"Good for you," I said. "What did you say?"

"Here, read it," she said handing me the letter.

After explaining the deplorable condition of the papers and her unhappiness with it, she asked the chief mucky-muck of the prestigious publishing house, "What kind of sleazeballs do you have working for you anyway?"

"Julia, I'm not sure you want to say 'sleazeballs' to the head of Knopf."

"Why not?" she said with that evil twinkle in her eye. Some years later, I asked Judith Jones if she'd ever seen that letter, and she didn't remember it. So I'm not sure if Julia changed her words or if the Knopf mucky-muck enjoyed reading it as much as Julia enjoyed writing and called the "sleazeballs" on the carpet.

It was during our taping of *In Julia's Kitchen with Master Chefs* that Julia and I had the first and only fight we ever had. I think it surprised us both.

Johanne Killeen, chef-owner of Al Forno restaurant and cookbook author, prepares for her segment in Julia's kitchen turned TV set. Me checking out the details of her recipe.

Each episode of the series showed Julia cooking in her kitchen with the featured chef, who demonstrated a few signature restaurant dishes. After taping, Julia and I reworked the recipes until we found them doable for home cooks and then passed them on to Kathleen Anino, a professional recipe tester who did the major amount of testing. Chef Jacques Torres appeared on the show and demonstrated his recipe for chocolate soup, just one of the many innovative desserts he created for New York's Le Cirque. He lined a soup tureen with rum-flavored caramelized bananas, poured on a semisweet chocolate sauce, covered it with meringue, and baked it in a water bath. The "soup" was served warm, and its deliciousness still haunts me.

Julia wanted to write the recipe for individual ramekins rather than one large tureen, and we were having trouble. Reducing dessert recipes is particularly difficult because baking involves a lot of chemistry and the balance of ingredients has to be just right. Perhaps, with that particular dessert, the changed ratio of moisture from the bananas to starch in the chocolate was disturbing the balance in the smaller dishes. Who knows? We couldn't get the recipe to work just right. Kathleen was away for a few days, but before she left she made several suggestions to me, and I was alone in the kitchen testing the recipe once again. I don't *love* to bake. I'm happiest as a top-of-the-stove cook, simmering and braising my way through sauces, soups, and stews, so I wasn't particularly enjoying the testing and I just wanted it finished. Julia walked into the kitchen.

"I think we should wait until Kathleen gets back and she can test it again," she said.

"Well, she left some good notes, and I think I can work from those. I definitely think less chocolate is the answer."

"No, let's wait."

I could tell that she was digging in her heels, but I was close to working out the problem. I just didn't want to leave it in limbo. "But everything is measured and ready to go."

"Doesn't matter. We should wait."

I recognized the firm stance and definitive tone. What was her problem? Why couldn't I just finish what I was doing and be done with it? "Okay. I'll just put this one in the oven. If it doesn't work, I'll leave it for Kathleen."

She raised her voice and her finger. "No. Stop now. We'll wait for Kathleen."

Never had she made me so angry, and I stormed out of the kitchen and upstairs to "my room," where I paced in a circle, muttering misery. "She's acting like . . . like . . . like her aunt Theodora." It was the worst I could think of. Julia used to tell us about her monster aunt

Theodora and once described her in a letter to me: "She looked nice as pie, a really impressive upper-class duchess type, and acted sweet as pie until she was crossed. And then, the little digs, the pricks, the scratches, and how she would tear people apart down to the bone—but so delicately done."

Within ten minutes, an agonizing feeling of regret swept away my anger. I knew I had to apologize for storming off the way I had. I didn't know what I would face, but I dragged myself remorsefully downstairs. Julia was standing at the bottom of the steps.

"I'm sorry, dearie," she said before I could get my apology out.

"So am I."

"I behaved badly."

"Me too. I was going to tell you that you reminded me of your aunt Theodora."

"I wanted to tell you that you reminded me of you-know-who." I knew whom she meant. It was someone we had worked with who annoyed Julia by always doing things so quickly, and just annoyed me all around. It was an insult equal to my aunt Theodora one.

I laughed, she smiled, and our fight was over. By saying that I reminded her of you-know-who, she let me know that I had been plowing through one test after another in a mad dash just to get it done, and that was not her style. No matter how pressured the situation might be, cooking was always to be careful, meticulous—and fun.

At the end of one of the weeks of taping, I packed my small bag and returned to Providence. It was May 12, 1994. I remember the date exactly because it was the day Paul Child died. His health had been so poor that, foolishly, I was certain Julia was prepared for it. But the depth of her pain was so extreme that I did wonder if this time something would break inside her. Her long, sobbing phone calls broke my heart. "It is the end of an era," she kept repeating, and I was struck by the immensity of feeling that an entire period of one's life was simply finished. I found it so difficult to comfort her, especially since she did not believe in God or an afterlife, as I did, so it was useless to offer such comforts as "He's in a better place" or "He will always be there watching over you."

Three days after Paul died, I sat with Julia at her kitchen table before going to the nursing home to collect his belongings. She and Paul had long ago joined the Neptune Society, and they made all the arrangements for his cremation.

"Do you plan to be cremated?" she asked me.

"No. I think I want to be buried. I don't really care where, but I don't want the funeral procession to travel on a highway. I want to ride on back country roads."

"It doesn't matter. When you're gone, you're gone. You wouldn't know."

"Well, I think I would, so if you're around, make sure I ride through the country."

"Won't matter," she said.

We went to the nursing home, gathered Paul's belongings—including the ties he'd still worn there and his weathered baseball cap—and returned home. I was sensitive to Julia's emotional state, but she was more pensive than despondent, so she startled me when she stopped on the sidewalk in front of her house and gasped.

"Look," she said, staring at the yard.

I didn't see what she saw, so I asked, "At what?"

"The wisteria is blooming."

"Oh, yes, it's lovely," I responded, completely unaware of the significance until she told me that it had never bloomed before—never in the thirty years that the Childs had lived there. Paul had planted and nursed it and Charlie the gardener had pampered and fed it, but they'd finally given up hope, deciding that the location was much too shady for the plant ever to flower. That day, the blossoming pale lavender flowers struck Julia to the quick.

Back in the kitchen, I said, "Don't you think that's a sign that there is a life afterward? That it's a message from Paul?"

Julia took this photo of me with David about to serve her lunch.

I could see that she was trying to make sense of it, and she spread her arms wide, trying to wrap them around something she could not describe. "Perhaps there is a greater . . . something," she said, struggling for the words. She never said "God" or "afterlife," just "something," but we both felt that the something was from Paul, and we cried quietly together. We never discussed the possibility of an afterlife again, but I like to think that if she could be here, she would make sure that my funeral procession would travel by country roads.

We resumed taping of *In Julia's Kitchen* after Paul was cremated but before his ashes were scattered in Maine. I again moved into her house, and although she rallied during the daily activities, I was heedful of her emotions when the crew left at the end of the day. Even though Paul had not lived at home for many years, he was still there, and I wanted to keep Julia's spirits buoyed as much as possible. To that end, I had an exceptional ally. Her nephew David McWilliams, her brother's son, was living in the third-floor apartment while studying for his graduate degree in business at Boston University. David was a constant delight. Moreover, he had an insatiable appetite, so we could count on him to bound into the kitchen smiling and happy whenever Julia called up the stairs, "Boop-boop. Hungry, David?" Not only did his presence soothe Julia's spirits, but his good counsel made me realize I didn't need to walk on eggshells; I found I could easily talk to Julia about Paul without making her sad. In fact, mostly it made us laugh.

Julia always kept an ironing board open in her bedroom during shoots so she could quickly press a blouse or skirt if necessary. One day, I noticed that along with the iron, the board held a bowl of fresh peaches and one of ripe garden tomatoes. They were gifts from Charlie the gardener, and Julia wanted to keep them for family meals rather than have them gobbled up by the production crew. In between the bowls sat what I quite suddenly realized was an urn, although I had never actually seen one up close.

"Is that Paul?" I couldn't help asking.

"Yes," Julia said.

"On the ironing board, Julia?"

She smiled that wonderful big, twinkling smile of hers. "Oh, I think he's very happy with the peaches and tomatoes. He loved both."

Close to the end of the shooting schedule, Julia's sister, Dorothy, came to visit. She slept in the room next to mine and was always up and dressed, ready to walk down to breakfast with me, at six. But one morning, instead of joining me in the hallway, she called me into her room. She was sitting on the corner of the bed, with her hands folded in her lap. I could tell by the look on her face that she was grappling with something.

She patted a spot on the bed next to her. "Can you sit for a minute, Nancy?"

"Of course. Is there anything wrong? Are you okay?"

"I wanted to talk to you about Julia. What do you think about her doing these shows?"

"In what way, Dort?"

"Julia made me promise to tell her when she should stop. You know, when she was too old to do it anymore. She didn't want to appear a fool. Is she?"

I knew what Dorothy was asking and why. Julia did of course look older on the programs. She was more stooped, she sat more, and sometimes displayed a rare lack of energy. But it was more than that. The culinary genius who so expertly communicated the intricacies of French cooking to generations of cooks was often left asking chefs a third her age how they chopped their onions. On my own tours, students often asked me what was going on. They described Julia's co-hosts as being patronizing and condescending.

"I don't think it's Julia, Dort. I mean, look at the Norway show Russ Morash did with her. That was only a few years ago, and Julia was absolutely classic Julia. I just think this is bad producing and a bad format for her unless she's with someone like Jacques, who excites and stimulates her to perform her best."

"Do you think I should tell her to stop?"

I don't know if Dorothy made her decision based on my response, but I told her what I felt. "This is her passion, Dort. I think asking her to give it up would be more damaging than any criticism she receives for keeping at it."

Dort and I never discussed it again, and Julia agreed to do another series in 1996, *Baking with Julia*. Thank heavens, for that series neither of us had to write the book. Dorie Greenspan, author of a number of superb baking cookbooks and a master baker if ever there was one, wrote the beautiful book that accompanied the show. Julia appeared on camera with the chefs, and I was culinary producer.

Her television work was not all that kept Julia busy in the mid 1990's. She continued to give demonstrations, attend conferences, and teach classes from California to Italy. There was simply no turnoff switch for the passion she had for what she was doing. In late February 1996, Julia and I spent six days at the Highlands Inn in

Carmel, California, where Julia was the guest of honor at a truly posh culinary extravaganza. The Masters of Food & Wine event is held yearly for no reason other than the celebration of the finest in food and wine. Three hundred guests from around the world enjoyed gala dinners, truffle and foie gras lunches, wines of great distinction, and buffet tables laden with the world's premium unpasteurized cheeses. Food luminaries mingled with elegant, passionate gourmands, who paid an obscene amount of money to experience the best of the world of gastronomy. Vineyard owners from France, California, Italy, Spain, and Australia, to list but a few, were there with a handpicked selection of their productions. There was even a beer maker from Germany whose family had been making the brew for seven hundred years.

Julia agreed to give a demonstration as well as do several radio and television interviews. Somehow, at Julia's insistence, we also found time to cut out and tour the area. She especially wanted to see if we could find the whales that were in the Pacific waters running by the inn. So we drove to a number of popular lookout sites and did indeed see them. We were both in great spirits. Julia was in California, and there was no place on earth that she loved more. And I was in love. Earlier that month, I'd met Roy Bailey. I knew as soon as I met him that he was the one, but I wonder if I would have realized it if I hadn't already known Julia so well. Roy was just as bold and outspoken, just as outrageous and naughty, and just as funny if not funnier than Julia was. His personality might well have overwhelmed me if I had not had so many Julia years to prepare for it.

I told Julia that I was pretty sure I had met "him," and she was delighted. Up until then, she had been supportive of the few boyfriends I had, but although she didn't come right out and say it, I could tell that she didn't think they were right for me. The day we arrived in Carmel, there was a card from Roy waiting for me at the hotel desk.

"It's from Roy," I said, all smiles, holding it up for her to see.

"Let's see," she said taking the card and examining the address. "He has a strong, fine hand. I approve."

I don't know if it was because Roy was a professional artist and she felt a connection because of Paul's art or if she just sensed that all the pieces fit, but from the get-go she liked him. The day I introduced them to each other, I let us into Julia's house and yelled hello as Roy and I walked up the back stairs. Julia met us at the top and Roy put out his hand to shake hers, but instead Julia reached her long arms around him and gave him a huge, warm hug. "Anyone who is with our Nancy deserves a hug," she said. Approval noted.

So Julia and I floated happily through our days at the Highland Inn. For the gala meals, the inn invited twenty or so well-known chefs, including Julia, to each prepare a course. Knowing what a hectic schedule she planned for herself, she might have chosen to prepare a simpler dish for her contribution to the gala dinner, but she didn't. She decided to prepare her Designer Duck, which involved roasting the duck until the breast meat was just "springy rather than squishy to the touch" then skinning and disassembling the bird so the breasts could be pan-sautéed briefly to finish cooking and the legs and thighs breaded and sautéed a longer time in another pan.

The day of the dinner, Julia spent the morning doing a television interview and the afternoon giving a demonstration. Cooks from the inn were supposed to get the ducks ready for the sauté stage, but when we arrived, we saw that nothing was finished beyond the roasting. With the dinner hour perilously close, there was no time to lose, so Julia and I grabbed knives, donned aprons, and began removing breasts, legs, thighs, and skin from enough ducks to make hunters weep. Bless the late chef Jean-Louis Palladin, who, realizing what was happening, called to all chefs who were not up their necks in their own preparations to grab their knives and get to our table. He had alerted the kitchen to our needs in French, so the entire brigade that came to our aid was French. Julia explained in French what we were doing, and I sincerely regretted that my knowledge of the language was so limited. I had no trouble, however, translating Julia's statement when she looked up from her duck, knife poised in front of her, smiled, and said in perfect French, "Cooking together is such fun." *Oui* a hundred times over.

Even with all that expert help, we were not finished by the time the guests began to arrive for the evening festivities. Julia and I were expected to join the guests in the dining room in time for the cocktail hour, but she didn't want to leave the kitchen and I had to chase her out.

"We still have so much to do," she said.

"I'll stay and make sure it gets done," I told her. "No one will miss me, but you *have* to be there." Reluctantly Julia left the kitchen, and when I finally made it into the dining room in time to sit down for the first course, she caught me by the arm. "How'd it go?" she asked.

"Great," I said. "They're all set to be sautéed."

"I wanted to stay," she said resolutely, and I knew she meant it. Schmoozing over cocktails did not come even close to boning ducks with a group of friends. Cooking was her passion, and I never saw it wane. Nothing ever eroded her energy or joy for being in front of a stove. It was a wise choice for Dort not to tell her to stop. And Julia never did.

She continued to do what she had always done with all the energy and passion she'd always had. But our work together did stop. In 1997, I signed a contract with Knopf for another book, which was larger and more involved than my first. Roy and I were juggling our lives in homes in Nantucket and Providence, and for me that was enough.

Julia and I did continue, however, to play together, and keeping up with Julia was no less of a challenge than it had ever been. In 1997, when she was still living in her Santa Barbara condominium at Montecito Shores, she invited Roy and me to stay with her for a few days over New Year's. We didn't need any reason to go other than to celebrate with her, but she had a specific one on her mind: she had decided to sell her Montecito unit and move to the retirement community of Casa Marinda. The apartment at the Casa was considerably

Roy Bailey, Sally Jackson, and Joann Warren partying at the Wine Cask.

smaller and she was in the process of furniture downsizing. Much of Paul's painting equipment was still in the condominium, and she wanted to see if there was anything that Roy would like. And she wanted to show us what would be her new digs. As she warned, they were much smaller, and when she gave us the tour, she said that the man living in the unit next door to hers was not well. Perhaps "when he slips off the raft, I can buy his place and break down the wall," she told us.

New Year's Eve itself presented a dilemma to Julia because there were two parties that she really wanted to attend. Russ and Marian Morash were hosting what sounded like a fabulous bash at the Santa Barbara Biltmore, a breathtaking resort in a magical setting. And our good friend from Boston, Sally Jackson, and her husband, Paul Mace, were celebrating their wedding anniversary at the Wine Cask, a fine Santa Barbara restaurant, where they had had their wedding dinner a few years earlier.

Roy and I did our best with hats and noses to keep up with Julia at Russ and Marian's New Year's party.

Julia decided we should join Sally and Paul along with their honor attendants, Jack and Joann Warren, also friends of Julia's, at the Wine Cask since we had missed their actual wedding. We began the evening at the Warrens', where Sally and Paul gave *us* anniversary gifts: silver wine coasters inscribed with Julia's favorite toast, "Here's to us. None better." Then we moved on to the Wine Cask, where Sally and Paul were obviously well remembered as the good-time couple they are. We were feted admirably, and our glasses remained full until long after midnight, when we shook the confetti from our hair, grabbed a handful of the bobbing balloons, and said goodnight.

Roy, Julia, and I climbed into our car and headed home. "That was such fun," I said, sated, tired, and a little tipsy.

"We can still make Russ and Marian's party," Julia said.

I didn't need an interpreter to translate the look on Roy's face when he turned to me: *Is she serious?* Most of us have had a number of evenings of party-hopping that last until the sun comes up, but will we still want to do it when we're eighty-four?

Julia's ability to rally and her energetic, determined mind-set remained a part of who she was even in her nineties, when health issues threatened to compromise them. I was planning to visit her in August 2004 for her ninety-second birthday, but Sally Jackson called me in May to say that she had just spoken to Stephanie and learned that Julia's health had failed.

"I don't want to spread gloom and doom, but I think we should go out to see her as soon as possible," she said. "Can you go next week?"

"Absolutely."

"I'll tell Stephanie and Julia that we're coming. I think we should be prepared for the worst."

I began to think of how difficult it was going to be to see Julia bedridden. I had spoken to her recently on the phone, and she told me how delighted she was with her new kitten that slept on the bed with her. She e-mailed me photos of the wee black-and-white kitten, or *poussiquette,* as she referred to all felines. *Poussiquette*'s given name, like the Childs' cat in France, was Minou, French for "kitty cat." I tried to picture Julia in bed playing with the kitten and not simply lying supine, dozing in and out of sleep.

A few days later, I received an e-mail from Sally giving me our flight schedule, sleeping arrangements, and a packed itinerary from Julia that filled just about every minute of the time we would be in California. None of it involved playing on the bed with a kitten. So much for keeping vigil.

The following week, Sally and I arrived at Julia's small apartment in the lovely Casa Miranda, an above-average assisted-living facility in Santa Barbara. Julia was thinner than I'd ever seen her and in a wheelchair. I think the common expression is "resigned to a wheelchair," but there was no resignation; she was rigorously undergoing physical therapy to help her walk again following hip surgery some months before. She was also eager to get going, and for the next three days Stephanie, Sally, and I wheeled her to breakfasts with her Casa buddies, into restaurants for lunches and dinners with good friends, and through the local Costco, where a girl of about twelve approached her shyly for her autograph. We gobbled down Double-Double burgers at the In-N-Out drive-through and took in a movie, *The Day After Tomorrow*, which Julia thought sounded like fun. In spite of cat-napping through some of it, she found the action exciting.

Julia and I had good talks during that visit. Roy had passed away a year and half before, and she knew how much I missed him. She wanted to know if I was okay, really okay. I told her that I was following her example and keeping busy by working. I was writing a novel, which was loosely based on the television work we did together. She wanted to know all about it, and as I told her what was in it we began to talk about the years we had spent together and what fun we had.

On the way to the airport on the morning we left, Sally and I drove by the apartment. Julia was in the middle of her therapy, and the therapist wheeled her out to the car so we could say our good-byes. We chatted and promised to ring each other up often, and then Julia took hold of my arm. With her other hand, she gripped the walkway railing, pulled herself up and out of the wheelchair, and walked briskly and resolutely down the path to her front door.

That was the last time I saw Julia, and my image of her on that day is the same as it always was: an exceptional woman who had the energy and determination to accomplish whatever she wanted to do, whether it was to change the way we thought about eating or get up out of that wheelchair and walk on her own two feet to her front door.

Postscript

$\mathcal{I}$ miss my unique friend. I miss the cooking knowledge that I trusted so completely and that she so readily shared, the wise mentoring she so generously offered. The culinary world as a whole is poorer for her loss, certainly less colorful, and I think less focused on her vision of uniting professionals and nonprofessionals in the common goal of enlightening and enriching American kitchens—sensibly, with moderation in all things. It has lost that strong, positive voice of reason that weighed in on food fads, the food police, nutty nutrition, and dangerous diets, and did so for the benefit of sound enjoyable dining, not for the sound bite.

More than that, I miss the friend who made me laugh and showed me that having a good time sometimes meant breaking the rules. I chuckle when I recall her quick witticisms, such as the time I was trying to explain jam bands and in particular Phish to her.

"Jam bands usually have large groups of fans who follow them around from concert to concert. You've heard of the Grateful Dead? Well, their fans were called Deadheads, and they went practically everywhere the band did."

"So the Phish have fish heads," she logically concluded.

I'd love to hear that warbling "woo-hoo" or "boop-boop" across a crowded room alerting me to where she was, or her typical nighttime request to "knock me up" in the morning. I'd love to answer the phone and hear, "It's *Ju-u-lia,*" as though it could be anyone else, or hear her characteristically welcoming response to my calls to her: "Is that *Nancy?*" I want to see that index finger raised in indignation or feel it poking me in jest. I think of walking into her office and seeing her sitting at her huge plain oak desk with a teakettle on a nearby hot plate and books everywhere. I'd love to cook with her once more in her kitchen alone and then with a group, because "cooking together is such fun."

I miss the familiar, comfortable things: the Post-it notes, the kitchen table clothed in a padded vinyl tablecloth. I miss setting that table with her colorful round raffia placemats, the slightly chipped Provençal dishes, the blue-and-white breakfast bowls. I miss the cow.

Foolish things, I suppose, and like the lyrics from her favorite song say, they remind me of Julia. When they pop into my mind, in spite of how much I miss her, they compel me once again to say "souf-*flé*" and smile.

Resources

BOOKS

Child, Julia. *Mastering the Art of French Cooking.* New York: Knopf, 1961.

———.*Mastering the Art of French Cooking, Volume II.* New York: Knopf, 1970.

———.*The French Chef Cookbook.* New York: Knopf, 1968.

———.*From Julia's Kitchen.* New York: Knopf, 1975.

———.*The Way to Cook.* New York: Knopf, 1989.

———.*Cooking with Master Chefs.* New York: Knopf, 1993.

Child, Julia, and Nancy Barr. *In Julia's Kitchen with Master Chefs.* New York: Knopf, 1995.

Child, Julia and Jacques Pepin. *Julia and Jacques Cooking at Home.* New York: Knopf, 1999

Fitch, Noël Riley. *Appetite for Life: The Biography of Julia Child.* New York: Doubleday, 1997.

PERIODICALS

Apple, R. J. "Oyster-Loving Idealist." *New York Times,* August 18, 2004.

Hersh, Stephanie. "A Full Measure of Humor." *Gastronomica: The Journal of Food and Culture,* summer 2006.

Hudgins, Sharon. "A Conversation with Julia Child, Spring 1984." *Gastronomica: The Journal of Food and Culture,* summer 2006.

Julier, Alice. "Julia at Smith." *Gastronomica: The Journal of Food and Culture,* summer 2006.

Lawson, Carol. "Julia Child, Boiling, Answers Her Critics." *New York Times,* June 20, 1990.

Pépin, Jacques. "My Friend Julia Child." *Gastronomica: The Journal of Food and Culture,* summer 2006.

Schrambling, Regina. "Julia Child, the French Chef for a Jell-O Nation, Dies at 91." *New York Times,* August 13, 2004.

Whittemore, Hank. "Julia and Paul," interview with Julia and Paul Child. *Parade*, February 28, 1982.

INTERNET RESOURCES

Kummer, Corby, and Marilyn Mellowes. "PBS: 'Julia! America's Favorite Chef,' American Masters Series." *Washington Post*, June 16, 2005.

COLLECTIONS

Julia Child Papers. Arthur and Elizabeth Schlesinger Library on the History of Women in America, Harvard University.

Index

Page numbers in italic refer to illustrations